VIDEOGAMES

and

Education

History, Humanities, and
New Technology

Series Editors:
David J. Staley, Ohio State University,
Dennis A. Trinkle, Valparaiso University,
Jeffrey G. Barlow, Pacific University

Sponsored by
The American Association for History and Computing

COMPUTERS, VISUALIZATION, AND HISTORY
How New Technology Will Tranform Our Understanding of the Past
David J. Staley

TEACHING HISTORY IN THE DIGITAL CLASSROOM
D. Antonio Cantu and Wilson J. Warren

**DIGITAL SCHOLARSHIP IN THE TENURE, PROMOTION,
AND REVIEW PROCESS**
Edited by
Deborah Lines Andersen

VIDEOGAMES
and
Education

HARRY J. BROWN

M.E.Sharpe
Armonk, New York
London, England

Significant portions of Chapter 3 are drawn from Harry J. Brown,
"Malleable Mythologies: Competing Strategies for Adapting Film
Narrative to Video Games in Star Wars and The Lord of the Rings" in
Works and Days 22, nos. 1 and 2 © 2004, edited by Ken McAllister
and Ryan Moeller, by permission of David Downing; and from "Dream
Worlds: Film-Game Franchising and Narrative Form" in *The Business of
Entertainment,* vol. 1 © 2008, edited by Robert C. Sickels, by permission
of Praeger Press, Westport, CT.

Significant portions of Chapter 9 are drawn from Harry Brown and
Michael Oren, "Living Art: Commercial Modding and Code-Illiterate
Gamers" in *Digital Gameplay: Essays on the Nexus of Game and Gamer*
© 2005, edited by Nate Garrelts, by permission of McFarland & Company,
Jefferson, NC.

Library of Congress Cataloging-in-Publication Data

Brown, Harry J. (Harry John), 1972–
  Videogames and education / Harry J. Brown.
    p. cm. — (History, humanities, and new technology)
  Includes bibliographical references and index.
  ISBN 978-0-7656-1996-9 (cloth : alk. paper)
  1. Video games—Psychological aspects. 2. Learning, Psychology of.
  3. Video games and children. I. Title. II. Title: Video games and education.

GV1469.34.P79B76 2008
794.801'9—dc22   2007048929

❖ Contents ❖

❖ Acknowledgments ❖

To David Staley, for his enthusiasm and for his guidance in this project's early stages; to Steve Drummond, for his advice and encouragement in its later stages; to M.E. Sharpe, for their advance contract, which motivated my writing; to my colleagues at DePauw University, especially Meryl Altman, for their valuable institutional support; to Ben Frederick, for compiling the Glossary and the Videogame Bibliography, and for building me a bigger, faster machine for playing games; to Jacob Garbe, for his research assistance in summer 2006; to my students in ENG 155D (spring 2005) and HONR 300A (fall 2007), for their discussions, which have informed this project; to Richard Lynch and Twin Oaks, for depriving me of videogames for twenty-one days in January 2006; to my dad, who has never played a videogame, for his insight and dialogue on the project; to my mom, for her visits to Indiana in the summers of 2006 and 2007, which provided necessary relief from writing; to my brother, for doing the dirty work; to my sister, for compiling and distributing my Christmas list every year; and to my wife, for her patience, hard work, and love day in and day out: thank you.

To my daughters: regret that I would not take you to the pool while writing this book. No school tomorrow.

❖ Introduction ❖

Of Orangutans and Cyborgs

In spring 2007, visitors to the orangutan habitat at Zoo Atlanta enjoyed the curious spectacle of two lanky apes playing videogames. While four-year-old Bernas poked a touch screen mounted in a simulated tree trunk, his mother, Madu, swung carelessly in the vines overhead. Later, Madu herself descended and examined the screen, as an Associated Press (AP) photographer took her picture.[1]

The games, designed by primate researchers, challenge the orangutans to match sounds and images (right answers are rewarded with food pellets) or to make pictures using simple colors. Researchers at the zoo hope to use the games to gain insight into the animals' memory, reasoning, and socialization, which can aid efforts to protect endangered orangutans in Borneo and Sumatra. Tara Stoinski, a zoo conservationist, explains, "The more we understand about orangutans' cognitive processes, the more we'll understand about what they need to survive in the wild." Elliott Albers, a neuroscientist, adds, "Hopefully we can get the animals to find better sources of food more easily"[2]—better, presumably, than the food pellets at the zoo.

In addition to providing new information about orangutan cognition, Stoinski and Albers hope that the videogame experiment will serve the subtler but no less important purpose of raising awareness and sympathy for the animals, which will soon face extinction. Stoinski says that exhibiting Bernas and Madu while playing games "enables us to show the public how smart they are." The reaction of visitors seems promising. As Bernas drew splashy, colorful images on the screen, a woman watching with her three daughters marveled, "That's so cool. He can't get enough!"[3]

While allowing the orangutans to play videogames yields useful data, putting this experiment on public display is part of conservationists' strategy to make the apes seem more playful, more intelligent, and more creative—more like us. The picture produced by Bernas strikes us as a rudimentary work of art signaling the awakening of a creative imagination; it looks like something our own toddlers might make with magic markers or finger paints. Watching these shaggy orange creatures doing something so familiar to us draws them closer to us and recalls the Paleolithic evidence of our own creative awakening in the caves of Lascaux, France, and Altamira, Spain. The AP photograph of Madu touching her finger to the screen with the quiver of curiosity on her lips, circulated widely with the report of the experiment, also recalls the iconic moment from Stanley Kubrick's 1968 film, *2001: A Space Odyssey* (based on Arthur C. Clarke's novel) when brutish hominids, barely upright, confront the unknowable monolith and, touching their hands to its black surface, receive both the will to know and the will to power.

In Atlanta, a videogame consciously deployed by conservationists has served as a vehicle for fellow feeling with captive orangutans. By blurring the difference between the human and the animal, the display not only makes us care for the apes' survival but also places us, to our amazement or discomfort, in the borderland between the human and the "non-human," where the apes seem more like us, and we seem more like them. From a perverse viewpoint, Bernas and Madu at their touch screen seem less like primeval beings reaching toward sentience than modern troglodytes hunched in dimwitted fascination at their videogame consoles.

In the last decade, public discourse on videogames has made the opposing claims that the emergent medium will either elevate us, making us faster, more creative thinkers, or degrade us, making us illiterate, socially isolated, and pathologically violent. For their part, videogame advocates invoke cognitive theory and classroom evidence to argue that games may enhance human (as well as orangutan) learning. Marc Prensky, a prolific designer and promoter of business and educational simulations, argues in his 2001 book, *Digital Game-Based Learning,* that "it is possible to combine computer and videogames with a wide variety of educational content, achieving as good or better results as through traditional learning methods in the process." For Prensky, what makes games effective as pedagogical tools is their structure of goal-oriented tasks and rewards. "Opportunities for success," Prensky claims, lead to "a sense of purpose . . . fascination . . . [and] competence."[4]

In his 2003 book *What Video Games Have to Teach Us About Learning and Literacy,* education researcher James Paul Gee likewise argues that games help us to develop versatile cognitive skills. They teach us "to experience (see and act on) the world in a new way" and to develop "resources for future learning and problem solving." Gee concludes that games "operate with—that is, they build into their designs and encourage—good principles of learning, principles that are better than those in many of our skill-and-drill, back-to-basics, test-them-until-they-drop schools."[5] In other words, games may not only teach content, as Prensky shows, but they may also teach us to learn, accelerating cognitive development. Science writer Steven Johnson takes up Gee's argument and proffers it to mainstream readers in his book *Everything Bad Is Good for You: How Today's Popular Culture Is Actually Making Us Smarter,* published in 2005. Johnson claims that videogames teach us to probe an imaginary world laced with puzzles and hidden meaning, to form hypotheses based on our discoveries, to test these hypotheses in the game world, and to adjust our understanding of the game world according to the results of our tests. "When gamers interact with these environments," Johnson concludes in his book, "they are learning the basic procedure of the scientific method."[6]

Johnson hesitates to call videogames art, however. Their content, so often juvenile and offensive, is secondary in importance to the "cognitive challenges" they present. They are, he says, less like novels than the complex logic problems we find in standardized tests. But he hints that games might represent something more sublime than mere mental calisthenics. On the deepest level, he suggests, playing videogames is "about finding order and meaning in the world, and making decisions to help create that order." Johnson also suggests that educational technology advocates like Prensky and Gee hold a shallow view of the potential of videogames to transform human consciousness. "When I read these ostensibly positive accounts of video games," he writes, "they strike me as the equivalent of writing a story about the merits of the great novels and focusing on how reading them can improve your spelling. It's true enough, I suppose, but it doesn't do justice to the rich, textured experience of novel reading."[7]

In a 2006 *Wired* editorial, game designer Will Wright, creator of *SimCity, The Sims,* and *Spore,* writes even more lyrically of videogames as a fertile field for our innate creativity:

> The human imagination is an amazing thing. As children, we spend much of our time in imaginary worlds, substituting toys and make-believe for the real surroundings that we are just beginning to explore and understand. As we play, we learn. And as we grow, our play gets more complicated. We add rules and goals. The result is something we call games.[8]

Wright's vision of videogames as prosthetic enhancements of the human imagination recalls Donna Haraway's influential 1985 essay, "A Manifesto for Cyborgs: Science, Technology, and Socialist Feminism in the 1980s," in which she describes the cyborg, or cybernetic organism, as a revolutionary figure:

We are all chimeras, theorized and fabricated hybrids of machine and technology; in short, we are cyborgs. The cyborg is our ontology; it gives us our politics. The cyborg is a condensed image of both imagination and material reality, the two joined centers structuring any possibility of historical transformation.[9]

For Haraway, the cyborg, as a "hybrid of machine and organism," is "oppositional" and "utopian" in its resistance to biological, economic, or technological determinisms. It has "no origin story in the Western sense," no father or mother. It does not feel the "seductions" of "organic wholeness" or "higher unity." It "would not recognize the Garden of Eden; it is not made of mud and cannot dream of returning to dust."[10] The cyborg, essentially, is a posthuman entity. Videogames, likewise, are the first widely disseminated posthuman art form, emerging from the synthesis of human and artificial intelligence. While Haraway does not directly address videogames in her manifesto, we can recognize the videogame avatar as a species of cyborg and a manifestation of the revolutionary potential that Haraway senses in the convergence of human and machine. My avatar is a projection of my consciousness into the virtual world. Like my mirror image, my doppelganger, or my soul, he is both my other and myself. I travel, talk, and trade through him, but he is stronger, more beautiful, and more menacing than I am. He conceals and reveals my personality. He may serve as a means to channel my instinctual aggression, acquisitiveness, or lust, but he gives me no sensible pleasure or pain. He is immune to death, and in this he is most desirable and most distant from me. Our fables of creation, from the Golem and Pinocchio to Shelley's *Frankenstein* and Spielberg's *A.I.,* tell us that human artifice reaches, at it height, to recreate ourselves, and, in doing so, to match or to surpass the achievement of God. Videogame avatars, like Haraway's cyborgs, reflect these utopian dreams.

Still, the specter of the 1999 Columbine tragedy in Littleton, Colorado, looms and confronts utopian dreamers like Wright and committed advocates like Prensky, Gee, and Johnson with a troubling prospect—the prospect that games, while they foster learning and creativity, also foster sloth, misogyny, depression, disengagement, and, in extreme cases, ultraviolence. As Gee admits, "We can learn evil things as easily as we can learn moral ones."[11] Eric Harris and Dylan Klebold, the Columbine High School shooters, were avid gamers and amateur game designers, a fact that has bolstered arguments for government regulation of videogames. In a March 2005 broadcast, *60 Minutes* reported the story of a teenage triple murderer who, when captured by police, told them, "Life is like a video game. Everybody has got to die sometime." In the broadcast, Ed Bradley explains that Devin Moore, a neglected foster child, played *Grand Theft Auto III* "day and night for months." When Fayette, Alabama, police arrested him on suspicion of stealing a car and brought him to the station for questioning, Moore snapped, swiping a Glock from one of his captors, killing two officers and a police dispatcher, and fleeing in a stolen squad car. As he relates the details of the crime, Bradley walks through the rooms and corridors of the Fayette police station, tracing Moore's path as he killed the three men. A scenario in *Grand Theft Auto III,* he explains, likewise takes the player into a police station, where he frees a jailed convict, guns down cops, and escapes in a stolen squad car. This segment of the game, juxtaposed by *60 Minutes* editors to Bradley's walk through the actual killing zone, demonstrates an uncanny similarity between the rooms and corridors in the game and those where Moore killed three men.[12] In response to such cases, an American Medical Association (AMA) committee proposed in 2007 to designate videogame addiction as a diagnosable mental illness.[13]

Like the monolith in *2001,* videogames seem to promise enlightenment and destruction, cognitive enhancement as well as mental illness. Like the sentient shipboard computer HAL 9000, another memorable figure from Kubrick's film, games seem to play us as much as we play them, soothing us with soft tones as they eject us into the vacuum and seal the airlock. Yet even with its ominous notions of an abyssal alien monolith and a pathologically murderous supercomputer, *2001* remains a fable of humanism. The fashioning of animal bones into the first jagged weapons gives way to the fashioning of elegant interplanetary cruisers. The fearful monolith, in the end, does not represent an alien, antihuman malevolence, but rather a challenge that nurtures human evolution and urges us to higher states of being. Technology transfigures us.

In a more practical sense, videogames challenge us to define our humanity in relation to rapidly evolving technologies, which complicate our notions of identity, creativity, and moral value. This book situates videogames between the primitive and the posthuman, heeding both the dire warnings and the utopian promises, but searching for more reasonable and more specific ways to interpret the medium in the context of human experience and in the field of humanities research. I mean to continue an endeavor that has only begun in the last decade. In 2000, media scholar Henry Jenkins and the MIT Program in Comparative and Media Studies convened "Computer and Video Games Come of Age: A National Conference to Explore the Current State of an Emerging Entertainment Medium," the first summit between academics interested in the study of videogames and professional game designers. The following year, a group of like-minded media scholars led by Espen Aarseth, now a researcher at IT University of Copenhagen, founded the online journal *Game Studies,* one of the first forums dedicated exclusively to the emerging field of ludology, the study of games. In July 2002, at the end of the journal's first year, Aarseth reflected on its significance:

> As beginnings go, 2001 was a success: it was the year we could finally imagine and conceptualize a new academic field focused on the aesthetics, cultures,

and technologies of computer games. Not just as a part of media studies, or digital culture studies, or as educational technology, but also as an autonomous discipline of teaching and research, with an agenda not subjected to the rules of a condescending (or hostile) established academic field.[14]

I propose not to colonize the emergent field of game studies for the humanities but to build a bridge between the two fields and establish their common interests. While games have indeed gained a foothold in the academy, they have been adopted mostly in courses on applied technology and media studies. As we will see, videogames can be brought to bear on disciplines that have until now remained indifferent or, as Aarseth suspects, hostile to them. Works such as Prensky's, Gee's, and Johnson's have approached videogames from the perspective of cognitive science, regarding them as a means to learn other things; scholars like Aarseth have attempted to define game studies as a discrete discipline within the larger fields of cultural and media studies; I approach games from the perspective of the humanities, regarding them not only as the subject of a new discipline, but also as inventions that may inform or transform our work in a much wider range of disciplines.

I hope to make this cultural watershed intelligible to thinking persons who care about contemporary culture, but do not understand videogames or understand them only vaguely. We have heard too much, I think, that they play a part in youth violence and alienation. We have heard too much that they have conquered global markets and eclipsed film as the world's most profitable form of entertainment. We have heard too little, on the other hand, that they have begun to transform fundamental concepts in literature and the visual arts, as I discuss in Part I; that they have become a powerful form of political, ethical, and religious discourse, as I discuss in Part II; and that they have already influenced the way we teach, learn, and create, as I discuss in Part III.

I am broadly interested in the interrelations between the major trends in game design, the public controversies surrounding videogames, and the predominant critical positions in game studies. I do not mean to argue for or against these positions as much as I mean to explain them to readers who do not know whether to argue for or against them. I hope to draw games into mainstream critical discourse without undermining the recent efforts of videogame scholars, like Aarseth, to distinguish their discipline from literary and film studies. I speak to educators, scholars, and others who have limited experience with videogames but sense an intellectual responsibility to understand this significant cultural phenomenon. For initiated readers, I simply gesture to a broader relevance for their work. While I hope my ideas interest videogame specialists, I intend primarily to increase game literacy and expand the ranks of those who can talk about games, teach them, and teach with them, in order to increase our collective appreciation and understanding of them.

As the researchers at Zoo Atlanta have found, our fascination with Bernas and Madu arises from the sense of watching ourselves, not with detachment or mockery but with sympathy. We watch them learn as we watch our children learn. Many who read this book, though, have less skill with an Xbox 360 than Bernas has with his touch screen; I have you mind, not to convert you but to put a tool in your hand. I hope that you will approach this monolith with an orangutan's natural curiosity.

❖ Chronology ❖

c. 345 B.C.E. Plato composes *Laws,* describing play as a form of prayer

c. 330 B.C.E. Aristotle composes *Poetics,* outlining elements of dramatic storytelling

c. 398 Augustine composes *Confessions,* describing both his love and his revulsion for violent gladiator games

c. 975 *Exeter Book,* introducing the riddle poem to the English literary tradition, compiled

c. 1270 *Poetic Edda,* containing the wisdom contest between Odin and Vafthrudnir, compiled

c. 1415 Early Renaissance painters develop linear perspective

1516 Thomas More imagines a game for moral instruction in *Utopia*

1790 English printer creates *The New Game of Human Life,* a board game with moral lessons

1860 Milton Bradley creates *The Checkered Game of Life,* introducing moral choice into gameplay

1937 J.R.R. Tolkien writes *The Hobbit,* conceiving the imaginary realms that inspire later game designers

1938 Johan Huizinga writes *Homo Ludens,* theorizing gameplay as a fundamental component of civilization and human experience

1939	World War II begins
1943	U.S. Army develops Electronic Numerical Integrator and Computer (ENIAC), one of the earliest computers
1945	United States drops atomic bombs on Japan; World War II ends; Cold War begins
1947	Transistor introduced; cellular phone system conceived by military
1950	Alan Turing proposes the "Turing test" for artificial intelligence, a basis for later word-parsing programs like ELIZA
1952	Alexander Douglas designs Tic-Tac-Toe game on Electronic Delay Storage Automatic Calculator (EDSAC)
1954–1955	Tolkien writes *The Lord of the Rings* trilogy
1957	U.S.S.R. develops Intercontinental Ballistic Missiles and launches Sputnik
1958	William Higinbotham designs *Tennis for Two,* the first graphical videogame and forerunner of *Pong,* on oscilloscope computer
1959	United States develops Intercontinental Ballistic Missiles
1961	Integrated circuit, or microchip, introduced
1962	Cuban Missile Crisis; Steve Russell designs *Spacewar!* on PDP-1 mainframe
1965	United States escalates Vietnam War; Gordon Moore proposes "Moore's Law"
1966	Joseph Weizenbaum designs ELIZA, a program that inspires later text adventure games like Will Crowther's *Adventure*
1967	Roland Barthes publishes "Death of the Author," a seminal essay for new media theory

1968   Microprocessors introduced, leading to the development of the personal computer (PC)

1969   U.S. moon landing; Advanced Research Projects Agency Network (ARPANET), later the Internet, goes online

1971   Ralph Baer designs Magnavox Odyssey, the original home videogame console; Nolan Bushnell designs the original coin-operated arcade game, *Computer Space;* Gary Gygax creates *Chainmail,* forerunner of *Dungeons & Dragons*

1972   Floppy disc introduced; Bushnell designs *Pong* and founds Atari

1973   Minnesota Educational Computing Consortium (MECC), designers of first "edutainment" software, founded

1974   Gygax creates *Dungeons & Dragons,* a tabletop role-playing game that provides a formal and thematic model for later adventure and role-playing videogames; MECC develops *Oregon Trail*

1976   Will Crowther and Don Woods design *Adventure,* the original text adventure game, on PDP-10

1977   Atari 2600 released; the motion picture *Star Wars* premiers

1978   Richard Bartle and Roy Trubshaw design the first Multiuser Dungeon (MUD) on PDP-10; Taito develops *Space Invaders;* Warren Robinett designs *Adventure,* the original graphical adventure game, for Atari 2600

1979   Iran Hostage Crisis begins; commercial cellular phones introduced; Activision founded; Infocom founded; Atari develops *Asteroids;* Richard Garriott designs *Akalabeth,* the original graphical role-playing game for PC

1980   Operation Eagle Claw fails to rescue hostages; United States Special Operations Command (USSOCOM) founded to coordinate Special Forces operations; James Dallas Egbert III commits suicide, raising public concern about the effects of role-playing games; Atari secures copyright for games as intellectual property; Atari develops *Battlezone,* the first three-dimensional videogame, and *Missile Command,* a Cold War allegory; Namco develops *Pac-Man,* sparking the first videogame craze

1981 Iran Hostage Crisis ends; Nintendo develops *Donkey Kong,* introducing the videogame character Mario

1982 Compact disc (CD) introduced; Commodore 64, a PC widely used for gaming, released; Electronic Arts (EA) founded; Sega develops *Zaxxon,* the first isometric videogame; David Crane designs *Pitfall!* for Atari 2600; the motion picture *E.T.: The Extra-Terrestrial* premiers

1983 Ronald Reagan refers to U.S.S.R. as an "evil empire" and proposes Strategic Defense Initiative (SDI), or "Star Wars"; U.S. Marine barracks in Beirut bombed; Atari develops *Star Wars: Episode I; Robot;* and *E.T.: The Extra-Terrestrial;* Infocom develops *Planetfall;* the motion picture *WarGames* premiers

1984 Atari goes bankrupt; "Great Video Game Crash"; Alexey Pajitnov designs *Tetris,* the first widely addictive puzzle game

1985 Nintendo Entertainment System (NES) released; Quantum Computer Services, later America Online (AOL), founded; Origin develops *Ultima IV: Quest of the Avatar,* the first role-playing game emphasizing moral choice

1986 Chernobyl disaster; Internet opens to commercial use; Sega Master System released; Infocom develops *Trinity,* a work of interactive fiction portraying nuclear holocaust; Activision acquires Infocom; Lucasfilm Games launches *Habitat,* the first graphical online environment

1989 World Wide Web introduced; Nintendo Game Boy and Sega Genesis released; *Hot Circuits* exhibition at the American Museum of the Moving Image, the first venue to present videogames as cultural artifacts; Peter Molyneux designs *Populous* and Will Wright designs *SimCity,* the original "god games"

1991 Gulf War; U.S.S.R. dissolves; Cold War ends; Rodney King beating in Los Angeles; Super NES released; Sid Meier designs *Civilization; Neverwinter Nights,* the original massively multiplayer online role-playing game (MMORPG), launched on AOL

1992 Los Angeles riots serve as the thematic inspiration for *Grand Theft Auto: San Andreas;* id develops *Wolfenstein 3D,* the original first-person shooter

1993 Acclaim develops *Mortal Kombat,* raising public concerns about videogame violence; Cyan develops *Myst,* using CD technology to enhance graphic design of computer games; id develops *Doom*

1994 First congressional hearings on videogame violence; Entertainment Software Rating Board (ESRB) established; Independent Game Developers Association (IGDA), later Electronic Software Association (ESA), founded to protect the creative and commercial interests of the videogame industry

1995 Digital Video Disc (DVD) introduced; first Electronic Entertainment Expo (E3) held in Los Angeles; Nintendo 64, Sega Saturn, and Sony PlayStation released; LucasArts develops *Dark Forces,* a videogame sequel to *Star Wars: Episode VI: The Return of the Jedi,* an early instance of transmedia storytelling

1996 U.S. Marine Corps develops *Marine Doom,* a combat training program modified from *Doom;* rise of "military-entertainment complex"

1997 Origin launches *Ultima Online,* the first "synthetic world" with a dynamic in-game economy and sociology; id releases *Doom* source code to the public; Eric Harris distributes *Doom* mods on AOL

1999 Columbine High School shooting; Sega Dreamcast released; Verant launches *Everquest;* the motion picture *The Matrix* premiers

2000 Federal Trade Commission declares that violent videogames cause young people to "behave more violently"; Sony PlayStation 2 released; "Computer and Video Games Come of Age" conference at MIT draws media scholars and videogame developers into conversation; Raphael "Raph" Koster proposes "Declaration of the Rights of Avatars"; Valve appropriates *Counter-Strike,* a *Half-Life* mod created by hackers; Smilebit develops *Jet Set Radio,* the first game using cel-shaded animation; Will Wright designs *The Sims*

2001   September 11 attacks; War on Terror begins; Microsoft Xbox and Nintendo GameCube released; *Game Studies,* an online scholarly journal devoted to videogame studies, established; Afkar develops *Under Ash;* Lionhead develops *Black and White;* Rockstar develops *Grand Theft Auto III*

2002   *Blacksnow Interactive v. Mythic Entertainment* brings issue of gold farming before court; *Game On* exhibition at the Barbican Art Gallery; Bioware releases Aurora Toolkit with *Neverwinter Nights;* Westwood Studios convenes Mod College; Zipper develops *SOCOM: U.S. Navy Seals;* U.S. Army launches *America's Army*

2003   Devin Moore, an avid *Grand Theft Auto* player, kills two policemen and a police dispatcher in Fayette, Alabama; Routledge publishes *The Video Game Theory Reader,* bringing videogame studies closer to the critical mainstream; simultaneous release of *The Matrix: Reloaded* film and *Enter the Matrix* game; Linden Labs develops *Second Life;* Bioware develops *Star Wars: Knights of the Old Republic;* Hezbollah releases *Special Force; Red vs. Blue,* the first widely distributed machinima, premiers

2004   Education Arcade develops *Revolution;* Lionhead develops *Fable;* Persuasive Games develops *The Howard Dean for Iowa Game;* Rockstar develops *Grand Theft Auto: San Andreas;* Valve develops *Half-Life 2;* The History Channel implements the *Rome: Total War* game engine in its *Decisive Battles* series; *The Strangerhood* premiers

2005   Lucasfilm, Industrial Light and Magic, and LucasArts consolidate in San Francisco; Microsoft Xbox 360 released; "Hot Coffee" controversy; Lee Seung Seop dies after playing *World of Warcraft* for nearly fifty hours straight; U.S. senators Hillary Clinton, Joe Lieberman, and Evan Bayh introduce Family Entertainment Protection Act (FEPA) in response to "Hot Coffee"

2006   Nintendo Wii and Sony PlayStation 3 released; Bethesda develops *Elder Scrolls IV: Oblivion;* Left Behind Games develops *Left Behind: Eternal Forces,* the first mass-marketed evangelical videogame; Susana Ruiz, with support of MTV, designs *Darfur Is Dying* to raise awareness of humanitarian crisis

2007   Orangutans at Zoo Atlanta taught to play videogames; Manchester Cathedral controversy; American Medical Association (AMA) committee calls videogame addiction a mental illness comparable to alcoholism or gambling addiction; FEPA expires in committee

2008   Rockstar develops *Grand Theft Auto IV*; LucasArts develops *Star Wars: The Force Unleased*

❖ I ❖

POETICS

❖ 1 ❖

Videogames and Storytelling

In "Vafthrudnir's Sayings," part of the collection of Old Norse legends known as the *Poetic Edda,* Odin, the chief god of war and wisdom, seeks Vafthrudnir, the all-wise giant, in order to test the wisdom of the gods against that of their ancient adversaries. The two pose questions to each other until Odin wins Vafthrudnir's secrets, but the god does not revel in his triumph: Vafthrudnir foretells Odin's doom at Ragnarök. As bearer of the knowledge of the end of the world, Vafthrudnir is more than a giant. He is fate—all that is antagonistic or unknown to men and gods.

The dialogue between Odin and Vafthrudnir is a mythical expression of the wisdom contest, a game common in ancient cultures. The rules are simple: opponents swap questions or riddles until one fails to answer. In order to prove his wisdom superior to that of his opponent, the asker must know the answers to his own questions. Odin's answers to Vafthrudnir reveal the names of the horses that draw the sun and the moon, the name of the river that divides the realm of the giants from the realm of the gods, and the name of the field where the final battle between the gods and the giants will take place. Vafthrudnir's answers, in turn, reveal the history and the destiny of the world. In this sense, "Vafthrudnir's Sayings" is not only a game but also a story, a narrative collaboration between hero and antagonist that sketches the settings, characters, and plots comprising the Norse cosmos.[1]

As both contest and collaborative narrative, "Vafthrudnir's Sayings" is a literary archetype for current adventure and role-playing games, and it frames one of the predominant controversies among those who study the morphology and history of videogames. Are videogames games or stories? Are they primarily constituted by a system of rules, like tic-tac-toe or chess, or a sequence of imagined events, like a novel or a film? Adventure games and role-playing games that integrate cinematic storytelling with interactive problem solving stand at the center of the debate.

Ludologists, those who study videogames as games, insist that playing a game differs cognitively from reading a novel or viewing a film. While the emotional satisfaction we derive from a narrative relies on following a sequence of events and identifying with characters, the ludic or gameplay experience relies instead on the mastery of puzzles and problems. Markku Eskelinen pointedly writes, "If I throw a ball at you, I don't expect you to drop it and wait until it starts telling stories."[2]

Narratologists, those who study videogames as stories, draw a categorical distinction between puzzle games lacking narrative structure and adventure games with recognizable plots and characters. While they grant that interactivity radically complicates traditional concepts of plot and character, they claim that adventure games, like fiction and film, invite the audience to identify with characters and experience emotional catharsis. Media scholar and videogames advocate Henry Jenkins argues, "There is a tremendous amount that game designers and critics could learn through making meaningful comparisons with other storytelling media."[3]

The videogame industry reflects this theoretical divide, as development studios struggle to define the role of the videogame writer and, more broadly, to reconcile the tasks of game design and storytelling. What does the game writer actually write—the stories that frame the player's actions or the rules that govern them? Are these tasks connected or separate? Alexis Nolent, story designer for Ubisoft, differentiates game design from game narrative. "Game design," he says, "can be defined as establishing the rules for the game, what will make the game experience unique and addictive, while game writing is what will make it believable and worthwhile, from an emotional and quality standpoint." At the same time, Nolent admits that in the process of making of a game, game design and writing are closely related and perhaps "impossible to differentiate."[4] Technology writer Stephen Jacobs concludes that the growth of the industry depends on the theoretical reconciliation of game and story, as well as the more practical recognition and support of skilled writers: "In an environment where play drives story . . . the industry will need to learn how to identify, grow, and nurture these types of professionals."[5]

This debate about the nature of videogames is equally important for literary studies. While ludologists like Eskelinen, as well as more conventional literary scholars, believe that the study of games and the study of literature are separate disciplines, other scholars like Jenkins feel that videogames demand the scrutiny of literary scholars, and that literature, by the same token, demands the attention of game designers. Determining the relevance of videogames to literary studies, however, requires a new understanding of fundamental literary concepts. How can we craft a measured, emotionally compelling plot in a medium that grants the player control over the events in the story? How can we understand character development when the roles of reader and protagonist collapse into that of the player character, or avatar? If videogames are formed of both rule systems and narrative sequences, then what is the formal relation between rules and stories in games?

Like "Vafthrudnir's Sayings," videogames are both wisdom contests and narrative cosmogonies. They test our ingenuity and intellect while they immerse us in an imaginary world textured by narratives. By most accounts, however, the emergent genre still awaits its Shakespeare, Cervantes, or Dickens, one who can take a merely popular art form and make it transcendent. This chapter considers the craft and critique of narrative in relation to videogames and addresses the special problems that interactivity poses to established ideas of plot and character, particularly in adventure and role-playing games. Further, it evaluates game designers' recent attempts to synthesize narrative and ludic experiences through the development of new narrative models and more complex artificial intelligence (AI) systems— that aim not only to make games more successful on the market, but also more capable of transforming consciousness, in the way that great literature does.

Riddles, Rules, and Role-Playing

In their attempt to define their new discipline and defend it from colonization by literary scholars, ludologists sometimes reject literary analogues, in which puzzles serve as vehicles for the revelation of fictional worlds. In his book *Twisty Little Passages: An Approach to Interactive Fiction,* Nick Montfort surveys the cultural history of text adventure games and interactive fiction (IF), tracing the earliest synthesis of narrative and ludic experiences to riddle poems such as those in the *Poetic Edda* or in the tenth-century Anglo-Saxon codex known as the *Exeter Book.* Montfort suggests that these riddles posit a "metaphorical system" containing both a question and an answer. In order to find the answer, the reader must "inhabit" the system and engage it on its own terms. Likewise, Montfort concludes, adventure games invite the player to inhabit an imaginary world and, in playing the game, "to enact an understanding of that world."[6] Like riddles, adventure games begin with undiscovered meaning, a locked door, and the dark entrance to a cave. But they do not withhold the key from us. They only require us to search for it, and in order to do so, we must inhabit the world it evokes.

Gary Gygax seized on this idea of intellectual immersion as the premise of his 1974 tabletop role-playing game *Dungeons & Dragons,* in which players inhabit a Tolkienesque fantasy world, fight mythical monsters, and solve an array of problems—from disarming a trap to negotiating a diplomatic agreement between rival kingdoms. Gygax created the game by adapting the rules of his 1971 medieval strategy game *Chainmail* to encounters between individual characters. Instead of generic units of infantry and cavalry, *Dungeons & Dragons* players control avatars with simulated appearances, personalities, and skills that determine their capabilities within the game. Instead of flat, schematic battlefields, a verbally rendered fictional world, populated by other characters and deepened by subterranean labyrinths, provides the play environment. In short, Gygax transformed something like chess into something more like *The Hobbit*.

Because players may become dwarves, elves, wizards, rangers, and numerous other fantastic character types, Gygax, though he denies the charge, seems to have pilfered Tolkien and other popular fantasy writers.[7] But he also created something essentially new: not an epic narrative like Tolkien's, but rather a formal narrative system capable of generating an infinite number of stories. First, he conceived the "dungeon master," a player who assumes the role of the imaginary world itself, establishing the setting for the game, presenting quests and problems to the other players, and determining the results of player action within the game world. Second, he devised an intricate rule system governing player action, compiled in three core rule books: the *Player's Handbook, Monster Manual,* and *Dungeon Master's Guide.* In collaboration with the players, the dungeon master crafts an improvisational oral narrative to frame player action and applies the rule system, using die rolls and numerical tables to decide the outcome of exploration, combat, and attempted feats of skill. The rule books define the parameters for these collaborative narratives, setting the limits of what a dungeon master might contrive and what players might enact within that contrivance. As a contest of wisdom forming a mythic world, *Dungeons & Dragons* recalls "Vafthrudnir's Sayings" and the tradition of riddle poetry. As a system for generating stories through player interaction, it represents the first formal model for computer adventure games.

In 1975, programmer and role-playing enthusiast Will Crowther attempted to replicate the experience of playing *Dungeons & Dragons* on a PDP-10 mainframe computer at the technology company Bolt, Beranek, and Newman, synthesizing Gygax's dungeon master as a textual database containing descriptions of different game areas and a word parser to interpret the user input. Distributed on the ARPANET and modified many times by other programmers, including Don Woods, who shares credit with Crowther for the original game, Crowther's *Adventure* signaled the emergence of the text adventure. The game opens with a second-person description of the player's surroundings resembling one a dungeon master might offer at the beginning of a quest: "You are standing at the end of a road before a small brick building. Around you is a forest. A small stream flows out of the building and down a gulley." From here, we may issue a variety of commands, including directional movements and simple actions. The command "enter" takes us inside: "You are inside a building, a well house for a large spring. There are some keys on the ground here. There is a shiny brass lamp nearby. There is food here. There is a bottle of water here." We may "take" these useful items, "exit" the building, and go "down" into the gulley, where we find a metal grate. Using our keys, we "unlock" the grate and enter a small dark passage. Further exploration of the cave system beneath the grate uncovers treasures and monsters, including a pirate, who compulsively robs our collected tools and treasures. While the game is mediated by a machine instead of a dungeon master, it functions as a narrative system like *Dungeons & Dragons,* unfolding a story in response to player action, according to programmatic rules.

In 1978, Atari programmer Warren Robinett created *Adventure,* adapting Crowther's game to the graphical interface of the Atari 2600 console. Again, we face monsters, thieves, and puzzles in search of treasure. With a pixilated golden sword and small collection of tools, we scramble to slay three dragons, which replace the underground denizens in Crowther's game; evade a thieving bat, which replaces the pirate; and recover the magic chalice, which replaces Crowther's more varied treasures. Most significantly, Robinett's game, which we will examine more closely in the next chapter, gives a visible shape to the "you" in text adventure games. The small, plain square that flits across the screen is the first visual projection of the videogame player into the game world, the embryonic avatar, who has since assumed endlessly diverse proportions in current videogames.

Dungeons & Dragons, Crowther's *Adventure,* and Robinett's *Adventure* represent three of the most significant evolutionary leaps in the development of current adventure and role-playing games. Drawing from popular fantasy, Gygax created a narrative system comprised of rules for generating stories through player dialogue. Crowther, in turn, synthesized this narrative system on a computer, enabling solitary players to participate in dialogic storytelling. Robinett, finally, rendered Crowther's textual world in spaces, shapes, colors, and sounds, providing an archetype for subsequent graphical adventure franchises, such as *Ultima, King's Quest, Myst, Forgotten Realms, Final Fantasy,* and *The Elder Scrolls.*

The theoretical and practical difficulties of reconciling narrative and interactive gameplay arise from these same technical transformations. A computer cannot improvise in its programmed dialogue with a player, nor can it consider subtle nuances in its application of game rules, as a human dungeon master can. For these reasons, videogame plots often seem contrived, and characters often seem robotic. The industry recognizes that its own creations are, in a sense, Rube Goldberg machines that only awkwardly replicate the unmediated, organic dialogue at the core of *Dungeons & Dragons.* In the attempt to define an ideal form for interactive storytelling, the International Game Developers Association (IGDA) looks back, past the most popular and commercially successful games of the last three decades, to tabletop role-playing games: "The quest for interactive storytelling in games is a quest toward the perfect state that tabletop RPGs already had. . . . The problem is that a human GM [game master] can respond to any conceived action on the part of the player, but until artificial intelligence advances an astonishing degree, computer games are inherently limited in their flexibility."[8] Broadly speaking, then, the greatest challenge of game designers is to reconcile old ideas and new technology.

Narrative and Simulation

Composed in the fourth century B.C.E., Aristotle's *Poetics,* a classical basis for narrative theories, identifies plot as the "first principle" of tragedy, the key that unlocks the emotions of the audience. According to Aristotle, the beauty of a dramatic narrative, like a production of nature itself, exists in the essential unity of its parts. "Tragedy," Aristotle writes, "is an imitation of an action that is complete and whole. . . . A whole is that which has a beginning, a middle, and an end." Like a musician who excites emotion through the measured arrangement of notes, the tragedian arouses pathos through the careful sequencing of dramatic incidents: the "reversal," or twist, involving a sympathetic character whose tragic flaw leads him to crisis; the "recognition," or epiphany, that signals a "change from ignorance to knowledge"; and the catharsis or "purgation" of emotions sustained throughout the drama.[9]

Aristotle's dicta on tragic drama continue to guide our approach to the varied forms of modern narrative. In his influential 1983 handbook, *The Art of Fiction: Notes on Craft for Young Writers,* novelist John Gardner reinforces the Aristotelian notion of plot as the first principle of narrative structure. "Plotting," he writes, "must be the first and foremost concern of the writer. . . . Whatever the origin of the story idea, the writer has no story until he has figured out a plot that will efficiently and elegantly express it. . . . Though character is the emotional core of great fiction . . . [plot is] the focus of every good writer's plan." According to Gardner, effective narratives contain exposition, conflict, and resolution—a beginning, middle, and an end. While a writer may arrange and multiply these components in different ways, depending on the purpose and the length of the work, he cannot omit any of them without sacrificing the emotional engagement of the reader. Gardner advises that "working unit by unit, always keeping in mind what the plan of his story requires . . . the writer achieves a story with no dead spots, no blurs, a story in which we find no lapses of aesthetic interest."[10]

Narratologists suggest that adventure games feature a structure like that of a novel. As the story's hero, we progress through a series of conflicts and discoveries toward a gripping climax and an emotionally satisfying resolution. Awarded the 2004 Game Developers Choice Award for writing, Bioware's *Star Wars: Knights of the Old Republic* pits us against Darth Malak, an evil tyrant who plans to conquer the galaxy with the aid of the Star Forge, a hidden superweapon. After gathering allies and resources on the planet Taris, which is eventually besieged and destroyed by Malak, we flee to the planet Dantooine to learn the ways of the force and receive our quest from the Jedi Council: find and destroy Malak and the Star Forge. Our search for clues leads us to five different planets—Dantooine, Tatooine, Manaan, Kashyyyk, and Korriban—each containing its own stories and supporting characters. When we finally defeat Malak near the planet Rakata Prime, we have a choice: use the Star Forge to rule the galaxy alone, or destroy it and restore the Republic.

The game contains the necessary components of Aristotelian dramatic structure. It has a beginning, set on Taris and Dantooine, in which we become a Jedi. It has a middle, set on Dantooine, Tatooine, Manaan, Kashyyyk, and Korriban, in which we search for the Star Forge. And it has an end, set on Rakata Prime and the Star Forge, in which we defeat Malak. Our moment of recognition comes when we discover that our character is not merely a Jedi apprentice but Darth Revan, a powerful Sith lord thought to have been killed but secretly captured, purged of his identity and memories, and rehabilitated by the Jedi. As a potentially tragic hero, Revan—even as a rehabilitated Jedi—has requisite flaws: he lacks patience and feels the seduction of power. When the Jedi Bastila Shan defects to the dark side, she precipitates a reversal of fortune; Bastila, formerly our greatest ally against Malak, now becomes our enemy. We reach our resolution when we follow Bastila, return to the dark side, and usurp Malak—or when we remain with the light side and save the Republic. While the choice gives us nominal control over the outcome of the story, it does not undermine catharsis. In both cases, we destroy the antagonist Malak. Our decision to make Revan a tyrant or a savior simply determines whether *Knights of the Old Republic* is a tragedy or a romance.

Like novels and films, adventure and role-playing games contain subplots, known as side quests, but these subplots need not relate to the overarching narrative, and we may ignore them. On the other hand, we may also ignore the main plot in pursuit of myriad subplots. In *Knights of the Old Republic,* we may put off our search for the Star Forge and reconcile feuding families on Dantooine, hunt dragons on Tatooine, do *pro bono* legal work on Manaan, foment a slave revolt on Kashyyyk, or search for artifacts in the ancient tombs on

Korriban. Other games offer even greater potential for free play. In Bethesda's *The Elder Scrolls IV: Oblivion,* the central plot requires us to save the empire of Tamriel from an invasion of demonic forces and restore Martin Septim, the rightful heir to the imperial throne. We may ignore this quest, however, in order to pursue a hobby, such as collecting rare books, researching alchemical formulae, or robbing wealthy estates. In Rockstar North's *Grand Theft Auto: San Andreas,* we play Carl Johnson, a gangster who means to take control of the streets and avenge the murder of his mother. We may dally in our rise to power, however, by becoming a gambler, a pilot, a bodybuilder, a playboy, or a fast food junkie, wandering the vast game world of San Andreas seeking amusement wherever we may find it.

Aristotle and contemporary writers like Gardner represent the writer as a crafter whose art emerges through the diligent and expert assembly of narrative components. Videogames complicate this notion by giving the player control in assembling the events that unfold on screen, and in this sense, videogames seem to realize what Roland Barthes theorized as the "death of the author." According to Barthes, readers rather than authors create meanings from texts. The author "dies" in giving birth to the text, which becomes independent of the author in being read. This "death" frees the reader from having to interpret a text with reference to its authorial origin and multiplies its meanings.[11] In his influential book *Cybertext: Perspectives on Ergodic Literature,* however, Espen Aarseth claims that reader-response theory applies to videogames in only a limited way. "The performance of their reader takes place all in his head," Aarseth writes, "while the user of cybertext also performs in an extranoematic sense." In other words, when we read a novel, we make new meanings by interpreting the text. When we play a videogame, we make new texts by manipulating the words and images that appear on the screen. Aarseth's concept of "ergodic literature," or literature that requires the active participation of the user to unfold, underlies ludologists' skepticism about the possibility of narrative structure in videogames. In fiction and film, the author, screenwriter, or director constructs the reader's experience; in games, the player constructs his own experience, which is not necessarily narrative.[12]

Ludologists draw an important distinction between classical narrative structure and the "sandbox" style of play exemplified by *Oblivion* and *San Andreas.* In fact, Aarseth argues that what makes these games most enjoyable is not a cathartic experience, but rather the potential to escape from narrative constraints and freely explore the virtual environment. "The gameworld is its own reward," he writes.[13] Theorist and game designer Gonzalo Frasca elaborates on this distinction, describing the art of narrative as the structuring of events in a fixed sequence, and the art of simulation as the structuring of rules that players must follow as they determine events themselves. These rules may govern the way the game is played, the way the game is won, and even the way players themselves may manipulate the rules. Frasca envisions the game designer not as a storyteller but as a dungeon master, one who controls the conditions of play rather than assembling a narrative sequence.[14]

In narrative systems like *Dungeons & Dragons* and computer games, however, writing rules is inherently related to writing stories. The rules governing the ways we play the game enforce a narrative structure, especially when these rules stipulate a clear end to the game, a victory condition. While some games offer the potential for the sandbox style of play, these same games often integrate rules that compel our participation in the game's implicit narrative sequence. In Crowther's *Adventure,* for instance, our goal is to discover the pirate's horde and to escape the subterranean labyrinth, but if we become distracted or frustrated, the game sets us on the right path. If we enter the command, "kill myself," the game offers friendly counsel: "Violence isn't the answer to this one." Graphical adventure games like *Myst* simply do not allow us to manipulate objects in the virtual environment that are irrelevant to our goals, and most games include rules that make any disruption of the main plot impossible. In *Knights of the Old Republic,* several key components of the main quest to destroy Malak depend on Bastila: she devises the plan to seek the Jedi enclave on Dantooine; she discloses Revan's true identity; and she betrays us, prompting our own climactic decision at the end of the game. If we decide to kill Bastila early in the game, these narrative turns might never occur, but the combat system prevents us from attacking our companions. In *Oblivion* we may attack friendly characters, but if these characters, like Martin Septim, are essential to the game narrative, then we may only knock them unconscious, not kill them. In these cases, rules limit player action in order to preserve narrative structure.

In order to explain the difference between narrative and simulation in videogames, Frasca refers to the Greek distinction between *ludus,* the sort of play that "incorporates rules that define a winner and a loser," and *paidia,* the sort of play that does not.[15] While Aarseth insists that simulation, the free exploration of the game world, constitutes the essential appeal of videogames, some designers believe that games should offer us an Aristotelian sense of purpose and a promise of resolution. In *Black & White,* for instance, game designer Peter Molyneux has created a game in which we lord over the imagined world as a god, freely dominating our subjects for good or for evil. But he has also furnished us with a traditional conflict, an antagonist, and a purpose: defeat the rival god Nemesis. Even as he created a game that invites the player to question the conditions of the game world, Molyneux maintains that any game requires a victory condition to hold the player's interest. In an interview preceding the release of *Black & White,* Molyneux said, "I did god games before where you're regarding the world and you had to dominate. . . . What it missed was . . . an unfolding story that gave people objectives. Because it's all very well giving people untold powers, but unless they have a focus for these powers it soon becomes very boring."[16] Will Wright, creator of *SimCity* and *The Sims,* sees his games not as unfolding stories, but rather as tools that give players the means to create their own stories. "I'm thinking *The Truman Show,*" he says, "where you would allow the player to run around with a certain amount of free will, and the computer is like the director, who controls the envelope around Truman but can't directly affect his movements."[17]

The divergent views of Molyneux and Wright raise questions concerning the fundamental purpose of videogames. Should games, like novels or films, have narrative closure? Does the pleasure of playing a videogame reside in following a story or in making our own stories? Most videogame designers and critics consider both experiences vital and have sought a practical balance between *ludus* and *paidia,* a model that allows the player to roam freely through a vast and interesting world and, at the same time, to progress through an immersive storyline to a climactic ending—a model that has come to be known as the storyworld.

In her book *Narrative as Virtual Reality,* Marie-Laure Ryan envisions "the ultimate goal of art" as "the synthesis of immersion and interactivity," a seamless merging of narrative and simulation that preserves both a coherent narrative structure and the ability for the user to influence the progression of the story. For Ryan, this utopian vision of "total art" has taken shape in adventure and role-playing games that immerse us in the storyworld, a virtual space that serves as the frame for an array of potential stories emerging spontaneously through the collaboration of game designer and player. Ryan compares the structure of a storyworld to that of a theme park, with its discrete areas and attractions. Within this narrative Disneyland, the player navigates a network of semiautonomous settings and episodes, each one containing an assortment of nested narratives.[18]

We find literary analogues in collections of short stories or narrative poems such as Sherwood Anderson's 1919 short story collection *Winesburg, Ohio,* and in Edgar Lee Masters's 1915 poetry collection *Spoon River Anthology.* Each story or poem within these collections represents an independent narrative with a familiar Aristotelian contour. A thorough exploration of Winesburg or Spoon River and their citizens, however, reveals subtle connections, hidden or fragmentary narratives, and a larger story. The nature of this larger story, in part, depends on our choices of which nested narratives we read and the order in which we read them.

In the effort to reconcile narrative and simulation, game designers have adopted the storyworld as a paradigm. The IGDA calls its model for interactive narrative Dynamic Object-Oriented Narrative, which it describes as networks of scenes nested within a larger network of interconnected episodes or settings. Their terminology derives from the computer programming strategy of "composing the data space from objects, which contain other objects, which contain other objects."[19] Hal Barwood, a former designer for LucasArts, describes storyworlds in more practical terms: "We have elements of stories . . . scenes and locations that can be put together in various ways depending on how the player plays."[20]

The navigable galaxy in *Knights of the Old Republic* contains seven planets, each one containing an array of potential quests. Some of these quests are contained on a single planet; others require us to visit several or all of the planets. Likewise, the empire of Tamriel in *Oblivion* contains a network of seven cities radiating from the central Imperial City. While the surrounding wilderness contains hidden dungeons and random encounters with monsters and bandits, most of the quest narratives originate in the cities. *Oblivion* also includes many quests with longer and more satisfying dramatic arcs that take us to multiple cities, such as becoming a guild master, finding a cure for vampirism, and foiling the demon who has unleashed his minions throughout the realm. Set in a parallel California and Nevada, *San Andreas* contains three major cities—Los Santos, San Fierro, and Las Venturas—corresponding to Los Angeles, San Francisco, and Las Vegas. Each city contains a number of unique districts and sprawls outward into surrounding counties containing smaller towns and other landmarks. As in the other games, each location offers a range of discrete quests, but the main quest to restore Carl's gang takes us to all three cities.

In some ways, the storyworld guarantees the potential for a coherent narrative structure. Although we may choose to disrupt narratives, most adventure and role-playing games carefully script and constrain player action through limited dialogue options and the use of cinematic cut scenes to establish major narrative events and transitions. In her model of interactive narrative, Ryan emphasizes a necessary balance between active and passive player experiences, similar to Molyneux's design strategy:

> The implementation of dramatic narrative in an interactive environment requires a delicate coordination of the user's actions with the goals of the system. . . . It is by controlling the general path of the reader, maintaining a steady forward progression, limiting decision points, or neutralizing the strategic consequences of decisions that interactive texts can guarantee narrative coherence.[21]

In *Knights of the Old Republic,* for example, the events that provide a stable narrative contour emerge cinematically at programmed moments: Malak's destruction of Taris, Revan's discovery of his true identity, and Bastila's defection. Likewise, *Oblivion* opens with a cinematic sequence showing the assassination of Uriel Septim, emperor of Tamriel. Later sequences show the emperor's surviving son, Martin Septim, taking command of his father's loyal bodyguards in a mountain stronghold; the destruction of the city of Kvatch by a horde of demons; and Martin's transformation into a messianic figure who saves the empire. Through the combination of active and passive player experiences, these games allow the player to control events, but frames them within an established narrative structure.

At the same time, these storyworlds offer the potential for free exploration and enable what narratologists and game designers call "emergent narratives." Jenkins writes:

> Emergent narratives are not prestructured or preprogrammed, taking shape through the gameplay, yet they are not as unstructured, chaotic, and frustrating as life itself. . . . Game spaces are designed to be rich with narrative potential, enabling the story-constructing activity of the players. . . . It makes sense to think of game designers less as storytellers than as narrative architects.[22]

According to Jenkins, the synthesis of narrative and simulation in emergent narratives becomes practical if we conceive narrative not sequentially, as Aristotle did, but spatially. Game designers often create an imaginary landscape in which stories can occur before creating the stories themselves.

In his comprehensive and influential book *Designing Virtual Worlds,* Richard Bartle identifies geography as the first principle of game design, just as Aristotle and Gardner privilege plot: "Designers of virtual worlds often choose maps as the first concrete realization of their dreams. In any venture that has place or travel at its core, a map is the natural starting point. In constructing a map, not only are ideas given form, but new ideas are suggested. . . . Geography is therefore where designers turn their concepts into reality."[23] Confronted with these virtual worlds, players themselves become cartographers, gradually recording the dimensions of the imaginary world as it reveals itself. In text adventure games, we draw these maps ourselves; successful completion of the game demands an accurate understanding of the game space. More recent graphical games draw the map for us and feature an indispensable map mode, in which we can temporarily extract ourselves from the virtual environment and apprehend the storyworld as a whole. In *Hamlet on the Holodeck: The Future of Narrative in Cyberspace,* an exploration of the shape of narrative in cyberspace, Janet Murray, who has pioneered the exploration of literary studies and new media, writes, "The challenge for the future is to invent an increasingly graceful choreography of navigation to lure the interactor through ever more expansive narrative landscapes."[24] Whether we adopt choreography, architecture, or cartography as a model, the ascendance of videogames as a literary form, it seems, will rely on the understanding of gameplay as a form of navigation.

Character, Identity, and Sympathy

The difficulty we have in identifying with videogame characters poses another major problem for critics and game designers who would see videogames as a new literary form. Although current videogames employ richly detailed graphics, professional voice acting, and relatively nuanced artificial intelligence, critics often remark that game characters remain flat and automated. They look the same, repeat the same greetings, endearments, and insults, and walk the same programmatic paths through the virtual streets. Even the most sophisticated storyworlds are populated with characters that seem more like chatterbots rather than living actors.

While Aristotle and Gardner argue that plot is the first principle of drama and fiction, they also recognize the importance of character development. Aristotle argues that characters must possess "goodness," "appropriateness," and "consistency" in their actions, and that they should represent persons who are uncommon and noble but also near to the understanding of the audience.[25] Gardner likewise claims that "characters must stand before us with . . . such continuous clarity that nothing they do strikes us as improbable behavior for just that character." The writer must "make us see and feel vividly what his characters see and feel—to draw us into the characters' world as if we were born to it." In other words, characters should be sympathetic and coherently portrayed, exemplary but identifiable.[26]

Game designers have struggled to meet these standards of sympathy and consistency. In *Writing for Video Games,* game designer Steve Ince argues that "a game's important characters must be treated as . . . if they were being developed for a top film or TV series. They should be fully rounded with a relevant back story, clear motivation and a well-defined sense of what makes them tick." In many games, Ince observes a lack of dramatic tension in the dialogue, which serves mainly as an expository device to provide information, tools, or rewards to the player character.[27] Barwood also believes that game characters fail to engage our emotions. "Stories are really about humanity," he observes, "and hopes and fears of the players are what's in the balance. . . . Can a story game evoke tears? I've never encountered such a thing."[28]

Game designers like Barwood, Ince, and Nolent, as well as scholars like Jenkins and Montfort, suggest that the industry might address the lack of good characterization in videogames by raising the standards of game writing or by adding professional fiction writers or screenwriters to design teams. The digital medium, however, poses a problem that designers cannot solve simply by hiring better writers or by approaching games as if they were films or television shows. A digitally rendered character, after all, is categorically different from an image of a real person captured by a camera. Digital animator Steve Theodore suggests that the more closely a digital character resembles a real person, the more difficulty players have in forming an emotional connection with the character. Theodore refers to Masahiro Mori, whose research in robotics reveals that "as machines approach a more convincing human appearance, they stop being pleasantly anthropomorphic and quickly become . . . creepy." Carefully rendered game characters seem lifelike but not living, more like robots or animated corpses than people. Theodore sees them as "failed representation[s] of humanity . . . broken people," less appealing and sympathetic to audiences than "obviously cartoonish" characters like Mickey Mouse or "pleasantly anthropomorphic" robots like C-3PO in *Star Wars*.[29] More realistic rendering of human characters, in other words, is not the same as more sympathetic characterization. Theodore concludes that game characters should be sufficiently anthropomorphic to invite identification, but not so humanlike that they seem inhuman.

For this reason, perhaps, some of the most memorable game characters are nonhuman. Steve Meretzky's memorable science fiction text game *Planetfall*, for instance, features a likeable robot named Floyd, who assists the player character in the completion of puzzles and other tasks. Floyd is not simply a tool, an extension of the player's own capabilities, however. Near the end of the game, he sacrifices himself to save us. Mangled by "hideous mutated monsters," Floyd falls into our arms with only moments to live, in a highly sentimentalized scene:

> You drop to your knees and cradle Floyd's head in your lap. Floyd looks up at his friend with half-open eyes. "Floyd did it. . . . Floyd good friend, huh?" Quietly, you sing Floyd's favorite song, the Ballad of the Starcrossed Miner. . . . Floyd smiles with contentment, and then his eyes close as his head rolls to one side. You sit in silence for a moment, in memory of a brave friend who gave his life so that you might live.

In response to Barwood's claim that a videogame never moved him to tears, Patricia Peiser, only somewhat in jest, says, "I can confess, I cried when Floyd died. And the six guys who were in the room with me did, too!"[30] From a more critical perspective, Montfort cites Floyd as one of the first characters that caused players and designers "to think about what made for a good character in an interactive work."[31]

The "hunter-killer" droid HK-47, who appears in both *Knights of the Old Republic* and its sequel, *Knights of the Old Republic II: The Sith Lords,* is

Floyd's bad seed. He acts like our servant and addresses us as "master," but he clearly considers himself superior to organic "meatbags" and, like a twisted Mr. Spock, continually expresses exasperation and mockery for human foibles. While Floyd sacrifices his life to save ours, HK-47, as a manufactured assassin, holds no regard for any life form. At one point, he offer's an assassin droid's creation story:

> Query. . . . Why were we created? Do we have a purpose? Why are we commanded to assassinate and kill? Statement: It is a long story, but I will keep it short. Recitation: Once upon a time organic meatbags bred out of control and filled the galaxy. There are different meatbags across different planets, all bumping into each other. They talk a great deal and threaten each other for various reasons, mostly involving mating, survival, and resources. It is really quite tiresome. . . . We were created as a way of enforcing a certain galactic view of our masters, of imposing our masters' will on the galaxy through extermination of other organics.

For his dark comic relief, HK-47 won the 2005 Game Developers Choice Award for original game character.

Floyd and HK-47 are unmistakably mechanical, and they speak in a distinctly robotic style, making them pleasantly anthropomorphic but not uncannily lifelike. The two robots seem most human in the ways they relate to us, demonstrating that the potential for sympathetic characterization in videogames does not lie in more realistic graphics but rather in sharper artificial intelligence systems that simulate the nuanced, spontaneous dialogue of organic narrative systems like *Dungeons & Dragons*. Within these systems, characters would seem to remember past encounters, modify their behavior accordingly, and form an emotional relation to the player character rather than simply reacting to programmatic prompts.

Designers have recently sought to simulate memory and emotional response in game characters by creating "influence systems," in which our actions determine not only narrative trajectory, but also the appearance of our character and the tenor of our interaction with other characters. *Knights of the Old Republic* and its sequel implicitly pose the Machiavellian question of whether it is better for a leader to be loved or feared. We may coerce other characters through intimidation and violence or gain their trust through negotiation and aid. If we follow the path of the dark side, our healthy complexion gradually turns gaunt and ghastly. In Molyneux's *Fable,* we may likewise become a renowned paladin or a notorious scoundrel. When we happen upon a traveler in distress, we may escort him to safety or rob him; when a foe begs our mercy, we may spare his life or take it. When we enter a town, children either flock to us in admiration or flee our wrath. Our reputation rises and falls with every action, and both games encourage us to form romantic attachments with other characters. In these more recent games, narrative progression depends on the completion of tasks as well as the methods we employ, and the game world holds us responsible for our actions. By roughly simulating a social contract, these influence systems encourage us to consider our actions within the game world more carefully. Given the consequences, we tend to treat our game decisions like real decisions and come to identify more closely with our avatar. The longer we play, the more our character reflects our choices.

Just as the player's involvement in the videogame plot destabilizes narrative structure, the potential for the player to project his or her own identity on the avatar complicates characterization. Ince suggests that player characters with the same depth and detail as characters in fiction and film risk alienating the player. "Because no two players are the same," he argues, "the way they view the player character are going to be different. . . . The motivation and objectives of the character should never be at odds with those of the player."[32] By limiting information about the player character's motivation, personality, and background, game designers create blank slates, characterless characters, more easily adaptable to the player's own identity—such as Darth Revan at the outset of *Knights of the Old Republic,* a character purged of memory and personality. What makes a memorable character in fiction and film, in fact, stands at odds with what makes an effective player character.

Some designers see the potential not only for emergent narratives, but also for emergent characters. Just as plots might emerge spontaneously through player action, so too might personalities. Molyneux asks, "Why shouldn't we create a game that allows the game to look at the person who's playing it and change itself to cater to that one single person?"[33] The influence systems in *The Sith Lords* and Molyneux's *Fable* gesture to this vision of games that play us, and they promise that more advanced artificial intelligence, rather than improved graphical rendering, will give rise to better game characters. Just as interactivity invites us to think of narrative in spatial terms, it also begs a new understanding of characterization. While game characters should be classically sympathetic and consistent, they should also be capable of simulating spontaneous communication and psychological nuance.

Narrative and the Digital Divide

Although videogames draw from the fonts of mythology and a range of literary genres, we hesitate to speak of game writers in the way that we speak of screenwriters, playwrights, and novelists. Our image of game writers more closely resembles that of television staff writers: a team of overworked apprentices who, under stifling commercial constraints, slap together, in assembly-line style, a series of formulaic and often flawed products. To some extent, the ambivalence toward games as a narrative art form arises from the critical impulse to lump them together with other narrative art forms and to ignore the peculiar technical component that makes them essentially different from novels and films. Because interactivity compels us to reconsider fundamental notions of plot and character, we find that what makes a bad novel—flat characters, narrative inconsistency, or a lack of closure—does not necessarily make a bad game. Understanding the potential of videogames as literature depends on understanding the medium itself. What can writers achieve in the digital realm that would be impossible in text or film? The most intriguing concepts in interactive narrative—Ryan's storyworld, Jenkins's emergent narratives, and Molyneux's characters that change in response to player action—begin with this question. In practical terms, however, the rapid and continuing evolution of digital technology has made it difficult to establish clear aesthetic standards and critical approaches to interactive narrative.

In his essay "Games, the New Lively Art," Jenkins suggests that videogames exist in a stage comparable to that of film in the early twentieth century, still a novelty to be tinkered with rather than a medium to be crafted and studied. He suggests several trends that designers and literary critics should promote in order to ensure the future of games as a serious art form, including the pursuit of wider audiences, the development of psychologically nuanced game characters, and the discussion of the social and ethical impact of games from a more informed perspective. Jenkins argues that all of these things depend on the dialogue between the videogame industry and humanities scholars.[34] At the MIT Program in Comparative Media Studies' "Computer and Video Games Come of Age" conference in 2000, Jenkins himself brought these different constituencies together with some success, but the digital divide remains. Humanities scholars read and watch movies, but most do not own game consoles, content to leave those to their kids. If we would see videogames as something more than a juvenile art form, videogame technology itself must become more stable, more integrated into the human experience out of which literature emerges, and slower in its evolution, so that writers may develop a mastery of the digital medium, and critics may reflect on the significance of the technological and theoretical challenges it poses.

If videogames, like literature, would transform consciousness and enthrall both critical and popular audiences, its creators must be artists as well as artisans, trained in the craft of writing, as well as the use of the complex tools necessary to tell stories in this new medium. At present, we have writers who know how to tell compelling stories but lack the skill or the inclination to tell them in videogames. We also have technicians who are adept in digital technology, but lack the skill or inclination to tell compelling stories. Only within the last few years have game companies recognized the need to add professional writers to their development teams. Still, videogames await their Shakespeare, their Cervantes, or their Dickens. I think they would profit more, however, from a Ben Franklin, one equally capable of using a printing press and of crafting words to amuse, incite, and inspire. Without one of these skills, Franklin knew, the other is useless.

❖ 2 ❖

Videogame Aesthetics

On February 15, 1913, the International Exhibition of Modern Art opened at the Sixty-ninth Regiment Armory in New York City, featuring works by Claude Monet, Vincent Van Gogh, Pablo Picasso, Henri Matisse, and Marcel Duchamp. The Cubists, in particular, generated a critical furor. A *New York Times* critic famously described Duchamp's *Nude Descending a Staircase, No. 2* as "an explosion in a shingle factory."[1] Others questioned the talent and sanity of the avant-garde artists. In response to a similar exhibition in London in 1910, Virginia Woolf wrote, "about December 1910 human character changed."[2]

The advent of videogames, particularly when we speak of them as an emergent art form, has aroused a similar range of responses. Some believe that games signal a profound change in cultural consciousness. Game designer Denis Dyack, for example, makes the monumental claim that "video games are probably the most advanced form of art thus far in human history," because they synthesize text, image, sound, video, and the active participation of the audience into a unified aesthetic experience.[3] Others simply dismiss them as a crass novelty. In March 2000, *Newsweek* critic Jack Kroll riled the videogame community when he wrote that "games can be fun and rewarding in many ways, but they can't transmit the emotional complexity that is the root of art."[4] Kroll's article prompted media scholar and videogames advocate Henry Jenkins to respond in MIT's *Technology Review,* "Computer games are art—a popular art, an emerging art, a largely unrecognized art, but an art nonetheless."[5]

In November 2005, film critic Roger Ebert rekindled the debate, writing in his online column that games are "inherently inferior to film and literature." Ebert reasons that great art comes from the confident hand of a master, and that interactive games deny artists the necessary command of the medium. "Video games by their nature require player choices," he argues, "which is the opposite of the strategy of serious film and literature, which requires authorial control."[6] Writer and filmmaker Clive Barker publicly challenged Ebert at the Hollywood and Games Summit in June 2007, arguing that player control itself has aesthetic value, in that it allows us to "take ourselves away from the oppressive facts of our lives." Online, Ebert shot back: "Spoken with the maturity of an honest and articulate 4-year old." Although he admits that he knows games by reputation rather than experience, Ebert points out that in every game the player controls the outcome. "Art seeks to lead you to an inevitable conclusion," he argues, "not a smorgasbord of choices."[7] In Ebert's opinion, "video games can be . . . challenging and visually wonderful," but they ultimately "represent a loss of those precious hours we have available to make ourselves more cultured, civilized and empathetic."[8]

For the videogame community, these widely publicized debates have come to represent the deeper ideological struggle for videogames to claim legitimacy as an art form. Kroll and Ebert, it would seem, stand for the stodgy old guard, while Jenkins and Barker stand for the new and the visionary. This oversimplified view, however, misses what is really at stake in the argument: two contending theories of art, which disagree on the fundamental value of interactivity. On one hand, games, like novels and films, tell compelling stories. They provide for a deeply immersive experience, inviting us, as Barker observes, to transcend the "oppressive facts of our lives" and to escape to imaginary worlds. On the other hand, they allow us to take control of images and events on screen, inviting an interactive engagement with these imaginary worlds. For Ebert, the capacity for the audience to manipulate the content and structure of an artwork undermines its aesthetic potential. He asserts a classical aesthetic principle that recalls Aristotle's definition of drama as a skillful arrangement of key narrative components: a beginning, middle, and an end, revelation and catharsis. Any intervention by the audience inevitably destroys this underlying order. "To my knowledge," Ebert writes, "no one in or out of the [videogame] field has ever been able to cite a game worthy of comparison with the great dramatists, poets, filmmakers, novelists and composers."[9] For Jenkins and others, however, interactivity demands critical consideration as a dynamic new aesthetic principle. Duchamp's *Nude Descending a Staircase* looks like an explosion in a shingle factory only if we insist that a nude look fleshy, rosy, and ripe. Games, likewise, seem chaotic only if we insist they look like plays, poems, films, novels, or symphonies. Videogames, like Cubism, requires a basic adjustment in our critical perspective.

At the same time, even the most enthusiastic apologists claim that while videogames have the potential to revolutionize aesthetic consciousness, they remain, at present, an "infant" art form. Steven Poole, author of *Trigger Happy: Videogames and the Entertainment Revolution,* writes, "The aesthetics of the virtual spaces that videogames create . . . are still in a kind of infancy."[10] In his well-known essay, "Games, the New Lively Art," Jenkins compares the current state of videogames to the state of cinema in the early decades of the twentieth century, before film technology stabilized and legitimate *auteurs* began to develop the unique aesthetic capabilities of the medium. Jenkins cites game designer Warren Specter, who says, "We're just emerging from infancy. We're still making (and remaking!) *The Great Train Robbery* or *Birth of a Nation* or, to be really generous, maybe we're at the beginning of what might be called our talkies period."[11] Likewise, media critic Peter Lunenfeld compares current games to television in the age of *Mr. Ed, Combat,* and *Bewitched,* before contemporary video artists approached the medium with heightened critical awareness. Someday, Lunenfeld says, some "Game Boy" out there "will grow up and rock our world, for real."[12]

This conventional idea of videogames as an infant art form poses significant questions concerning videogame aesthetics, which this chapter addresses. First, who are its parents—what does it owe to painting, sculpture, architecture, photography, film, and animation? And what will it be when it grows up—what special aesthetic qualities will come to define the medium? Understanding a new art form naturally takes place in the context of our understanding of established art forms. Theorists' attempts to define the videogame aesthetic has consistently led them to search for games' sister art, to trace their cultural genealogy, variously, to film, painting, photography, performance art, animation, graphic art, or architecture. While these comparisons usefully situate videogames within better understood aesthetic traditions, we must also consider the original aspects of the new aesthetic of interactivity, hailed by designers like Dyack and critics like Jenkins. As visual art, videogames have followed the rapid parallel development of computer technology, and while they have borrowed concepts from other art forms, they have also evolved a unique aesthetic of presence and action, founded on the laws of motion and perspective and on our perceptual and psychological relations to space.

Abstraction, Representation, and Motion

As I ascend into the Jerrall Mountains northwest of Bruma, the forest thins into highland meadow and yellow wildflowers brush my leather greaves. A chill wind tousles the scrub grass. I reach the higher crags, where the setting sun casts a pink glow on the snow and glints on my silver armor. In the dying light, the exquisite marble of the Ayleid ruin rises before me, cracked and skeletal. I turn to gaze at the faint stars appearing in the purple sky to the east, as another day passes like a dream in Bethesda's beautifully rendered epic role-playing adventure, *The Elder Scrolls IV: Oblivion*, a game universally praised for its lush, finely detailed graphics. Moving within this immersive world is something like floating through a Hudson River School painting in a wash of serotonin. The landscape is animated, soft around the edges, and glowing. *Oblivion* does not quite overwhelm us with the sublime, but it does offer the same pleasure we feel experiencing a work of art. As Poole writes in *Trigger Happy*, "The inner life of video games—how they work—is bound up with the inner life of the player. And the player's response to a well-designed video game is in part the same sort of response he or she has to a film, or to a painting: it is an aesthetic one."[13] In part, our aesthetic response to games like *Oblivion* comes from our sense of presence in the virtual world, an experience intensified by such details as the rough texture of a pine tree's gray-brown bark, the play of tall grass in the breeze, and the nearly imperceptible changes in ambient light as the hours pass in the game world.

Oblivion vividly illustrates the two dominant trends in the graphical design of videogames over the last four decades: the movement from abstraction to photorealism; and the movement from a two-dimensional, third-person perspective to a three-dimensional, first-person perspective. Unlike the artists featured in the Armory exhibition, who embraced abstraction by choice, the first generation of game designers, limited by the capabilities of computer hardware, did so by necessity. Early arcade games such as Atari's *Asteroids, Battlezone,* and *Tempest* simulated objects in space using simple wireframe models rendered against a black background. Other games like Atari's *Breakout* and Taito's *Space Invaders,* as well as early console games, rendered images using bitmaps, simple arrangements of colored pixels. Current games like *Oblivion* construct three-dimensional virtual worlds using polygonal models; each image consists of a dizzying multiplicity of basic geometric figures such as triangles and squares. These shapes, interlocking with each other according to the rules of Euclidean geometry, compose the basic substance of virtual reality, just as interlocking atoms and molecules combine to form material reality. The greater the memory and processing power of the game platform, the greater the number of polygons designers can use in the construction and animation of the game world. The greater the number of polygons, the more lifelike the game world appears. Sharp, angular edges give way to fluid, organic forms, with surfaces mapped with realistic textures such as grass, brick, or flesh. A mathematical construct comes to life.

In this way, the level of visual detail and realism achievable in videogames corresponds directly to the level of technology used to create and run them. Videogame scholar Mark J.P. Wolf explains that the specifications of early consoles imposed strict aesthetic limitations on designers:

The Atari 2600 had only 128 bytes of RAM (and no disk storage), and a graphics clock that ran at roughly 1.2 MHz. Early cartridges for the Atari 2600 contained as little as 2 or 4 kilobytes of ROM. The television image produced for games had only 192 lines vertically and 160 color clocks, or pixels, across. Because the microprocessor was so slow, most games used only half of the 192 lines available, and roughly half of the resolution as well. . . . In addition to the low resolution, the graphics making up the playing field (or playfield) laid over the solid-color background were drawn only on the left side of the screen, and then duplicated on the right half of the screen . . . accounting for much of the horizontal symmetry found in early Atari games.[14]

Former Atari programmer Warren Robinett recalls the difficulty in realizing an artistic vision within the technical constraints of early game systems. When he discovered Will Crowther and Don Woods's original text adventure game, *Adventure,* he sought to recreate it as a graphical adventure, translating Crowther and Woods's imagined spaces, filled with monsters and magic, into the simple sprites and abstract playfields of the Atari 2600. He writes, "My main breakthrough, I think, was figuring out how to adapt the adventure game idea from its birth medium (with the player reading text descriptions and typing text commands) to the video game medium (with color, motion, animation, sounds, and joystick controllers)."[15]

Robinett's *Adventure,* released in 1978 and named after its textual predecessor, illustrates the player character, the "You" of text adventures, as a small square icon capable of movement within a network of screens, or "rooms," containing castles, labyrinths, monsters, and hidden items. Unlike the great majority of arcade and console games at the time, the game imposes no scoring system or time limit; our quest is simply to find the Enchanted Chalice and carry it back to the Gold Castle, our home base. Three roaming dragons threaten to gobble us at every turn, and a pesky bat tries to snatch whatever we carry. We have several tools at our disposal: a sword to kill the dragons, a bridge to leap the walls, keys to open the castle gates, and a magnet to grab other objects from a distance. We may, however, carry only one of these objects at a time.

The contrast between *Oblivion* and *Adventure* reveals that videogame aesthetics are subject to Moore's Law, the dictum presented by Intel Corporation cofounder Gordon Moore in 1965 that computing power would double about every two years. As a result of the accelerated development of microprocessors, the aesthetic possibilities of videogames have likewise grown exponentially, as if designers have moved from the caves of Lascaux to the Sistine Chapel in three decades. The Xbox 360, a console that runs *Oblivion,* contains a 120-gigabyte hard drive and three 3.2-gigahertz processors capable of handling 500 million polygons per second. The average size of Xbox 360 games is about four gigabytes, about 1 million times larger than the average Atari game; as one of the largest Xbox 360 games, *Oblivion* is almost 2 million times larger than *Adventure*. This vast technological difference is dramatically apparent on screen. In one case, we watch blinky pixels flit across a flat, gray playfield. In the other, we watch the sun set from a snowcapped mountain peak, or gothic cathedral spires loom over a fortified city, or a luminous specter rise from a finely engraved sarcophagus. In videogames, better technology results in deeper and more satisfying aesthetic experiences.

Adventure, nevertheless, introduces fundamental graphical concepts for successive generations of action-adventure games, including *Oblivion.* First, it substitutes scoring with a quest, a narrative. Second, it expands gameplay beyond a single screen, transforming the standard Atari playfield into a larger game world that reveals itself as we move within it. Third, it populates the game world with monsters with basic artificial intelligence; the dragons pursue us relentlessly, but if we carry the sword, they will flee. Fourth, it incarnates us as an avatar, a player character icon capable not only of single-minded combat, but also of exploration and problem solving. Finally, it encourages thinking and mapping rather than thumb twitching, providing us with tools that enhance our abilities and offer multiple ways to complete our task. When we enter the next room, we may take the sword to slay the dragon that lies wait, or the key to open the gate and make a run for safety. We may, in fact, win the Enchanted Chalice without slaying any of the dragons.

Notwithstanding the visual impressiveness of games like *Oblivion,* critics have begun to question designers' persistent efforts to create photorealistic graphics at the expense of experimentation with more abstract visual styles. In the late 1970s, limited technology dictated simple vector lines and bitmaps, but why should current designers categorically reject abstraction? Why have representational graphics become the aesthetic standard in videogames? The pursuit of photorealism, Wolf argues, hinders the analysis of videogame aesthetics, tethering critical criteria to game technology. Because we generally judge games by their graphics, we generally judge newer games to be better than older games, though we pay lip service to story design and gameplay. Games writer David Heyward colorfully describes the raw appeal of graphics to the vast majority of gamers: "We'll always stand by gameplay, but it's graphics that will be handcuffing us to the bed during our next 'business trip.'"[16] In spite of its great conceptual contribution to later videogame design, Robinett's *Adventure,* with its avatar composed of a single polygon and its trio of duck-like dragons, appears to most gamers merely a curiosity of a cruder age, like a cave painting. Because we fix our attention on graphics, we miss the critical importance of Robinett's work.

Aristotle believed that imitation, or *mimesis*, was an innate human tendency and therefore the basis of all learning and art. In *Poetics*, he writes:

> Imitation comes naturally to human beings from childhood (and in this they differ from other animals, i.e. in having a strong propensity for imitation and in learning their earliest lessons through imitation); so does the universal pleasure in imitations. What happens in practice is evidence of this: we take delight in viewing the most accurate possible images of objects, which in themselves cause distress when we see them.[17]

Wolf also recalls art theorist Wilhelm Worringer's 1908 treatise, *Abstraction and Empathy,* to explain the dominance of photorealism in videogame design. Abstract art, Worringer argues, resists the powerful aesthetic impulse to empathize with the figures or ideas represented in a work. For Wolf, this "need for empathy" explains the popularity of representational art and the general ambivalence toward more abstract forms. In games as in most media, abstraction remains "an acquired taste . . . relegated to a marginalized genre, created and seen only by a few."[18] The machinery representing player agents in early games, such as the missile base in *Space Invaders,* the spaceship in *Asteroids,* and the tank in *Battlezone,* soon give way to more identifiable player characters such as Pac-Man, Frogger, and Mario. The smallest dash of empathy, like fairy dust, transforms bitmaps into characters and cultural icons.

Wolf further argues that the photorealistic bias also arises from designers' imitation of the visual styles of other media. "Video games have come to rely on conventions from film and television," he writes, "allowing the depiction and navigation of their diegetic worlds to seem more intuitive and familiar to players." In their emulation of cinema, Wolf writes, designers "have neglected the realm of possibilities which abstraction has to offer." He calls for "a deliberate move back into abstract design that takes into consideration the unique properties of the video game medium."[19]

We can glimpse what such experiments with abstraction might yield in games such as Atari's 1984 *Marble Madness,* in which we roll a blue marble through perilous, Escheresque labyrinths, balancing on edges of black voids and dodging threats such as the malicious black marbles that would bump us off course and the hopping tubules that would envelop and digest us. The game's graphics, like a complex toy, have a tactile appeal. We take pleasure not only in the look of the mazes and the marbles, but also in the interplay of vectors, momentum, and gravity. Alexey Pajitnov's *Tetris,* designed in 1984 and popularized by the Nintendo Game Boy in 1989, similarly engages us with tumbling "tetronimoes" that we nudge and rotate as they fall through space into a linear order. In Namco's *Katamari Damacy,* released in 2004, we play a celestial prince who races to clump all of the clutter of the world into massive

27

bumble balls, or katamari, which our father, the King of All Cosmos, hurls into the sky to become new stars. The game represents an innumerable array of animals and real objects—from ladybugs and tiny thumbtacks to whales and colossal sports stadiums—but it depicts these real objects from a surreal perspective. Dislocated from their familiar contexts, they become elements in a dynamic game of reordering the universe.

These abstract detours in game design reveal something unique about videogames as an art form: their proper aesthetic is one of kinesis—of force, vector, and collision. In 1989, the American Museum of the Moving Image in New York opened a new exhibition, Hot Circuits: A Video Arcade, a retrospective display of arcade games including *Pong, Space Invaders, Asteroids, Battlezone,* and *Missile Command.* Museum director Rochelle Slovin suggests that these earlier, more abstract games not only have a "modernist feel" and a "poetic spareness," but also the beauty of "pure mathematics" that recalls their genesis on mainframe computers used for ballistics calculations.[20] The art of videogames, in other words, is an art of motion, of action rather than image. Media theorist Alexander Galloway explains, "Without action, games remain only in the pages of an abstract rule book. Without the active participation of players and machines, video games exist only as static computer code. Video games come into being when the machine is powered up and the software is executed; they exist when enacted."[21]

We find evidence for Slovin's and Galloway's ideas in the most rudimentary games. Informally designed by MIT programmers on a PDP-1 mainframe in 1962, *Spacewar!* depicts two tiny rockets, equipped only with canons and thrusters, facing off on opposite sides of a dim star. As the rockets spin and shoot, the star exerts its constant gravitational pull, drawing the two combatants inward to annihilation as they struggle to annihilate each other. But if we can maneuver our rocket at just the right angle and fire our thruster a split second before colliding with the star, we can slingshot outward, behind our opponent, in position for the kill. The game's artistry lies in its subtle revelation of the invisible forces governing the playfield: with calculation and coordination, we can convert gravity from a threat to an advantage. *Asteroids* likewise renders Newton's laws of motion in a weightless environment with elegance. Our spacecraft, a tiny delta, thrusts, spins, and counterthrusts, inertia itself hurtling us across blackness toward inevitable collision with other hurling bodies: and then—no spectacular pyrotechnics, only an instant and inglorious implosion—comes the "poetic spareness" of death in a vacuum.

Later iterations of *Asteroids,* nonetheless, show the steady movement away from an abstract art of motion toward heightened realism. In *Asteroids* for the Atari 2600, released in 1981, the space rocks become solid and colored red, green, lavender, blue, brown, and beige; deep space loses something of its deadly blankness. In Atari's 1987 *Blasteroids,* we clear the asteroid field sector by sector, tripping through hyperspace portals in search of the tentacled alien overlord Mukor. Our new spacecraft is more versatile, fitted with better thrusters, better armor, or better guns, as the situation demands. Our "modernist" struggle to stay alive in a treacherous void becomes a quest narrative like *Adventure,* with tools, antagonists, and a goal. In Styrox's 1998 adaptation of *Asteroids* for PlayStation, the boulders, all rough, pockmarked, and realistic, hurtle through three-dimensional space. Stark vector lines and vivid bitmaps give way to polygonal models; abstraction, finally, cedes to representation.

Poole speculates that photorealism, once achieved, will provide a platform for the exploration of alternate visual styles. "It's only recently," he writes, "that [videogames] . . . having mastered the creation of believably solid worlds, have begun to attempt interesting artistic stylizations of the underlying mathematical framework."[22] More recent adaptations of *Asteroids* seem to realize Poole's prediction. Iain McCleod's 2004 *Spheres of Chaos* and Binary Zoo Studios' 2005 *Mono* offer new, highly kinetic, abstract styles in which elementary forces and collisions are displayed in massive synesthetic blasts of pulsing colors, sound waves, and music. Even with its photorealistic makeover, Styrox's *Asteroids* pays homage to its predecessor. Blasting a suspiciously abstract boulder in level fifteen unlocks the old arcade game, which survives as an Easter egg buried in the code of new game, like a latent genetic link to an ancient ancestor. These games, perhaps, signal a growing aesthetic appreciation of earlier games as artifacts that may inform future design.

Perspective, Dimension, and Presence

Marie-Laure Ryan emphasizes Renaissance artists' crucial break from their medieval predecessors, when they discovered the laws of perspective and created the illusion of three dimensions in painting. Looking at these art works, Ryan explains, "the spectator experiences the depicted objects as virtually present, though the flat surface of the painting erects an invisible wall that prevents physical interaction."[23] For example, in Raphael's *School of Athens,* a fresco completed in 1510 to adorn the Vatican's Apostolic Palace, the great philosophers of the ages confer and dispute on a marble terrace. A succession of gilt archways rises over the company, measuring the span from foreground to background. In the space beyond, we see brilliant blue skies. The fresco seems to open heaven itself to us, inviting us to step into the scene and mingle with Pythagoras, Plato, and Aristotle.

While such paintings only entice the viewer to enter their sumptuous worlds with the illusion of three-dimensional space, videogames dissolve the "invisible wall" and allow the viewer to enter a simulated three-dimensional space. Virtual reality theorists describe this mediated experience of entering a graphical environment as immersion, a pleasurable sensation like diving into deep water. In her book *Hamlet on the Holodeck: The Future of Narrative in Cyberspace,* Janet Murray writes:

> We seek the same feeling from a psychologically immersive experience that we do from a plunge in the ocean or swimming pool: the sensation of being surrounded by a completely other reality, as different as water is from air, that takes over all of our attention, our whole perceptual apparatus. We enjoy the movement out of our familiar world, the feeling of alertness that comes from being in this new place, and the delight that comes from learning to move within it.[24]

This presence within a virtual world, Ryan explains, allows us "to explore an environment, and the ability to change it."[25] Like Baroque frescoes, videogames simulate a world beyond view, but as interactive environments, they also simulate a world that is responsive to the player, the illusion that our action as well as our vision extends into their world. In fact, they offer something more than photorealism—they offer phenomenology, not only the perfect image of a snowcapped mountain at sunset, but also the convincing sensation of climbing the mountain and gazing at the sunset from its peak. Ryan describes this experience of presence in a virtual world as "nothing less than the participation of the whole of the individual in the artistic experience."[26]

In videogame design, this vision of a fully immersive aesthetic experience has motivated the parallel development of photorealistic graphics and a first-person, three-dimensional perspective. Videogames invite us to step through the invisible wall that bars our entrance into the School of Athens by merging the point of view of the player with that of the avatar. Just as we trace the development of the pixilated playfields of Atari's *Adventure* to the lush landscapes of *Oblivion,* we can also trace game designers' advance into the third dimension. Atari's 1980 *Battlezone,* a tank simulation rendered in wireframe graphics, marks the first shift to first-person point of view, situating the player inside the tank looking outward to the battlefield through an aperture under the gun barrel. As we maneuver, boulders, hills, and enemy tanks grow smaller as they recede into the distance, and for the first time, we behold a game world subject to the laws of perspective. Sega's 1982 *Zaxxon* renders the game world through isometric projection, a visual style still widely used in games, that emulates architectural design by drawing horizontal lines at an angle of thirty degrees to the horizontal plane of projection. The player witnesses the action from an elevated perspective, as if looking into an animated diorama. Poole explains that isometric projection, while it does not merge the perspectives of player and avatar, enhances our sense of presence by creating the illusion of solidity lacking in wireframe games like *Battlezone.* "You could see three sides of an object rather than just one," he explains, "and now, crucially, the game screen was not just a neutral arena; it had become an environment."[27]

Wolfenstein 3D, created by id Software in 1992, affords us a first-person perspective of a three-dimensional game world for the first time. In our attempt to escape a Nazi prison, we race through dungeon labyrinths shooting soldiers and vicious guard dogs, grabbing weapons, loot, and health bonuses. The walls, mapped with rough textures, register our relative speed and progress as we move, enhancing our sense of presence within the virtual environment. As the original first-person shooter, *Wolfenstein 3D* reflects our incarnation in the game with a representation of our hands, clutching our weapon, at the bottom of the screen. Alison McMahan suggests that this "subjective, individual viewpoint . . . promised a degree of immersiveness that the God's-eye-view of isometric perspective could never deliver. . . . The gun is not used for aiming, but it does make the player feel more like they are incorporated in the space."[28]

More recent developments in game design have further enhanced our sense of virtual presence. High dynamic range (HDR) lighting, for instance, simulates the reflection of light on different surfaces. Valve's *Half-Life 2: Lost Coast* includes a tutorial demonstrating the subtle capabilities of HDR lighting, in which the designers call attention to the difference in the way sunlight strikes dry wooden planks and wet stones. We also notice the refraction of light through tinted class and feel the sudden glare as we emerge from a small dark tunnel on to a brightly lit cliff side. In their frenzy to slaughter alien thugs and radioactive abominations, most players will fail to notice the special care that *Half-Life 2* designers have taken in rendering ambient light, but these gradual steps in changing the way we sense virtual environments mark steady progress toward Ryan's vision of a simulated phenomenology, an aesthetic experience beyond photorealism.

Perspective, dimension, and presence in videogames not only delight our senses, as Murray and Ryan suggest, but also promise a kind of liberation of the player as viewer. Just as interactive narrative de-centers the author and grants the reader influence over imaginary events, three-dimensional modeling allows us to view a digitally rendered object from any vantage point we choose. The artist no longer frames and fixes our view. We may enter the School of Athens and freely take our place within it, perching at center stage with Plato and Aristotle, hunching downstage with Heraclitus, or leering with Zeno from stage left. Videogame scholar James Newman argues that this "mastery of space" by free movement is the "defining feature" of videogames as an art form:

Typically, videogames create "worlds," "lands," or "environments" for players to explore, traverse, conquer, and even dynamically manipulate and transform in some cases. . . . Progress through a particular game is frequently presented to the player as progress through the world of the game. . . . In this sense, gameplay may not only be seen as bounded in space, but also as a journey through it.[29]

This ability to journey through an artwork enables us to experience it from innumerable perspectives and liberates our view. As Poole explains:

By holding a mathematical model of its world in memory, the videogame can, moreover, offer the player a potentially infinite number of different views of the same object: the screen is continually redrawn according to where the player's character is looking. . . . Such a multiplicity of available viewpoints contributes to an undeniable voyeurism . . . [and] the liberated, democratized viewpoint of the spectator.[30]

For Jenkins, the feeling of total liberation within virtual space meets a desperate need in increasingly crowded, restrictive, urban spaces for an ideal of "complete freedom of movement." He writes, "Perhaps my son finds in his video games what I found in the woods behind the school on my bike whizzing down the hills of suburban back streets, or settled into my treehouse during a thunderstorm with a good adventure novel—intensity of experience, escape from adult regulation."[31]

Jenkins's nostalgic recollection of his tree house, however, evokes refuge and security more than it evokes adventure and liberation. For Ryan, the sense of rootedness, of close emotional identification with a place, has crucial importance in virtual worlds, perhaps more so than the liberation of movement. In other words, to feel present in videogames, we must feel at home in them, and while exploration and exercise contribute to our sense of presence in the game world, so too does being at ease there. Ryan draws from the philosopher Gaston Bachelard and argues that virtual worlds, in part, represent a "conceptualization of open spaces as cozy habitat, 'intimate immensity' and the 'universe as house.'"[32] Even in the largest videogame storyworlds, we find safe harbors, a place to escape the thunderstorm, dump our loot, reequip, and take stock of things. In *Star Wars: Knights of the Old Republic,* we can duck cosmic destruction in our trusty starship, the Ebon Hawk; in *Grand Theft Auto: San Andreas,* we can chill out at our little house on Grove Street; and in *Oblivion* we can purchase a stately residence in any of Cyrodiil's cities. In massively-multiplayer online games, we will see in Chapter 8, players often spend long hours acquiring enough gold to buy a deed and build a home in the game world, to claim one's homestead on the virtual frontier.

Like Jenkins, Ryan suspects that the emotional need to project ourselves into virtual environments and feel at home there arises from the conditions of modern life. She argues that the "nomadic, alienated space of postmodernism," where no one quite feels at home, has its compensation in the "sedentary dreams" of a virtual home. "Postmodern literature," she explains, "conceptualizes space in terms of perpetual movement, blind navigation, a gallery of mirrors, being lost in a not-always-so-funhouse, a self-transforming labyrinth, parallel and embedded universes, and discontinuous non-Cartesian expanses, all experiences that preclude an intimate relation to a specific location."[33] The aesthetic of interactivity is an art of motion, phenomenon, and direct experience, spatial construction and revelation, a way of animating art with a new and unfamiliar life. At the same time, Ryan suggests, we flee to the fantastic worlds of videogames in order to feel more at home, to rediscover a something familiar that modern life has denied us.

Videogames and the Art World

Rochelle Slovin, director of the Hot Circuits exhibition at the American Museum of the Moving Image, writes, "Looking back on it [the exhibition] today—when new media is an everyday subject, and early video games are enjoying not only increased critical attention but are being repackaged for nostalgic use on home computers—the exhibition seems to have been a decade ahead of its time."[34] As Slovin anticipated, a series of major exhibitions on videogames as a distinct art form followed Hot Circuits, attempting to articulate the emerging aesthetics of videogame design and explore their relations to other arts. In 1994, the Ars Electronica festival in Linz, Austria, featured lectures and works by European and North American artists exploring the potential for games to express philosophical and aesthetic concepts and to stimulate creativity. The event marked one of the earliest international forums where a diverse community of artists affirmed that games had transcended the status of technological novelty and had become a possible medium for artistic expression.

In 2002, the Barbican Art Gallery in London opened Game On, a videogame exhibition that surpassed the scope of both Hot Circuits and Ars Electronica. The Barbican announced the event as "the first major UK exhibition to explore the vibrant history and culture of computer games."[35] With more than 125 games and 10 platforms on display, the show emphasized the status of games as historical and cultural artifacts, as Hot Circuits did, and explored the potential of videogames as a medium for creative expression, as Ars Electronica did, but it also asserted the role of the game designer as artist rather than as programmer or engineer. It attempted, moreover, to situate games within the larger culture by demonstrating the relation between games, films, and graphic art and by framing social issues such as videogame violence.

Other exhibitions, including Game Show at the Massachusetts Museum of Contemporary Art in 2001, Blinky at Foxy Productions in New York in 2003, Radical Entertainment at the Institute for Contemporary Arts in London in 2003, and the Whitney Biennial in 2004, featured artists, adept in programming, who have modified commercially produced games as a mode of critique of videogame conventions and the broader culture of technology. Anne-Marie Schleiner, Brody Condon, and Joan Leadre's *Velvet-Strike,* for instance, embeds antiwar messages into the graphical battlefields of Valve's online combat game, *Counter-Strike.* On virtual walls, we find an image of two soldiers in loving embrace, a heart-shaped formation of iconic soldiers, and a slogan: "Give online peace a chance."

Art critic William Martin believes that videogame modifications, or "mods," such as *Velvet-Strike,* demonstrate the potential for game designers to answer the persistent criticism that games are socially disengaged, a commodity rather than an art form. "Using the popular culture phenomenon of the videogame to deliver this group's antiwar stance," Martin writes, "*Velvet-Strike* addresses the mass commercialization and distribution of the videogame as an effective and viable modus of transmission for both a commercially and politically subversive message."[36] Lunenfeld compares the aesthetic awakening represented by the mod artists to the renaissance in graphic novel design of the late 1980s:

> During that period of remarkable creative activity, readers had the sense that collective icons and memories were being fractured and recombined to create something novel that nonetheless drew from the same wellspring of generic pleasure that had fed them from pimpledom up. These artists refracted the language and the culture of comics through a new set of sensibilities, creating something that could draw in . . . a large audience that loved the medium as much as they did, and wanted to see it taken to a new place.[37]

As we will see more clearly in Chapter 9, modders have begun to take videogames to a new place, approaching the medium with the same volatile blend of adoration and critique.

Other artists have seized on the distinctive visual style of videogames as the basis for a new form of pop art, in which photographic images are adapted as videogame images. Cory Arcangel's *NES Home Movies: 8-bit Landscape Studies* transfers photographs of the artist's hometown of Buffalo, New York, into the Nintendo's 8-bit cartridge format, transforming real landscapes into images one might find in a classic NES game. Art critic Christiane Paul explains that the work "fuses traditional landscape photography with gaming aesthetics, creating a scenery that effectively transcends the media from which it borrows and seems to evolve into a new manifestation of pop art."[38] Jon Haddock's *Screen-*

shots achieves a similar fusion by rendering iconic photographs or film scenes in isometric projection, inviting us to review them from a three-dimensional, remediated perspective. We witness the assassination of Martin Luther King, the Columbine High School shooting, or the murder of Fredo Corleone in *The Godfather Part II* as if reenacted in *The Sims*. Poole observes that "the hyperreal style of videogame representation isolates and preserves the iconic structure of historical imagery with which we are familiar from news photographs and CCTV videos, while abstracting it from the messy impedimenta of the actual."[39] As games have taken hold of the culture, artists such as Arcangel and Haddock have adopted the videogame as a means of reflecting the hyperreality of modern life and blurring the boundary between simulation and experience.

Videogame designers, in turn, have increasingly referred to the visual arts in their ongoing exploration of more stylized forms. Games such as SmileBit's *Jet Set Radio,* Nintendo's *The Legend of Zelda: The Wind Waker,* and Ubisoft's *XIII* employ cel-shaded animation, a synthesis of conventional polygonal modeling with the visual styles of graphic novels and manga that yields lively, interactive cartoons. Clover Studio's celebrated *Ōkami,* an adventure game based on Japanese mythology, uses a unique style of cel-shading that imitates traditional Japanese *suibokuga* ink and wash painting. On the other hand, Lonnie Flickinger's *Pencil Whipped* recreates the first-person shooter using pencil doodles scanned into the three-dimensional game world as objects, monsters, and environmental textures. Playing the game, we feel like we have slipped, nightmarishly, into the sketchbook of a demented seventh-grader. Other games emulate more traditional styles. Sega's *Rez,* a cybernetic adventure set inside a computer brain, reproduces the geometric abstractions of the Russian painter Wassily Kandinsky. By synchronizing the hypnotic soundtrack to our flight through these vertiginous spaces, the game induces a synesthetic feeling for shape and color. *Rez, Pencil Whipped,* and *Jet Set Radio* do not simply substitute one derivative aesthetic for another, jilting cinema for manga, *suibokuga,* Bauhaus, or classroom doodle; they demonstrate, rather, that games may animate rather than imitate these visual styles, shocking them to new life with the kinetic forces that motivated *Spacewar!* and *Asteroids.*

The Problem of Videogame Criticism

Even as they find their way into major art galleries, videogames struggle against the predominant critical view that they are not high art. Churned out by massive entertainment conglomerates rather than inspired creative consciousness, they seem fettered to profit motive. Art critics Ellen Sandor and Janine Fron, for instance, view *Screenshots* as an example of the ways games may promote critical discourse, but they observe that the game industry "exists to attract an audience for the sake of commercialized entertainment" and fails to manifest "interest in other art forms, respect for history, and awareness of social responsibility."[40] Lunenfeld says more bluntly that most games are created by designers "whose frame of reference extends no further back than *Pong, Pac-Man,* and *Donkey Kong.*"[41] Exhibitions like Hot Circuits and Game On might signal the recognition of videogames among the cultural elite, but games remain more at home in the living room than in the art gallery.

At the same time, the awakening self-consciousness of videogames as art, the use of games as vehicles for critique, and the ongoing cross-fertilization between games and other art forms signal that they are coming out of their infancy, nurtured by an increasingly coherent discourse of game studies. In his vision of the emergence of games as a new art, Robinett describes the parallel development of the game industry and game criticism. Following an early period of technical and aesthetic experimentation, Robinett explains, critics and critical theories emerge. "The critics and theorists cannot get started without a body of works to winnow and analyze," Robinett explains, "and their work is meaningless without a stream of new works being created, presumably informed (somewhat) by their efforts. The wolf keeps the caribou strong. The players, the designers, the critics, and the theorists are natural members of a healthy ecosystem."[42]

Robinett expresses the consensus among designers and critics, who sense the need for productive dialogue between them. As we have already seen in relation to games and literary studies, however, the inherent dynamism of the medium has proven an obstacle to the development of the critical idiom that Robinett sees as a crucial link in the "ecosystem" that sustains the art of game design. The accelerated technological advance of the medium has, on one hand, yielded stunning developments in graphics, enabling photorealistic, three-dimensional rendering that gives us a sense of presence in imaginary worlds; however, it has also guaranteed the perpetual instability of the medium itself, as well as the critical discourse that nurtures the development of the medium, which continually has to catch up with technology. In fact, Jenkins considers Moore's Law a major obstacle for game studies:

> Game designers . . . have confronted dramatic shifts in their basic tools and resources on average every 18 months since the emergence of their medium. This constant need to respond to a shifting technological infrastructure has shifted attention onto mastering tools which could otherwise have been devoted to exploring the properties and potentials of the medium. . . . We have not had time to codify what experienced game designers know, and we have certainly not yet established a canon of great works that might serve as exemplars. There have been real creative accomplishments across the first three decades of game design, but we haven't really sorted out what they are and why they matter.[43]

In other words, without a stable development platform and common frame of reference, we can have neither mastery nor critique.

But the difficulties of developing a discourse that shows us why games matter should not be taken as proof that games, as Kroll and Ebert suggest, do not matter. Cultural history shows that what seems degenerate at first often contributes a new vitality to our experience and critique of culture. Cubism has not destroyed our ability to understand art; it has led to a new understanding of form and perspective. Cinema and television have not made us illiterate; they have introduced a new literacy based on the complex and dynamic interrelation of word, image, sound, and motion. Likewise, videogames now compel us to reconsider accepted notions of art. Embracing them, as some gamers do, without a critical view of their form, their emotional and intellectual appeal, and their relation to other art forms encourages the philistine consumerism that Sandor and Fron sense in the game industry. At the same time, dismissing them as a fad encourages a snobbish ignorance of a growing force in the cultural life of the twenty-first century.

❖ 3 ❖

Videogames and Film

On June 11, 1982, Universal Pictures released Steven Spielberg's film *E.T. the Extra-Terrestrial*, a story of friendship between a misfit boy and a benevolent alien stranded on Earth. The film charmed audiences, generating $11 million in its first weekend and more than $350 million in its first year. Ronald Reagan and Princess Diana cried when they saw the film, and the United Nations awarded Spielberg the Peace Medal for his work. Looking back on the film twenty years later, Roger Ebert writes, "This movie made my heart glad. It is filled with innocence, hope, and good cheer. . . . *E.T. the Extra-Terrestrial* is a movie like *The Wizard of Oz*, that you can grow up with and grow old with, and it won't let you down. . . . *E.T.* is a reminder of what movies are for."[1]

In July 1982, Warner Communications, the parent company of Atari, secured the rights to create an *E.T.* videogame for the Atari 2600 console. The deal promised a happy marriage between Hollywood and the burgeoning videogame industry. At the time, Atari led the games market, and by landing *E.T.* they acquired the hottest film license since *Star Wars*. Anticipating massive sales, Atari rushed to complete the game in time for the 1982 holiday season, manufacturing 5 million game cartridges, about one for every two Atari consoles owned in the United States.

The game flopped spectacularly. Warner stock plummeted, and Atari claimed more than $500 million in losses in 1983. In September of that year, Atari buried tons of unsold merchandise in a landfill in Alamogordo, New Mexico, including (rumor had it) almost 4 million *E.T.* cartridges. Within a year, Warner dismantled and sold Atari. Although employee dissatisfaction, inefficient distribution practices, and increasing competition with home computer games contributed to Atari's crash, *E.T.* has come to signify the creative and commercial bankruptcy of the industry in 1983.

On June 25, 2005, a long way from Alamogordo, George Lucas welcomed 2,000 guests to the gala opening of the Letterman Digital Arts Center (LDAC) in the Presidio of San Francisco, where Lucasfilm and its special effects and videogame divisions, Industrial Light and Magic (ILM) and LucasArts, had just moved into their new, shared headquarters. Lucas's guests included California Senators Barbara Boxer and Dianne Feinstein, House Minority leader Nancy Pelosi, and four San Francisco mayors. The city's most esteemed chefs prepared a buffet of gourmet fried chicken and stuffed vegetables, while Chris Isaak and Bonnie Raitt entertained the crowd. Joan Baez, also in attendance, surveyed the crowd and reflected, "There's something to be said for having a billion bucks."[2]

Actually, the Letterman Digital Arts Center cost only $350 million. It covers twenty-three acres of the Presidio and stands on the site of the former Letterman Army Medical Center, demolished in 2001 to make way for the four main buildings of the LDAC. Located in the Golden Gate National Recreation Area, the Lucasfilm campus is open to the public. While the buildings themselves are tightly secured, visitors may stroll, and gawk, and have their picture taken with the bronze statue of Yoda perched on the fountain near the entrance of the LDAC.

Lucasfilm boasts that the new facility features "the largest computer network in the entertainment industry, a high-performance system designed to deliver large volumes of data and high-resolution images to artists' desktops, encouraging interactive collaboration on the creation of synthetic scenes and characters. . . . Distance boundaries have been eliminated, and digital artists can collaborate internally throughout the campus, as well as with creators of entertainment anywhere in the world."[3] While the visual effects designers at ILM and the game designers at LucasArts sometimes collaborated prior to their consolidation, they did so in separate facilities, without the advantages of proximity and a shared database. Now they work on the same campus and in the same virtual studio. At an International Game Developers Association (IGDA) meeting in San Francisco in December 2005, Lucasfilm representatives explained, "Developers are now 'right down the hall' from each other, developing on the same code base, staffing projects with crew from both divisions, and tackling problems with the best techniques either side has to offer. It's not just about sharing assets. . . we're building a unified set of technology to produce both movies and games, and give both companies unique competitive advantages."[4] Lucasfilm's press release announcing the opening of the LDAC echoes the millennial narrative of the *Star Wars* films. The triumphant alliance of Lucasfilm filmmakers and game designers heralds a "new vision" for the entertainment industry, in which the "seamless integration of entertainment technologies . . . represents a new way to work . . . [and] recognizes the convergence of movies, videogames, visual effects, animation, and online, and brings Lucasfilm to the forefront of that movement."[5]

In more practical terms, the consolidation signals a more deliberate approach to media convergence. In 1982, when Warner bought the *E.T.* license and commissioned Atari with an adaptation for the Atari 2600, the videogame industry followed Hollywood's lead, waiting for someone to make a blockbuster film and then buying the rights to the film. Lucasfilm now facilitates the simultaneous production films and games. In his keynote address at the 2005 Siggraph digital arts exposition in Los Angeles, Lucas explained, "It used to be an assembly-line process: One person would do one thing, then the next person would do the next thing. But now, we're going to push the envelope and get everybody to work simultaneously on the same thing." Lucas calls this new production model "the future of entertainment."[6]

Beyond Lucasfilm's corporate proselytizing, what does all this talk about a "new vision" and the "future of entertainment" really mean? How has the relation between the film and videogame industries changed in the two decades between 1982, when the adaptation of *E.T.* to the Atari 2600 cost Warner $500 million, and 2005, when George Lucas has reconfigured his $15 billion-dollar–empire in order to maximize the potential for film-game franchising? This chapter considers the influence of film-game franchising on the way artists create films and videogames, the way audiences consume them, and the way scholars interpret them.

Hollywood and the Videogame Industry

Videogame enthusiasts and media scholars often claim that games will overtake—or have already overtaken—film as the dominant entertainment medium. In a WNYC New York Public Radio interview in 2003, *New York Times Magazine* writer Jonathan Dee hailed the ascendance of videogames, predicting, "I can see a future in which when the technology gets a little better . . . I would be hard-pressed to think of a reason why anyone would pay to go see, for instance, a new James Bond movie as opposed to playing the new James Bond game."[7] In a *Gamasutra* interview, game designer Denis Dyack made the more monumental claim that games are not only more sophisticated and popular than films, but also nothing less than "the most advanced form of art thus far in human history," in their synthesis of text, image, sound, video, and the active participation of the audience into a unified aesthetic experience.[8]

As film studios and games consolidate their interests, however, the traditional rivalry between film and game producers dissolves in corporate synergy, and the fortunes and creative interests of the two industries fall into harmony, as they have at Lucasfilm. Predictions of videogame supremacy like Dee's and Dyack's often ignore the fact that games and films share largely in each other's commercial success. Videogame companies have grown rapidly, but they have not usurped movie studios as much as they have become viable subsidiaries capable of functioning in financial and creative concert not only with film but also with television, publishing, and sports entertainment. Consumers are not conflicted, as Dee imagines, by a choice between the new Bond movie and the new Bond game, but more likely will go see the movie and buy the game, with the sense that their experience of one is enhanced by the other. The future probably will not witness more games and fewer films, but rather more games, more films, more games based on films, and more films based on games, with the integrated production and marketing of film-game franchises.

In one of the most celebrated ventures in media convergence, Larry and Andy Wachowski, creators of *The Matrix* trilogy, produced the game *Enter the Matrix* simultaneously with the last two films of the trilogy, shooting scenes for the game on the movies' sets with the movies' actors, and releasing the game on May 15, 2003, the same day as *The Matrix: Reloaded*. Likewise, on September 21, 2004, Lucasfilm jointly released a new DVD box set of the original *Star Wars* trilogy in 2004 with *Star Wars: Battlefront*, a combat game in which players could reenact battles from all six *Star Wars* films. In 2005, Peter Jackson likewise produced his blockbuster film *King Kong* in tandem with a successful *King Kong* game designed by Michael Ancel and published by Ubisoft. In the last several years, numerous licensed videogame adaptations of major summer and holiday blockbusters were released a few days before or a few days after their respective films, including: all three *Star Wars* films (1999–2005); all five *Harry Potter* films (2001–2008); all three *Spider-Man* films (2002–2007); *Hulk* (2002); *The Lord of the Rings: The Two Towers* (2002); *The Lord of the Rings: The Return of the King* (2003); *The Chronicles of Narnia: The Lion, the Witch, and the Wardrobe* (2005); *The Chronicles of Narnia: Prince Caspian* (2008); *Pirates of the Caribbean: Dead Man's Chest* (2006); *Pirates of the Caribbean: At World's End* (2007); *Transformers* (2007); and *Ironman* (2008). These multimedia franchises have made it more difficult to distinguish the production of films and videogames as separate enterprises.

The LDAC is the first factory designed primarily to make film-game franchises. In the same press release announcing a "new vision" for the entertainment industry, Lucasfilm offers more specific "facts and figures" describing its technological infrastructure, which includes 10,000 gigabytes of storage, image and sound editing systems, a render farm for processing digital images, a media center for format conversion and duplication, a 300-seat movie theater, and, most importantly, the largest data network in the industry with fiber optics connecting to every desktop computer to LDAC resources and to each other.

In practical terms, images and visual effects created by ILM for the *Star Wars* films can be immediately appropriated and repurposed by game designers. Steve Sullivan, head of research and development at ILM, explains, "An example would be, ILM is doing a shot for a film, but LucasArts artists can have that exact same shot sitting on their desk, and they can start building a game environment around it."[9] LucasArts' *Star Wars Episode III: Revenge of the Sith*, a game based closely on the 2005 film, marked the first time a *Star Wars* film shared specific images data with a *Star Wars* videogame. LucasArts designers have likewise contributed integrally to ILM. "Previsualization," a form of animated storyboarding developed through the collaboration of ILM and LucasArts, has adapted game design tools to filmmaking. Sullivan describes previsualization as

> a tool that directors would use to quickly mock up the ideas of a story and see what's going to work. It's really like building up a preview of a movie in a video game world. Instead of using static story boards, you can really just get in and create 3D content and camera moves directly. It's the best example of the kind of collaboration we've got going on. It came from George [Lucas]— it didn't come from either division. But it requires things that both divisions have expertise in.[10]

Lucas said at Siggraph, "Cinema is not the art of the image; it's the art of the moving image." Previsualization is not simply a faster or flashier way of planning a shot. Rather, it enables filmmakers, for the first time, to edit the interplay of image and motion in the earliest stages of production, to control more deliberately what eventually appears on screen even before shooting begins.

Lucas cites *Star Wars Episode II: Attack of the Clones* as the "first film to be completely shot digitally."[11] While he waits, somewhat frustrated, for Hollywood to catch up, he believes that digitization represents the future of cinema:

> We're hoping that at some point the theaters will switch over to digital projection, and the filmmakers will start using the new digital cameras so that we as an industry can advance technically and make everything much easier. Right now, Sony, Panavision, Fujinon and a lot of other companies are investing tens of millions of dollars into this idea, and the industry isn't backing it. . . . At some point, I know it will all happen.[12]

He predicts that digitization will "democratize" the industry, enabling amateur filmmakers to shoot with a handheld camera purchased from a local Wal-Mart, edit on a desktop computer, and distribute and publicize their work on the Internet. On a more fundamental level, however, the reduction of cinema to image data means that films and videogames can be created with the same tools, as we already see in ILM's use of previsualization. If, as Lucas predicts, "it will all happen," then the relation between the two industries will move beyond licensed adaptations and franchises; they will, as they have in Lucasworld, merged into a single industry.

Film-Game Franchising and Transmedia Storytelling

The development of previsualization technology and the franchising of blockbuster films and videogames suggest that the increasing collaboration between the two industries will influence the creation of films and games at every phase, from pre-production to post-release publicity, and that the gradual digitization of filmmaking will facilitate film-game franchising by giving filmmakers and game designers a common medium and common tools. But what kind of story will be produced by companies like Lucasfilm, equipped to produce films, games, and television shows simultaneously?

In his adaptation of *E.T.* to the Atari 2600, designer Howard Scott Warshaw sought to capture the suspense and sentimentality of the film by creating an adventure game that simulated E.T.'s quest to "phone home." Players, however, found the game slow and repetitive, with neither the emotional impact of the film, nor the engaging puzzles of earlier Atari adventure games like *Adventure* and *Raiders of the Lost Ark*. Recent critics routinely cite Atari's *E.T.* as the worst game ever made, attributing its aesthetic and commercial failure to Atari's rush to ship the game before Christmas, but the game reveals a deeper theoretical uncertainty among game designers at the time about strategies for the adaptation of a story from one medium to another. As the first great failed attempt to convert a blockbuster film to a videogame, *E.T.* proved that a film's popularity alone could not buoy a bad game.

In the decades since Atari's bust, highly improved technology has, as we have seen, enabled designers to make their games look more cinematic. More importantly, filmmakers and game designers have learned from earlier failures and developed subtler and more calculated strategies for spinning stories across multiple media. In *Convergence Culture: Where Old and New Media Collide*, Henry Jenkins describes *The Matrix* franchise as an "entertainment for the age of media convergence, integrating multiple texts to create a narrative so large that it cannot be contained within a single medium." Jenkins observes that the Wachowskis "plant clues [in the films] that won't make sense until we play the computer game. They draw on the back story revealed through a series of animated shorts, which need to be downloaded off the Web or watched off a separate DVD." Jenkins calls this emergent narrative structure "transmedia storytelling":

> In the ideal form . . . each medium does what it does best—so that a story might be introduced in a film, expanded through television, novels, and comics; its world might be explored through gameplay or experienced as an amusement park attraction. Each franchise entry needs to be self-contained so you don't need to have seen the film to enjoy the game, and vice versa. Any given product is a point of entry into the franchise as a whole.

According to Jenkins, collaborative authorship and the process of "world-making" define these new narrative franchises. He quotes an experienced screenwriter, who says, "When I first started, you would pitch a story because without a story, you didn't really have a film. Later, once sequels started to take off, you pitched a character because a good character could support multiple stories. And now, you pitch a world because a world can support multiple characters and multiple stories across multiple media."[13]

Two television commercials, one produced by LucasArts to promote the game *Star Wars: Bounty Hunter*, and the other produced by Electronic Arts (EA) to promote their adaptation of Peter Jackson's *The Lord of the Rings: The Return of the King*, provide sketches of two competing strategies for transmedia storytelling. LucasArts' advertisement, released during the 2002 holiday shopping season, opens with an animated close-up of a snorkel poking from the surface of a swampy, extraterrestrial pool. As nervous breathing hisses from the tube, a gauntleted fist grips the snorkel and plugs the airway with a thumb. A gasping, bug-eyed alien springs to the surface to find that the obstructing thumb belongs to Jango Fett, the most ruthless bounty hunter in the galaxy. Jango seizes his quivering prey and in his gruff, mercenary's voice, jokes, "Did you miss me?"

The commercial represents another example of the collaboration between Lucasfilm special effects engineers and LucasArts game designers that Lucas hopes to maximize at the LDAC. Although created at ILM, we do not find this scene in any of the *Star Wars* films. The game's appeal, in fact, derives from its clear departure from the 2002 film, *Episode II: Attack of the Clones*, in which Jango, the game's hero, is a significant but nonetheless supporting character, who in the end is summarily beheaded by a Jedi lightsaber. The game narrative itself follows this strategy of departure from the film narrative, representing an interactive prequel to *Attack of the Clones* in its story of a secret bargain between Jango and the Sith Lord Count Dooku to create the clone army already in existence at the outset of the film.

EA's advertisement, released during the 2003 holiday season, represents a different strategy. As the commercial opens with the New Line Cinema and

Wingnut Films logos set to the haunting soundtrack of *The Lord of the Rings* films, we expect to see yet another commercial for the last film in Jackson's trilogy. In fact, as we watch the Nazgûl glide above Minas Tirith, the giant Oliphaunt thunder across the Pellinor Fields, and the stalwart fellowship of Gimli, Legolas, Aragorn, and Gandalf in pitched battles with armies of orcs, we see that we are not wrong; these are indeed tantalizing scenes from the upcoming film. But then something strange happens: the filmed scenes transform fluidly and subtly into the photorealistic digital animations for EA's new game. In contrast to the *Bounty Hunter* commercial, the spot simultaneously advertises the movie and the game, which derives marketability from its nearly perfect mimicry of Jackson's film. Like LucasArts' game, EA's *The Return of the King* correlates this advertising strategy with an interactive narrative strategy, which offers players the chance to participate in scenes involving environments, characters, and battle sequences reproduced from those seen in the film. The commercial concludes with the invitation, "Be the hero! Live the movie!"

The two advertisements manifest fundamentally different narrative and marketing strategies in these two advertisements. *Bounty Hunter* offers consumers something new, something unavailable in theaters, while *The Return of the King* offers consumers something familiar, a chance to interact with something they have seen or soon will see in theaters. At the 2004 Game Developers Convention, veteran game designer Warren Spector urged fellow designers to use film narrative as a way to "draw in the casual gamer, who's used to having a story told to him in other entertainment mediums, particularly movies."[14] This strategy underlies game companies' exorbitant spending on film licenses, which represents the acquisition of a guaranteed audience and the probable success of the game among the same crowds who pack the cineplexes.

While both strategies have proven commercially successful, LucasArts' creation of game narratives that extrapolate rather than mimic the film narratives more freely explores the possibilities of transmedia storytelling that intrigue Jenkins. EA's mimetic approach in both *The Lord of the Rings: The Two Towers* and *The Return of the King* yields, on the other hand, missions that replicate action sequences from the films. In the first mission of *The Two Towers*, the player is Isildur in the midst of the ancient battle that first claimed the Ring of Power from a seventeen-foot, mail-clad Sauron; in the second mission the player becomes Aragorn defending the wounded Frodo from the Nazgûl on Weathertop Hill. Both scenes come from the first film of the trilogy, *The Lord of the Rings: The Fellowship of the Ring*. In the succeeding missions, adapted from *The Two Towers*, the player may choose to continue as Aragorn, Gimli, or Legolas, but, with the exception of a minor variance in the bonus missions, the choice of character has no bearing on the unfolding of the game narrative. As in the television commercial, animations and music in both *The Two Towers* and *The Return of the King* flow seamlessly into and out of sequences from the films, which are spliced into the game narrative. The game world has been designed directly from film sets, and actors from the film have been employed for animations and voiceovers, creating an overall play experience, as the advertisement indeed claims, in which one seems to "live the movie."

In its many adaptations of the *Star Wars* films since the release of *Episode I: The Phantom Menace* in 1999, LucasArts has adopted an elaborative approach in which multiple games, such as *Jedi Starfighter*, *Clone Wars*, and *Bounty Hunter* do not mimic the film narrative but rather follow independent narratives branching from the movie plots. Although familiar movie characters, in some cases, reappear in the LucasArts games, the games' animations, soundtracks, settings, and narratives are original. In contrast to the mimetic *The Lord of the Rings* games, the game narratives situate themselves outside the established chronology of the *Star Wars* films, becoming, in effect, interactive prequels and sequels to the films. In a 2006 interview LucasArts Project Lead Chris Williams said:

> We're not in a space right now where we just want to be cranking out movie games. To the extent that we did that with the *Episode III* game, we're kind of done with that. We want to be telling new stories, new experiences, and really taking advantage of the interactive medium. And not just rehashing or serving up a film experience in a sort of interactive way. We're not sitting here right now waiting for ILM to come to us with some big film project so we can just crank out a movie game of it. The goal is use these tools, techniques, and knowledge to make a really exciting, innovative, next-gen product.[15]

At the same time, *Star Wars* games reinterpret scenes from the films in ways that are recognizable to the established *Star Wars* audience but are, nonetheless, new. In *Star Wars: Knights of the Old Republic*, a role-playing game set four millennia before events depicted in the films, the player character liberates a comrade from slavery by winning a swoop bike race, a sequence that recalls *The Phantom Menace*, in which the young Anakin Skywalker must win his own emancipation in a pod race. In the same game, the central plot twist reveals that the player character, plagued by amnesia through more than half the game, finally discovers that he is a powerful Sith Lord thought to be dead and now psychologically reprogrammed by the Jedi Council to do good. The revelatory animation echoes the 1980 film *Episode V: The Empire Strikes Back*, in which Luke Skywalker, undergoing Jedi training with Yoda, beheads an apparition of Darth Vader only to discover his own face behind

Vader's mask. Finally, the closing animation of *Knights of the Old Republic*, in which an evil, celestial-sized superweapon is spectacularly destroyed, and a battle-weary but joyous crowd celebrates the motley band of heroes, recalls the familiar ending of the original 1977 *Star Wars* film, *Episode IV: A New Hope*, in which the Death Star is annihilated, and Luke Skywalker, Han Solo, Chewbacca, and the faithful droids are given medals before a happy assembly of rebels.

LucasArts has also adopted this strategy in its "Jedi Knight" series: *Dark Forces, Jedi Knight, Jedi Outcast*, and *Jedi Academy*. Each of these games represents a narrative sequel of the original *Star Wars* trilogy in which central characters from the films such as Luke Skywalker, Boba Fett, and Lando Calrissian recede to supporting and new characters, unseen in the films, take center stage. *Republic Commando* (2005), likewise, is set during the Clone Wars of Episodes II and III, but abandons the perspective of the elite Jedi heroes in favor of that of the faceless grunts, who appear in the films only as laser fodder.

In a March 2004 interview, Peter Morawiec spoke to *Game Developer* magazine about adapting genre fiction and film narratives to game design:

> As the videogame market matures, I believe it's natural for the story-driven games to be crafted within established narrative genres. With the age of today's average gamer pegged at something like 29, the audience welcomes greater thematic variety, as well as deeper and more mature storylines. I believe that people will instinctively want to play the same types of genres they like to watch or read.

Morawiec describes his own game designs as interactive narratives that move forward

> no matter how badly the player does, allowing even a total newbie to fumble his or her way through an entire storyline, without repeating missions or getting stuck. In a passive medium such as a movie, whenever the hero hits a low point mid-film, the story doesn't restart; rather, the hero recovers or finds another way to go on.

In terms of the interrelated strategies of designing and marketing film-game franchises, Morawiec's proposed script-imperative game narratives coax a player character along a relatively linear narrative path, limiting the "hybrid active-passive experience" in favor of replicating the traditional narrative structures of film. LucasArts has instead increased the potential of the player to participate actively within the mythic film-game universe, while sacrificing, perhaps, a measure of identification among the built-in film audiences.

For those who do not come to the games by way of a primary interest in the films, LucasArts' strategy explores the evolving possibilities of transmedia storytelling by giving the consumer, as Jenkins suggests, multiple points of entry into the franchise. While EA has created a game narrative more tailored to the massive audience of *The Lord of the Rings* films, a sort of interactive advertisement for the films, LucasArts has developed a true experiment in world-making, that allows game companies to adapt multiple game titles from a single film and allows the player to participate more actively within an expanding film-game universe.

EA has abandoned its mimetic approach in *Everything or Nothing*, a game that has gained critical favor as the first Bond game to offer a narrative independent of the Bond films. EA's elaboration of the Bond franchise compared to its replication of *The Lord of the Rings* suggests that their strategy with *The Two Towers* and *The Return of the King* has been determined, at least in part, by the existing mythology first created by J.R.R. Tolkien's novels. Because *The Lord of the Rings* games are third-tier adaptations—games based on films based on novels—and the *Star Wars* games are second-tier adaptations—games based on films—their respective designers have been bound by two different sets of rules. In a sense, Tolkien's novels have been canonized as a kind of immutable sacred text, and fans of the novels undoubtedly represent an established audience for the films who must, on some level, be acknowledged. As Peter Jackson has often spoken of his faithful intentions toward Tolkien and Tolkien's devotees, EA has similarly deferred to Jackson's films in order to avoid the risk of alienating the audiences who purchase the games based on their love for the films or the books. Neil Young, who oversees EA's *The Lord of the Rings* franchise, explains, "I wanted to adapt Peter's work for our medium in the same way that he has adapted Tolkien's work for his."[16]

One could not imagine Tolkien's *The Return of the King* ending with Frodo and Sam impaled on the ramparts of the Black Gate and Sauron's forces annihilating Gandalf and Aragorn and spreading eternal darkness over the World of Men. In *The Lord of the Rings* games, bound to some extent by the fixed narratives of Tolkien's novels and Jackson's films, such evil endings mean that the player has failed and must try again. *Star Wars*, on the other hand, is a more malleable mythology, and fans of Lucas' films, who sustain a cottage industry of derivative serial novels and fan fiction, seem more receptive to manipulations of their canon. In *Knights of the Old Republic*, for instance, the player may choose to reject the good counsel of the Jedi, slaughter loyal friends, and claim the galaxy in the name of Dark Side. The player, in a sense, may choose to fail according to the ethical standards established by the films and yet succeed in the game. *The Two Towers* and *The Return of the King* offer the player no such choice. LucasArts seems to have evaded criticism by *Star Wars* purists by disengaging from the film narratives, by letting the movies stand as they are and creating instead alternate stories partially unbound by the expectations of their established audience. Nonetheless, in their varying experiments in bringing interactivity to Middle Earth and that long ago, far, far away galaxy, EA and LucasArts have begun to create and to test these new modes of storytelling that have become possible in the wake of media convergence.

Homage, Parody, and Machinima

Woody Allen's 1985 comic fantasy *The Purple Rose of Cairo* features Mia Farrow as Cecilia, a waitress in Depression-era New Jersey who escapes her mundane job and loutish husband in the local movie house to watch the romantic adventure *The Purple Rose of Cairo* again and again. One day, while Cecilia sits transfixed, Tom Baxter, the film-within-the-film's dashing hero, notices her in the audience, steps out of the screen, and falls in love with her. When Gil Shepherd, the real-life actor who plays Tom, travels from Hollywood to New Jersey to try to convince his on-screen alter ego to go back where he belongs, he also falls for Cecilia. Courted by both suitors, one real and one imaginary, Cecilia finally chooses reality, only to be dumped by Gil once Tom has stepped back into the film.

Like the film, videogames visibly manifest the filmgoer's fantasy of "breaking the fourth wall" between the real and imaginary worlds. While *The Purple Rose of Cairo* imagines a film hero entering the woebegone world of an unhappy housewife, videogames—particularly those adapted from films—invite us to slip away from our world to become Neo, Aragorn, or James Bond. If *The Purple Rose of Cairo* were adapted as a game, Tom would likely pull Cecilia into his world rather than step into hers.

As we have seen in previous chapters, Jenkins compares current videogames to the cinema of the early twentieth century, an art form still in a stage of rapid technical development and radical experimentation, still awaiting coherent theories and critical approaches, and still lacking a tradition or a canon. Videogames, Jenkins believes, have almost unbounded commercial and artistic potential, but they need time to grow up.[17] Film critic Graham Leggat similarly describes the relation between games and film as Oedipal: "cinema's scrappy stepchild, the game world is . . . constantly competing with an idealized, phantasmic father for the love and attention of the mass market, yet never truly believing that it enjoys or deserves it."[18]

The videogame industry, likewise, views movies with an adolescent blend of infatuation and distrust. While it emulates the cinema in its pursuit of costly film licenses and transmedia franchises, it also manifests an acute awareness of cinema's artifices, visible in games that parody or pay homage

49

to Hollywood. For instance, in THQ's 2005 *Destroy All Humans!* we play as Cryptosporidium-137, a randy little alien bent on killing humans to harvest their DNA and, more generally, to exercise a healthy appetite for mass destruction. Set in the 1950s, the game takes its inspiration from cheap science fiction movies of the era. With his large head, gray skin, and black eyes, his flying saucer, disintegrator ray, "Zap-o-matic" lightning gun, and anal probe, Crypto fits the part of a B-movie alien. But the game refers to Tim Burton's 1996 invasion film parody *Mars Attacks!* more than it draws from films of an earlier era. We identify with the alien warmonger and share his glee in frying farmers, policemen, and government agents because the game portrays these people as shallow and stupid. The perverse humor of *Destroy All Humans!* relies on the sense that Crypto, full of wisecracks and impatience for the sexual repression and dullness of his victims, seems more human than the humans he destroys. The game overturns the moral sensibilities of the films it references, mocking the popular fears and fantasies of the Cold War and Hollywood's Golden Age.

Like *Destroy All Humans!* Capcom's 2003 *Viewtiful Joe* makes an affectionate mockery of the cinema, not by lampooning the lurid content of Saturday matinees but rather by calling attention to the artifice of what we see on screen in both films and games—something many videogames attempt to obscure in their quest for greater realism. Like *The Purple Rose of Cairo*, the game crosses the boundary between the real and the imaginary. While fan boy Joe and his girlfriend Silvia watch a Japanese superhero drama, the film's villain emerges from the screen and carries Sylvia away into Movieland. Joe follows, transformed in his alternate reality into Viewtiful Joe, a superhero clad in Power Rangers-style red tights and a crash helmet. At this point, the game departs radically from the simpler fighting games its design imitates. We defeat Joe's enemies not by executing increasingly complex attack maneuvers, but rather by manipulating the camera's perspective on these attacks through the use of "Viewtiful Effects." By zooming in on the action or rendering it in slow motion, Joe's attacks become more cinematic and therefore more powerful. In Movieland, action collapses into appearance. Joe must fight to rescue Silvia and, like his movie idols, he must look good doing it, or his efforts amount to nothing.

At the conclusion of *Viewtiful Joe*, the credit sequence displays a series of mock movie posters with Joe inserted into memorable scenes from classic Hollywood action films, including *King Kong*, *Jaws*, *Star Wars*, and *Gladiator*. Peter Molyneux's 2005 *The Movies* offers another way to become part of Hollywood tradition, placing us in the role of a movie mogul guiding a studio from 1920 to the present day. The simulation focuses on maintaining the studio itself, including set design and development of new filmmaking technology;

the hiring of actors and the nurturing their careers; and, finally, the shooting, editing, and marketing of films. The game couches its business simulation in a historical context. Different film genres vary in popularity from one era to the next. Comedies, for instance, are more successful in the Depression era, while science fiction flourishes during the Cold War. Like Molyneux's earlier god game *Black & White*, which promises free play but also compels us to defeat rival deities, *The Movies* pits us against rival studios, and the simulation gains its momentum from the drive to crush the competition.

In this way, *The Movies* follows the design of other tycoon, conquest, and sports franchise simulations, but the game is unique in its blend of simulation with tools that allow the player to create digital films that can be viewed and distributed online. Videogame critic Ryan Davis describes these tools as "a Playskool version of something like FinalCut or Premiere [film editing software]," mostly offering a selection of prefabricated sequences that we compile to make our film.[19] Still, the tool also gives us control over subtler details such as mise-en-scène, lighting, sound effects, camera angles, and the mood of our actors' delivery. With its mock historical context, *The Movies* parodies Hollywood history like *Destroy All Humans!* and by pulling back the curtain on the movie business, the game emphasizes the artifice of cinema like *Viewtiful Joe*. But *The Movies* emulates Hollywood in a way that other games do not, promising to make the player a real filmmaker with the first set of in-game tools designed to create and distribute machinima.

Machinima, derived from "machine cinema," refers to the creation of digital animation using videogame software, an amateur's alternative to the more sophisticated computer-generated imagery (CGI) rendering tools used by professional filmmakers. As the first game to allow players to customize playback of gameplay sequences, id Software's 1996 *Quake* introduced the potential for gamers to dabble in cinematic art. Subsequent games such as *Unreal*, *Halo: Combat Evolved*, and *The Sims 2* offered players even greater potential to record gameplay, add visual and sound effects, and create feature-length narratives using character models and sets from the games. Rooster Teeth Productions' independently produced 2003 series *Red vs. Blue: The Blood Gulch Chronicles*, for instance, portrays comic dialogue among the bionic marines featured in *Halo*, and The History Channel series *Decisive Battles* represents the first commercial use of machinima, using Creative Assembly's real-time strategy game *Rome: Total War* to simulate clashes between ancient armies.

While machinima represents another intriguing aspect of Jenkins's transmedia storytelling, it does not threaten to replace cinema or to unseat professional CGI animators. The appeal of the genre lies in the novel juxtaposition of game images with the witty dialogue of amateur voice actors. Machinima works are often less visually engaging than the games themselves, and the comedic snap in the dialogue only emphasizes the artificiality or absence of affect in game characters, a serious obstacle to characterization in videogames and machinima.

In this sense, actors represent an essential difference between traditional cinema and digitally rendered games and films, something games cannot fully replicate. As we have seen in Chapter 1, even the most carefully rendered digital characters lack something lifelike in their appearance. Moreover, the repetitive structure of gameplay limits our capacity to identify with videogame heroes. If emotional involvement in a story depends on the identification with characters and the inevitability of resolution—death, in tragic terms—then videogames hold us at a distance, draining the story of consequence by allowing us, if we die, to start again where we left off using "Save" and "Load" functions. Videogame writer Steve Ince identifies repeated character death as a formidable obstacle to writing compelling game narrative:

> Discussion tends to assume that the end of the story comes with the game's finale, but if the character dies before that point is reached, that is the end of the current story for the player. Starting the game again or restarting from a suitable save point is effectively the player trying to experience a different ending. . . . Because the players consider any death to be a failure, they generally want to push past it and start again, resetting their mind, almost, to cancel out the failure.[20]

Novels and films move us because they make death meaningful; videogames make death meaningless. The climactic scene of Mel Gibson's disembowelment in *Braveheart*, for instance, would seem deflated if we could restart, drive a claymore through the trembling heart of Edward Longshanks, and marry the French princess. While some game characters like Mario, Lara Croft, and Master Chief have become celebrities, they are not, like the most beloved film stars, projections of our own emotions.

Media Convergence and Media Criticism

LucasArts' *Star Wars: The Force Unleashed* is the company's first major "next-gen product" available for Xbox 360, PlayStation 3, and Nintendo Wii. The game realizes both the technical and the narrative aspirations of Lucasfilm. Like *Bounty Hunter* and *Knights of the Old Republic*, the game narrative extends beyond the films and introduces new characters. Set seven years after the events depicted in *Revenge of the Sith* and more than ten years prior to the events depicted in *A New Hope*, *The Force Unleashed* casts the player as Darth Vader's powerful apprentice, a figure who does not appear in the films.

The game dramatizes the "dark times" in which the Jedi Knights are hunted to extinction and Darth Vader is fully transformed into a "Dark Lord of the Sith," events only vaguely represented in the films. With a new game engine jointly developed by LucasArts and ILM, *The Force Unleashed* represents the latest fruit of the collaboration fostered at the LDAC. In his production diary, Project Lead W. Haden Blackman writes, "The groups within [LDAC] are separated by discipline, but nothing happens in isolation. . . . [T]he animation group bleeds into the design team, which is a stone's throw away from the cinematics team, who takes their work and directs the characters and settings to perform the cutscene animation that propels the story."[21]

With the considerable financial and technological resources of the film industry brought to bear on interactive entertainment, videogames like *The Force Unleashed* will look more cinematic, as Blackman promises. With game design tools brought to bear on moviemaking, films will look faster and more kinetic. But, from a critical standpoint, will these games and films be better? Just as media convergence has transformed the way artists create films and games, both in the tools they use and in the stories they tell, it has also influenced the way critics and scholars evaluate and interpret films and games.

Adopting film theory as a means of interpreting games, media scholars propose that what we see in film establishes precedents for what we see in games, in terms of both thematic content and visual perspective. Film critic Graham Leggat writes, "Just about everything video games know about visual language and narrative was learned from the movies . . . from camera angles to cuts and dissolves, from the deployment of original music to mise-en-scène."[22] Game scholar Mark J.P. Wolf likewise claims, "Theoretically, many of the same issues are present in video games and film: spectator positioning and suture, point of view, sound and image relations, semiotics, and other theories dealing with images of representation. . . . It is perhaps due to the desire to measure up to the standard of visual realism set by film and television that the video game evolved as it has."[23] Videogame evolution parallels cinematic evolution, for instance, in the construction of virtual spaces. Wolf compares the single, static frames of early games like Taito's 1978 *Space Invaders* and Atari's 1980 *Missile Command* to the early films of the Lumière brothers and George Méliès, which maintain a static point of view and make no use of editing to link different locations. Scrolling games like Activision's 1982 *Pitfall!* and Nintendo's 1985 *Super Mario Bros.* correspond to the early development of panning and tracking. Early adventure games like Atari's *Adventure* and *E.T.* simulate cutting and continuity editing through the use of distinct but contiguous game spaces. Finally, Wolf argues, the immersive three-dimensional environments of current games replicate the "space represented in classical Hollywood film . . . viewed from multiple angles and viewpoints."[24]

At the same time, the potential for the player to act within these virtual environments makes game spaces essentially different from film spaces. Wolf explains, "Whereas the cinema offered a window and positioned the spectator within the world it depicted, the video game goes further, allowing the spectator to explore that world and take an active role in its events."[25] Our success in a game depends largely on our knowledge of the game space, and game narrative often unfolds in spatial terms, as we discover new stories in different areas of the game world. Unlike films, most games offer a map, a symbolic representation of the virtual environment that aids our navigation. In this sense, game space is twofold, containing a diegetic world as well as a hyperdiegetic schematization of that world. Perhaps most important, game spaces must offer the potential for free exploration, and so must appear navigable and continuous. Alexander Galloway explains this essential difference between cinematic vision and "gamic vision":

> Gamic vision requires fully rendered, actionable space. Traditional filmmaking almost never requires the construction of full spaces. Set designers and carpenters build only the portion of the set that will appear within the frame. Because a direct or has complete control over what does appear within the frame, this task is easy to accomplish. The camera positions are known in advance. Once the film is complete, no new camera positions will ever be included. . . . By contrast, game design explicitly requires the construction of a complete space in advance that is then exhaustively explorable. . . . The camera position in many games is not restricted. The player is the one who controls the camera positon, by looking, by moving, by scrolling, and so on.[26]

Molyneux calls the player "the best camera man because he knows what he wants to see," but the challenge, he says, "is to allow people the flexibility to choose their own camera angles," while maintaining visual and narrative coherence in the game.[27]

This notion of a "camera" and the ability to control it forms a crucial part of the visual language of videogames and, on a technical level, enables the synthesis of films and games envisioned by Lucasfilm. The first-person perspective that has become conventional in current games, following models like id Software's 1992 *Wolfenstein 3D* and Cyan's 1993 *Myst*, has its origin in the "subjective shot" utilized in film. Galloway describes the subjective shot as "a rather extreme first person point-of-view shot, where the camera pans and tracks as if it were mounted on the neck of a character. . . . The viewer sees exactly what the character sees, as if the camera 'eye' were the same as the character 'I.'"[28] In films as in games, the subjective shot is marked by visual or sound effects that simulate the physical or psychological experience of the character: blurred or tinted vision to indicate injury, a binocular or magnified view to indicate peering through a lens or a scope, or panting and heaving to indicate fatigue.

Citing familiar scenes from the films *The Terminator, Predator,* and *The Silence of the Lambs,* Galloway notes that films most often use this specialized shot to represent "a sense of alienation, detachment, otherness, or fear . . . the vision of criminals, monsters, or killer machines." Games, on the other hand, more commonly use the subjective shot not to represent marginalized consciousness, but rather to "achieve an intuitive sense of affective motion," to simulate being and acting within a virtual world. The subjective shot has become a keystone of game design in a variety of genres, including first-person shooters, role-playing games, and driving games. In fact, Galloway concludes, the subjective point of view "is so omnipresent and so central to the grammar [of videogames] . . . that it essentially becomes coterminous with it."[29]

While games, according to Leggat, Wolf, and Galloway, are the progeny of cinema in terms of both content and visual language, the aesthetics of game design has also begun to exert an influence on filmmaking, as film becomes more digitized. Ridley Scott, who produced a series of live-action online short films in 2004 promoting the release of Atari's *DRIV3R,* finds greater creative potential in games. Scott told the *New York Times,* "The idea that a world, the characters that inhabit it, and the stories those characters share can evolve with the audience's participation and, perhaps, exist in a perpetual universe is indeed very exciting to me."[30] Leggat compares the fight choreography in the *Matrix* and *Kill Bill* films to the wild moves performed in fighting games, and Galloway calls special attention to the "bullet time" sequence in *The Matrix,* where time slows and Neo impossibly dodges a hail of gunfire, as "a brief moment of gamic cinema, a brief moment where the aesthetic of gaming moves in and takes over the film."[31]

The interactive nature of game narrative that intrigues Scott has also prompted more independent filmmakers to reconsider the ways a story can be told on film. Tom Tykwer's 1999 film *Run Lola Run,* for instance, portrays a young woman trying to aid her desperate boyfriend as he rushes to repay a debt to a crime boss. Even with its chic rapid-fire editing and animation sequences, *Run Lola Run* looks like a standard caper film until Lola, surprisingly, is shot dead about twenty minutes into the action. Rather than accept this outcome, however, she simply opens her eyes and says, "No," transporting herself back in time as if restarting the game, which she replays twice throughout the film until she achieves the desired ending. *Run Lola Run* reveals that interactivity has begun to destabilize the way filmmakers view their craft, even at the fundamental level of narrative structure. Tykwer's film is not nonlinear but multilinear, like a game that a player can complete or fail to complete in any number of ways.

For some critics, however, media convergence, particularly this increasingly visible influence of videogames on cinema, signals an aesthetic and intellectual corruption. In a survey of films about the Second World War, film critic David Thomson calls Michael Bay's 2001 film *Pearl Harbor,* "not just a colossal bore, but a defamation of popular history that leaves you in despair of the cinema."[32] Thomson believes that videogames have obscured filmmakers and audiences' understanding of the complexity of history and the reality of violence. He writes:

> It's what you get when the kids in the audience and the kids in charge have spent two decades playing video combat games. . . . Virtually every set-up [in *Pearl Harbor*] puts the camera in the best position not just to see the explosion but also to be it. The essential Bay shot is the POV from the bomb that falls on the *Arizona*; it has all the gravitational zest, and the denial of damage or tragedy, that's built into the trigger-jerking spasms of video games.[33]

For Thomson, gamic vision in films does not signify the exciting potential of media convergence, but rather reduces cinematic art and marks a shallow fascination with the hyperactive images of violent action rather than the causes or consequences of such action.

Although fans of *Star Wars* and *The Matrix* might accuse Thomson of being old-fashioned, Thomson rightly observes that films, when they try to copy games, look silly. Even as *The Chronicles of Riddick: Escape from Butcher Bay* proves that good games can be made from bad films, and *The Godfather: The Game* proves that good games can be made from good films, Hollywood has not yet discovered a way to make a good film from a good game. Early attempts to do so have been ridiculous or merely forgettable, including *Super Mario Bros.* (1993), *Street Fighter* (1994), and *Mortal Kombat* (1995). *Final Fantasy: The Spirits Within* (2001), rendered entirely in CGI, lost more than $120 million and bankrupted Square Pictures. *Lara Croft: Tomb Raider* (2001), *Resident Evil* (2002), *Silent Hill* (2006), and *Hitman* (2007) have done well at the box office but utterly disappointed film critics with their glossy violence, inane dialogue, and shallow characterization. In other words, they seem too game-like.

Angelina Jolie's attempt to embody the iconic Lara Croft has raised critical awareness about the different virtues of each medium. In his book *Trigger Happy*, Steven Poole argues that Lara Croft, as she appears in the games, "is an abstraction, an animated conglomeration of sexual and attitudinal signs . . . whose very blankness encourages the (male or female) player's psychological projection."[34] Film critic Kate Stables likewise questions the methods for adapting iconic game characters to films:

What kind of pleasures can the filmmakers offer through live-action Lara that could rival [videogame Lara's] immersive, interactive charms? . . . Jolie can make Lara flesh, but [Lara] cannot be fleshed out. Just as Lara's iconic appearance must be recreated, so her thin, static back-story must be retained and respected. Film Lara can't grow, change, or perform the simplest movie-character arcs without damaging the original franchise.[35]

The most spectacular failures in film-game franchising, from Atari's *E.T.* to Square's *Final Fantasy: The Spirits Within*, occur when filmmakers attempt to replicate the grammar of videogames in films and game design-ers attempt to replicate the grammar of films in videogames. In a review of Jackson's *The Return of the King*, film critic Anthony Lane writes, "As I watched the film, an eager victim of its boundless will to astound, I found my loyal memories to the book beginning to fade. It may be time to halt the endless comparisons between page and screen, and to confess that the two are very different beasts."[36] As the fusion of the film and game industries continues and transmedia franchises emerge, designers of film-based games must similarly acknowledge that games and films, despite their convergence, are also two very different beasts. Though some may try to make games that play like films, or movies that play like games, we find that the narrative forms governing one genre do not quite fit the other. Like the Matrix itself, transmedia narrative is an expansive and perpetually expanding simulated dream world, a new sort of beast born in the age of convergence.

❖ II ❖
RHETORIC

❖ 4 ❖

Politics, Persuasion, and Propaganda in Videogames

In November 2005, three U.S. senators—Hillary Clinton (D-NY), Joe Lieberman (I-CT), and Evan Bayh (D-IN)—proposed the Family Entertainment Protection Act (FEPA), a law that would allow the Federal Trade Commission (FTC) to police the sale of games containing graphic violence or explicit sexual content. The National Institute on Media and the Family listed the five most offensive games targeted by FEPA, with terse descriptions of content:

1. *Far Cry.* Lots of blood and intense violence.
2. *F.E.A.R.* Graphic cannibalism.
3. *The Warriors.* Gang warfare against police.
4. *Stubbs the Zombie.* Lead character eats the brains of humans.
5. *True Crime: New York City.* A rogue police officer guns down people.[1]

The bill expired in committee in January 2007, lacking support and interest, but Clinton, Lieberman, and Bayh are justified in their concern about the destructive effects of videogames on young people. In their attempt to protect children from coercive messages, they show a realistic awareness of the persuasive power of interactive entertainment. But in their fixation on cannibals and cop killers, they demonstrate only a narrow appreciation of the rhetorical potential of videogames. They see only the harm they might do and only the most lurid forms of violence they represent. Games like *Doom,* the gory fantasy favored by the Columbine shooters, merit serious scrutiny, but legislators, educators, and parents should remain wary of games that present more subtle dangers, such as those disguised as a call of duty.

In fact, the government has capitalized on the lure of simulated violence as surely as the entertainment industry has. In 2002, the U.S. Army released *America's Army,* a game designed as a recruiting tool for the War on Terror and distributed for free on the Internet. In 2004, Syrian developers followed with *Under Siege,* a game, also available for free online, intended to propagandize Palestinian resistance. Videogames certainly have destructive potential, but their influence, as we will see, reaches far beyond living rooms and home-rooms, reaching as far, perhaps, as Hebron and Haditha.

At the same time, videogames have more constructive potential as a rhetorical device. In 2003, for instance, the Howard Dean campaign released *The Howard Dean for Iowa Game* to attract voters and promote the candidate's platform online—the first effort to integrate videogames into an American presidential campaign. In 2006, mtvU commissioned *Darfur Is Dying,* a game designed to raise awareness of the humanitarian crisis in the Sudan and to spark political action on college campuses.

Unfortunately, shocking incidents like the Columbine massacre and near-sighted legislation like FEPA have obscured the importance of these experiments and polarized public discourse about videogames. As we will see, many experts argue that games teach us to kill; many others claim that games teach us to think faster, more critically, and more creatively. Yet, these entrenched camps agree on one thing: games can influence our thinking and our actions, and in this sense, games can persuade and teach. In their capacity to influence the way we think and act, videogames have become intrinsically rhetorical, not only as a hobbyhorse in debates about free speech and child welfare, but also as a tool to inform and to manipulate public opinion.

Videogame designer and theorist Gonzalo Frasca, whose research emphasizes the potential of games as tools to raise social consciousness, argues that "videogames could indeed deal with human relationships and social issues, while encouraging critical thinking." Frasca, in fact, proposes that games might emulate Augusto Boal's notion of the Theatre of the Oppressed, using interactive simulations to enact an "oppressive situation, where the protagonist has to deal with powerful characters that do not let her achieve her goals."[2] In fact, many games already implicitly raise questions about the legitimacy and exercise of power.

Having considered the formal aspects of videogames as a narrative and visual art in the first part of the book, we turn to their influence as a form of public discourse in the way that Frasca describes them. This chapter reviews the public controversies created by videogames and considers the use of games as a mode of persuasion, both as activism and as propaganda. Finally, it considers the special rhetorical appeal of interactive entertainment, examining the ways our virtual participation in a conflict may influence our understanding of the larger political conflicts the games represent. What the courts, Congress, and the larger culture once viewed as an "inconsequential" diversion we now recognize as a gravely important medium. The controversies generated by videogames in the last three decades raise fundamental questions about the nature of creative expression, civil liberty, and commerce, and they invite us to examine these familiar issues through a new lens. Students likely spend much more time playing videogames than thinking about the Constitution, but in classrooms, one need not exclude the other.

Videogames and Public Controversy

While advocates and scholars often herald the industry's expanding revenues as primary evidence of the cultural ascendance of videogames, we find a more revealing measure of their status in their gradual recognition as a form of free speech. Today, defenders of the industry routinely invoke the First Amendment, and judges routinely decide in their favor, striking down laws restricting the distribution of videogames. Twenty-five years ago, however, even the most zealous civil libertarian would have hesitated to claim constitutional protection for *Space Invaders, Asteroids,* or *Pac-Man.*

In the early 1980s, the law generally viewed videogames not as a mode of communication but as a mode of conduct, differentiating expressive entertainment, such as music and film, from recreational entertainment, such as pinball and ping-pong. Because early arcade games lacked an obvious narrative or rhetorical component and required coordination and quick reflexes, courts reasoned that they were not a new medium but rather newfangled mock-ups of familiar game room diversions—more like pinball than film. This view still underlies the view of critics, like Roger Ebert, who persistently argue that videogames are like sport, in that they lack an intellectual or an aesthetic component. In 1982, the case *America's Best Family Showplace v. City of New York* concluded that videogames are "pure entertainment with no informational element." In 1983, the Supreme Court of Massachusetts likewise decided that "any communication or expression of ideas that occurs during the playing of a video game is purely inconsequential." Unprotected by the First Amendment, videogames fell victim to restrictive local ordinances, such as a 1982 law in Des Plaines, Illinois, that barred individuals under the age of twenty-one from visiting an arcade without a parent.[3]

Contrary to these precedents, David Goroff, in his 1984 *Columbia Law Review* analysis, claimed that videogames indeed merit constitutional protection. The game developer, he argues, is a kind of artist who presents an "expressive creation" to an audience, those who play the game. This new understanding of the videogame as something more than a gadget, as a "creation" capable of transmitting ideas, signals an important interpretive shift that has guided public discourse about videogames since the late 1980s.[4] Since the courts in New York and Massachusetts judged videogames "purely inconsequential," American legal thinking has generally reversed and followed Goroff's reasoning, consistently granting videogames First Amendment protection, even under the most difficult circumstances. In 2001, advocates for William Sanders, a teacher slain in the Columbine shooting, filed a product liability suit against several software companies, charging that videogames desensitized and provoked the killers to violence. Colorado judge Lewis Babcock dismissed the case, affirming the First Amendment rights of videogame developers in spite of his personal sympathy for the plaintiffs.

Since videogames have gained constitutional protection, advocates against media violence have adopted a different legal strategy, effectively changing the subject of debate from civil liberty to public welfare. Games, they say, may be a form of free speech, but if they pose a danger, like the man who calls "Fire!" in a crowded theater, then they are subject to regulation.

Congress first addressed the controversy in June 1994, convening a House subcommittee to assess the problem of videogame violence. Spurred by public concern about Midway's *Mortal Kombat* and Digital Pictures' *Night Trap,* two games containing graphic violence, the subcommittee sought measures to protect children from the insidious moral dangers arising from rapid technological change, especially those arising from the newly hatched World Wide Web. Chairman Edward Markey declared:

> Just as the technological developments that enable a game to portray graphic death scenes have led to plans for a rating system, technological advances that will bring these games directly into people's living rooms by way of cable or phone systems underscore the need to strengthen the ability of caregivers to protect young children from excessive and gratuitous video violence.[5]

Two months earlier, in April 1994, a group of leading software publishers founded the Interactive Digital Software Association (IDSA; renamed Entertainment Software Association [ESA] in 2003) to represent the interests of the videogame industry in the face of these increasingly serious inquiries. As its founding principles, the IDSA affirmed that videogames constitute a form of free speech and that the videogame industry must remain independent of government regulation. At the House subcommittee hearing, IDSA president Doug Lowenstein said, "It is our belief that neither the IDSA nor the government can constitutionally regulate content, nor should they try. That should remain the responsibility of individual publishers and platform manufacturers."[6]

While Congress has never really sought to "regulate content," as Lowenstein suggested, it has repeatedly attempted to restrict the distribution of violent or sexually explicit videogames, most recently with FEPA. Deflecting allegations of censorship, legislators have condemned game companies' apparent neglect of child welfare in their pursuit of expanding profits. In 1994, however, Lowenstein and Markey found common ground in their plan to implement a rating system independent of Congress and the publishers, the Entertainment Software Rating Board (ESRB). Ultimately, the formation of the ESRB was the most significant result of the 1994 hearing and still exists as the most practical compromise between the industry's right to free speech and the government's mandate to protect the public good. The rating system meets legislators' demands for a useful guide for parents but does not subject the industry to federal regulation. More significantly, it demonstrates a sense of social responsibility by the videogame industry and a willingness to work with Congress to address public concerns—attitudes not manifested prior to 1994.

By 2000, however, the context of videogame controversy had changed drastically, and the initial cooperation between Congress and the IDSA deteriorated into mistrust and antagonism. In the horror and confusion following Columbine, public scrutiny of videogames intensified. Eric Harris, one of the shooters, played *Doom* obsessively, and he maintained a Web site containing levels he had designed for the game, descriptions of homemade explosives, and hit lists naming fellow students. Online, he called himself "Rebldomaker," or Rebel Doom Maker. Harris's AOL member profile also indicated a link between his interest in the game and his destructive impulses, identifying one of his hobbies as "professional doom and doom2 creator," his occupation as "DOOMING the hell out of my computer (playing doom, a lot)," and his personal quote as: "Shut up and shoot it. . . . Kill Em AALLLL!!!!"[7] The public widely speculated that the *Doom II* levels designed by Harris corresponded to the halls and classrooms of Columbine High School, a connection that would have lent proof to the widespread allegation that videogames serve as murder simulators.

As further evidence of the killers' interest in violent videogames surfaced, President Bill Clinton ordered the FTC to investigate the marketing practices of entertainment companies, in order to corroborate the charge that the media bears some responsibility for transforming Eric Harris and Dylan Klebold into homicidal maniacs. The report concluded that the film, music, and videogame industries actively subvert their own parental advisories and rating systems by aggressively marketing graphic violence to children. More generally, the government called into doubt the basic ethical standards of the entertainment industry, as well as their professed willingness to cooperate with Congress and with independent rating boards.

In March and September 2000, a Senate committee convened to respond to the FTC report and to hear evidence from physicians, researchers, and educators who testified to a causal relation between videogame violence and antisocial behavior in children and adolescents. Craig Anderson, an Iowa State University psychologist, plainly expressed the consensus of the medical community that "playing violent video games can cause increases in aggression and violence. . . . Young people who play lots of violent video games behave more violently than those who do not."[8]

To many, this medical conclusion represented the smoking gun connecting the videogame industry to Columbine and other school shootings. Attorneys across the country filed product liability suits against game companies, demanding accountability from an industry, as they saw it, unjustly insulated by the First Amendment. Sabrina Steger, the distraught mother of a victim of a school shooting in Paducah, Kentucky, pleaded with the committee: "Our lawsuit is not about free speech. It is about product liability, plain and simple. Any person or company that makes a product is responsible for the harm that comes from its use."[9] Joe Lieberman, then a candidate for vice president, supported the allegations in vivid, alliterative rhetoric. He declared, "Columbine was a warning that the culture of carnage surrounding our children may have gone too far, and that the romanticized and sanitized visions of violence that our children are being bombarded with by the media has become part of a toxic mix that has actually now turned some of them into killers."[10]

Besieged, the videogame industry regarded these proceedings as an effort to leverage public fears against its constitutional right and to exploit Columbine for political gains. Lowenstein protested that Congress invited only those experts who supported their own position and submitted a report that challenged the research methods of Anderson and the others and called attention to researchers with dissenting views. Peter Moore, president of Sega of America, accused Senate committee members, including Lieberman, John McCain (R-AZ), and Sam Brownback (R-KS), of making "political stump speeches" at the expense of the industry's reputation.[11]

In June 2005, a new scandal confirmed for many legislators that videogame companies were working to undermine the ESRB, as the FTC alleged in 2000. Users discovered hidden content in Rockstar's *Grand Theft Auto III: San Andreas:* a scenario that portrayed the game's central character, Carl Johnson, having sex with a girlfriend, who invites Carl into her house for "coffee." Distributed by users on the Internet, the "Hot Coffee mod" unlocked the hidden content in the game's code and allowed players not only to witness an explicit sex scene, but also to control Carl's position and rhythm during the encounter. Rockstar pleaded that the scene emerged only as a result of user tampering, but industry critics assumed that the developers had concealed the scene in order to deceive the ESRB—an "Adults Only" rating would have severely restricted sales.

Hillary Clinton, who has now risen as a preeminent crusader against videogame violence, proposed FEPA in response to the "Hot Coffee" scandal, claiming that the industry cannot effectively police itself and requires federal intervention. As Clinton said on the floor of the Senate, FEPA would "put teeth" into the ESRB rating system, prohibiting businesses from selling "Mature" or "Adults Only" games to anyone under seventeen. It would also subject the ESRB to the FTC, which would oversee annual reviews of ESRB standards, investigate misleading ratings, respond to consumer grievances, and conduct secret audits of retailers to gather evidence of violations.[12] Following further House subcommittee hearings in June 2006, congressional representatives Cliff Stearns (R-FL), Jim Matheson (D-UT), and Mike McIntyre (D-NC) have proposed the Truth in Video Game Rating Act, a measure that targets not retailers but the ESRB itself, subjecting its practices to scrutiny by the Government Accountability Office (GAO).

Opponents identify a basic constitutional flaw in these proposals: an entertainment rating system created in the private sector cannot be used to enforce government policy. Clinton's rhetoric in support of the bill eschews this legal knot, emphasizing instead her commitment to family values. On the floor of the Senate, she said, "This is about protecting children. . . . Media culture is like having a stranger in your house, and it exerts a major influence over your children. It is this attack on the sensibilities of our children that is the subject of the bill I introduce today. It is a bill that I consider to be of tremendous importance to our families."[13] FEPA did not pass into law, confirming the belief of Lowenstein and others that its value was mainly rhetorical. Like the Senate hearings in 2000, they suggest, FEPA represented an attempt by Democratic leaders to position themselves more favorably with conservative voters at the expense of an industry already under public suspicion.

In 1982, when the Des Plaines City Council barred minors from arcades, legislators worried that videogames encouraged children to spend their allowances irresponsibly and to neglect homework. Now they worry that videogames may influence fundamental patterns of thinking and behavior. The sustained and increasingly aggressive efforts by Congress to regulate the industry demonstrate the widespread consciousness that videogames, in the course of their development, have gained immense rhetorical power.

Activist Games

We can broadly define rhetoric as the art of persuasion: any speech, text, or image that sways an audience toward a point of view. The Greeks understood it more narrowly as a forensic exercise and defined its conventions in terms of the relation between a speaker and an audience. In *Gorgias,* Plato makes little distinction between rhetoric and sophistry; Socrates advises, "The orator need have no knowledge of the truth about things; it is enough for him to have discovered a knack of persuading the ignorant that he seems to know more than the experts."[14] Aristotle elevated and formalized argumentation strategy by emphasizing the importance of proof: appeals to the character or the credibility of the speaker, the sympathy of the audience, or the merit of the speech itself. More than Plato's confidence game, persuasion, for Aristotle, ideally represents a kind of contract between the speaker and the audience, in which both seek a common good or a probability of truth, if absolute truth is elusive.[15] From Aristotle's time to our own, this principle has girded democratic societies. Where citizens are free to speak their case in public, the art of persuasion assumes primary importance. It becomes necessary to represent oneself or others before the law, to maintain one's position as a citizen or to rise to prominence, and to influence decisions and effect change.

While the fundamental purposes of rhetoric remain as relevant for us as they were for Aristotle, the means of achieving them have multiplied. Because the courts now grant protection to videogames as a form of free speech, videogames, as speech, may function as an essential mechanism of democracy. In his testimony to the Senate in March 2000, education researcher Eugene Provenzo explained that violent videogames cause "adolescents to assume a rhetorical stance that equates violence with style and personal empowerment."[16] In other words, videogames are not like a full moon or a hypnotic suggestion, driving children to madness. Rather, they are like a sophist's seductive argument, persuading children with skewed but subtle reasoning. Researchers have hesitated, however, to acknowledge that videogames might present a "rhetorical stance" other than that of a sociopath.

As Frasca suggests, however, videogames invite us to enlarge our understanding of the nature and function of rhetoric. Within this larger understanding, distress about violent images must sometimes give way to interest in the more constructive rhetorical possibilities of videogames, especially for educators. Ian Bogost, a videogame researcher at the Georgia Institute of Technology and cofounder of Persuasive Games, views the game developer today as both artist and activist. In their coauthored essay, "Videogames Go to Washington: The Story Behind *The Howard Dean for Iowa Game,*" Bogost and Frasca argue, "Videogames can and should inspire player action in the real world."[17] In a December 2003 review of simulation and strategy games in the webzine *Slate,* Steven Johnson ventures: "The [2004] U.S. presidential campaign may be the first true election of the digital age, but it's still missing one key ingredient. Where is the videogame version of Campaign 2004?"[18] By August 2004,

Lantern Games and Ubisoft had developed, respectively, *Frontrunner* and *The Political Machine.* Both games cast us as campaign manager for John Kerry, George W. Bush, or another candidate, simulating strategy in the months leading to the 2004 election. We manage budgets, secure endorsements from influential organizations, and schedule debates and talk show interviews in the frantic effort to boost our candidate's exposure and approval rating in each state.

But while their theme is political, these simulations offer no motivation for real political action. We may assume ideological stances on many different issues, and these stances realistically influence our candidate's support in each state, but these games are essentially self-contained fantasies of power, like sports games that allow us to manage our favorite teams or strategy games that allow us to build empires. In fact, these games encourage us to disengage from the political reality of 2004 by allowing us to make a run for the White House ourselves or to manage campaigns for historical candidates such as Abraham Lincoln, Franklin Roosevelt, or Ronald Reagan. *Frontrunner* designer Paul Schuytema says that he incorporated "ideological leanings" not to raise awareness or to provoke political action but mostly because "it makes the game . . . a little more fun."[19]

Ian Bogost and Gerard LaFond founded Persuasive Games in 2003 to create videogames with clearer rhetorical objectives. Their Web site defines their purpose:

> We design, build, and distribute electronic games for persuasion, instruction, and activism. Our games influence players to take action through game play. Games communicate differently than other media; they not only deliver messages but also simulate experiences. While often thought to be just a leisure activity, games can also become rhetorical tools.[20]

Bogost acknowledges that videogames, like the television sound bite, might "erode political speech while replacing it with mere entertainment," as do *Frontrunner* and *The Political Machine,* but in his own work he means to demonstrate that they might also "become a useful tool for fostering debate and critical thinking."[21]

In December 2003, the Howard Dean campaign hired Persuasive Games to develop *The Howard Dean for Iowa Game,* a game designed by Bogost and Frasca to help rally supporters in the weeks preceding the Iowa caucus. Bogost explains, "The intention of the game was to teach current and potential constituents about the power of grassroots outreach," the core principle of Dean's campaign strategy.[22] The game opens by displaying a map of Iowa divided into electoral districts, where we place icons representing Dean's supporters. The object of the game is to generate as many supporters as possible before the date of the caucus, but we begin with only one supporter, "You."

Placing "You" in one of the districts opens one of three minigames in which we wave a sign, distribute pamphlets, or canvas a street—activities the Dean campaign identified as crucial means of grassroots outreach. The higher we score in the minigames, the faster additional supporters are generated on the main map, and each additional supporter generates even more supporters.

Bogost articulates several problems designing activist games: "How do we tailor a videogame to convey an endorsed political message? How do we craft it so that the public does not dismiss it as trivial? How does it integrate with the rest of the campaign?"[23] In some ways, *The Howard Dean for Iowa Game* successfully conveys Dean's ideal of grassroots outreach. By design, the game argues that a single supporter, through old-fashioned legwork, can muster a small army of caucus-goers. As the game itself declares, "One person can make a difference!" In other ways, the game fails to persuade. While it teaches us the principles of grassroots campaigning, it does not outline Dean's platform. In other words, it tells us how to support Dean but not why we should do so. For this reason, Bogost admits, the game shares the stigma of Dean's ultimate failure in the Democratic primary.

In two subsequent projects, *Activism,* a game commissioned by the Democratic Congressional Campaign Committee, and *Take Back Illinois,* commissioned by the Illinois Republican Party, Bogost emphasizes policy issues rather than campaigning. Both games use integrated minigames corresponding to specific issues such as security, education, and the economy, illustrating the dilemmas of resource allocation. If we give too much attention to one issue while neglecting another, we lose the game and, perhaps, the election.

In response to Persuasive Games' work with Howard Dean, the Republican National Committee released *John Kerry Tax Invaders,* a parody of the arcade classic *Space Invaders* created by Web designer Jeremy Kenney. In the game, the player moves the disembodied head of George W. Bush, firing projectiles at advancing numeric phalanxes representing Kerry's proposed tax increases. Before the action begins, the game announces, "Only you can stop the tax invader! Save the USA from John Kerry's tax ideas!" Despite its crude design and obvious clownishness, the game presents a subtle argument. Drawing from linguists George Lakhoff and Frank Luntz, Bogost suggests that the game rhetorically frames tax increases as an invasion by hostile forces intent on seizing one's property. It "reflects an underlying logic at work in conservative politics . . . namely that [taxation] is a theft rather than a contribution to the common social good."[24] *John Kerry Tax Invaders* does not offer a lesson in tax policy any more than *Activism* addresses the complexities of education reform. Rather, it teaches one to think like a conservative, just as *Activism* teaches on to think about the problems of resource allocation.

More recently, activists have used videogames to address more global issues. In April 2006, mtvU commissioned *Darfur Is Dying,* a game developed by University of Southern California graduate student Susana Ruiz to inform players about the humanitarian crisis in Sudan and to encourage political action. We begin the game by selecting a character from a group of men and women, ages 10 through 30, to retrieve water for our village. Even this preliminary choice, however, confronts us with the perils of Darfur. The game tells us, "You risk being attacked and possibly killed by the Janjaweed militias when you leave the confines of your camp, but you must do it in order to provide water for your community." We dash across a barren landscape toward the well, hiding from trucks carrying armed militia. If we fail, we learn that boys captured by the militia face torture and death, while girls meet with kidnapping and rape. If we succeed, we enter another phase of the game, in which we perform a variety of tasks to keep our village supplied with food, water, and shelter. We may interact with other refugees, who tell us their stories and provide individual glimpses of the Darfur crisis. While humanitarian aid lends some relief, Janjaweed bandits frequently raid the settlement, undoing our work. Most significantly, perhaps, *Darfur Is Dying* features a prominent button inviting us to "Take Action." By pressing the button, we gain advantages within the game, such as increased medical aid or temporary protection from the Janjaweed. A menu offers us a variety of ways we might work to end the crisis, such as writing to our local congressional representative or starting a divestment movement on our campus.

Many political thinkers, including those enthusiastic about new media, see videogames like these as nothing more than interactive cartoons, amusing but too shallow to provoke critical thinking or active political response. Andrew Rasiej, an information technology advisor to the Democratic Party, told the *New York Times,* "They're cute and nice, and people will send them to each other, but they're not going to capture their imagination."[25] Even Bogost and Frasca hesitate to make grand claims for their work. "A campaign videogame is merely one message within an ecology of other messages," Bogost writes. "Games may . . . reinforce ideas, but they can hardly decide the fate of an election."[26]

But Rasiej, in his dismissal of activist games, seems like the jurists, twenty-five years ago, who called videogames "inconsequential." While they still lack the explosive potential of powder kegs like Michael Moore's film, *Fahrenheit 9/11,* educators and political scientists should not dismiss videogames simply because they are the most recent element in the media "ecology" that sustains modern politics. Persuasive Games touts its achievement as creator of "the first official videogame ever commissioned in the history of the U.S. presidential elections," and credits Dean as "the first candidate to use a videogame as endorsed political speech."[27] In future campaigns, videogames will enhance rather than replace traditional means of informing ourselves or our students about candidates, issues, or crises. After her game was launched at a Save Darfur rally in Washington, DC, Ruiz said, "Even just the idea that there is a game out there, that makes people say, 'Oh, there's a problem in Darfur,' even if it provokes that kind of discussion, we're miles ahead of where we were."[28] Although games like *Activism* and *Darfur Is Dying* may oversimplify the issues they mean to represent, they function, as both Ruiz and Bogost suggest, as entryways to greater understanding and more consequential political action.

Propaganda Games

Both political activism and propaganda attempt to sway an audience. Yet, while we bless activism as a vital service to democracy, we despise propaganda as an insidious tyranny of the mind. The word itself innocently suggests the dissemination of ideas, but its connotations are more sinister. Propaganda does not rely on proof, as Aristotle's rhetoric does. It agitates or massages our emotions with specious logic and false conclusions. It does not inform. More frequently, it deceives, disguising opinion and disinformation as objective truth. It does not invite inquiry or invite us to consider different points of view. Rather, it bombards us with an incessant repetition of doctrine. It coerces us with threats, even as it claims to have our best interest at heart.

In their influential 1988 book, *Manufacturing Consent: The Political Economy of the Mass Media,* Edward S. Herman and Noam Chomsky propose that capitalist propaganda rather than free discourse drives contemporary Western culture. They identify a systematic bias in news reporting, arguing that the mass media purvey audiences to advertisers as a commodity, suppressing information that might destabilize the profitable partnership between large corporations and government. They explain further that "the raw material of news must pass through successive filters, leaving only the cleansed residue fit to print." These filters determine which events are newsworthy, frame our interpretation of these events, and, in the end, refract raw information as propaganda. Among these filters, anticommunism functions as a "national religion," framing issues "in terms of a dichotomized world of Communist and anti-Communist powers, with gains and losses allocated to contesting sides, and rooting for 'our side' considered an entirely legitimate news practice."[29]

The dissolution of the Soviet Union has forced Herman and Chomsky to revise their ideas, but the principles of their propaganda model remain relevant. Since 1991, Islamic terrorism has replaced communism as our dominant anti-ideology, reflected in videogames even more conspicuously than in the news. In the wake of the invasions of Afghanistan and Iraq, antiterrorism games have flourished. Red Storm has defined the genre with their *Tom Clancy* franchises, *Splinter Cell, Rainbow Six,* and *Ghost Recon.*

Zipper and Pandemic have followed, respectively, with their *SOCOM* and *Full Spectrum Warrior* series.

Although these games have superficially distinct narratives and pit us against a colorful range of real and imagined rogue states and terrorist organizations, their essential drama is the same: Some barbarian, bent on toppling a friendly government or wreaking anarchic genocide, compels quick, covert action from a U.S.-led multinational force. Inserting behind enemy lines, a small, highly trained team uses discipline, cooperation, and the most advanced military technology to defeat a larger though undisciplined enemy force. Covert operations rule out any public recognition of the team's heroism, but they are not in it for the glory—it's all in a day's work.

Replayed in dozens of games, this drama persuades us not only by the emotional excitement of gameplay but also by a rhetorical repetition packaged as the latest releases: America cooperates with international allies and supports peaceful governments. We resort to military intervention only in response to unprovoked aggression, and never to preempt a threat or to secure resources for our own use. We cannot wait for the approval of politicians too entangled by bureaucracy to take decisive action. We do not intervene with overwhelming force, which might inflict collateral damage, but with nearly invisible operatives whose victory depends on training, precise intelligence, and the continual development of new military technologies. We do not occupy. We extract when the mission is completed and allow foreign governments to settle their own affairs. We expect no thanks from the American public or from liberated peoples, both necessarily ignorant of global realities. Defending freedom is its own reward. The games claim to offer the most realistic portrayal of military action, simulating actual weapons and tactics and incorporating the most advanced artificial intelligence. But their convincing veneer of realism masks the contradiction between the heroic drama the games enact and the reality of American foreign policy. Their narrative of the War on Terror is appealing but deceptive.

We hesitate, however, to accuse Red Storm, Zipper, and Pandemic of spreading propaganda. As commercial developers, they may admit that their business is fiction, not truth. Critics, in fact, have become more disturbed by the new partnership between the Pentagon and the videogame industry to spread an officially endorsed, militaristic ideology, an alliance that Stanford researchers Tim Lenoir and Henry Lowood describe as the military-entertainment complex.[30] While the Department of Defense, Lenoir and Lowood argue, has supported the development of its own war games since the beginning of the Cold War, they have only recently begun to use commercially developed videogames as training and recruiting tools. Since 1996, the Pentagon has adapted *Doom II* as a combat simulator, licensed two games from the *Rainbow*

Six series for the same purpose, and consulted with Zipper and Pandemic in their development of *SOCOM* and *Full Spectrum Warrior.*

In Lenoir and Lowood's view, these collaborations signal the transformation of videogame consoles, personal computers, and the Internet not merely into channels of propaganda, but into "the training ground for what we might consider the post-human warfare of the future."[31] Their prediction has been realized most strikingly in *America's Army,* a game developed by the Navy's Modeling, Simulation, and Virtual Environments Institute using programming derived from the popular first-person shooters *Half-Life* and *Counter-Strike.* Released on Independence Day 2002, and distributed for free online, the game is unique as the first designed as a recruiting tool rather than a combat simulator. Its creators propose to reach young people where, they presume, they spend most of their time—on the Internet, playing videogames.

Since 2002, only the *Grand Theft Auto* series has stirred more controversy than *America's Army.* As critics suggest, using a videogame as a recruiting tool presents the government with a conflict of interest. While Congress has worked for more than a decade to protect young people from the influence of violent videogames, the Pentagon has now adopted violent videogames to lure the same young people to recruitment offices and war zones. A young man with an automatic rifle gives us pause in Columbine and Compton; in Kabul and Karbala he gives us pride.

Conscious of the cultural ambivalence toward violence, the army carefully presents its brand of virtual gunplay as conscientious and constructive. On a "Parents Info" page, the *America's Army* Web site assures us that the game is a reliable source of information:

> The *America's Army* game provides civilians with an inside perspective and a virtual role in today's premier land force: the U.S. Army. The game is designed to provide an accurate portrayal of Soldier experiences across a number of occupations. . . . As such, it is part of the Army's communications strategy designed to leverage the power of the Internet as a portal through which young adults can get a first hand look at what it is like to be a Soldier. The game introduces players to different Army schools, Army training, and life in the Army.[32]

The game itself begins with a series of basic training missions before we skirmish against other players online. By offering more specialized training and enforcing "Rules of Engagement" that prohibit players from ignoring mission objectives or attacking friendly units, the game intends to convey an ethos of teamwork and organization. The *America's Army* Web site further counsels parents:

> In elementary school kids learn about the actions of the Continental Army that won our freedoms under George Washington and the Army's role in ending Hitler's oppression. Today they need to know that the Army is engaged around the world to defeat terrorist forces bent on the destruction of America and our

freedoms. The game provides a virtual means to explore a variety of Soldier experiences in basic training, advanced training, and training missions in real world Army units, so that young adults can see how our training builds and prepares Soldiers to serve in units in defense of freedom.[33]

Or, in the words of President Bush in a 2002 speech, "when we're talking about war, we're really talking about peace."[34]

The ideological message of *America's Army* is more forceful and direct than that of commercial combat simulators, urging us to consider the game as an initiation into a historic confraternity engaged in a vital struggle. In its invitation to get involved, *America's Army* resembles *The Howard Dean for Iowa Game* and *Darfur Is Dying* more so than it resembles its own forebears, *Half-Life* and *Counter-Strike;* it attempts to persuade us. But its purposes are more hidden and coercive, and its rhetoric, laced with truth claims, indirect threats, and the compulsive repetition of virtue words, bears the hallmarks of propaganda: History is clear. Without us, tyranny would destroy your freedoms.

Critics worry that the army is sowing confusion among young men who exchange their DualShock controller for an M-16A2 and find that the game, in fact, does not "provide an accurate portrayal of Soldier experiences," as the army promises. Alexander Galloway challenges the U.S. Army's repeated claim that the game presents useful information about military service. He argues, "One cannot claim there to be a fidelity of context between an American teenager shooting foreign enemies in *America's Army* and the everyday minutia of that teenager, the specificities of his or her social life in language, culture and tradition."[35] In other words, the game renders virtual combat in photorealistic detail but remains detached from the complex web of experience that constitutes "life in the Army." It does not represent separations from family, tedious routines, or potential conflicts between duty and personal values. More significantly, it removes combat action from a social context to vacuum-sealed virtual battlefields, where enemies do not masquerade as civilians, innocents do not get in the way, and wounded buddies do not bleed. Games like *Counter-Strike* and *Rainbow Six* may ignore experiences that do not lend themselves to entertaining gameplay, but *America's Army,* by pretending to be a legitimate source of information, perpetrates a deception in doing so, according to Galloway.

In response to *America's Army* and other antiterrorism games, Arab groups have developed their own interactive propaganda. In 2003, Hezbollah's Central Internet Bureau released *Special Force,* a game that anticipates the 2006 Israel-Lebanon conflict by casting us as a member of the Islamic resistance in southern Lebanon. Mahmoud Rayya, a Hezbollah official, declared that the game is designed to compete ideologically with American videogames and to introduce the principles of resistance. As their Web site explains, "This game is resisting the Israeli occupation through the media." Like *America's Army, Special Force* proposes both to indoctrinate and to offer training for the real world. Hezbollah's game is likewise packaged in propaganda. The Web site further tells us, "The designers of Special Force are very proud to provide you with this special product, which embodies objectively the defeat of the Israeli enemy and the heroic actions taken by heroes of the Islamic Resistance in Lebanon. Be a partner in the victory. Fight, resist and destroy your enemy in the game of force and victory."[36] More recently, the Global Islamic Media Front, an organization linked to Al-Qaeda, released online *Quest for Bush,* a first-person shooter in which we stalk and assassinate the president.[37]

Although their rhetoric lacks the militancy of that of Hezbollah and the Global Islamic Media Front, Afkar Media, a Syrian developer, identifies similar purposes in releasing a series of games celebrating the heroism of anti-Zionist resistance. Like President Bush and the U.S. Army, Afkar talks about peace when they are really talking about war. Their Web site declares their intentions to share the "peaceful truth and tolerance of our civilization" and to spread "justice, acceptance, and love," but their most notable game, *Under Siege,* dramatizes the violence of the Second Intifada between 1999 and 2002.[38] We confront the brutal Israeli Defense Force with little more than our wits, as we dash through the rubble, outmaneuver tanks and deadly snipers, infiltrate a fortified building, and tear down the Israeli flag planted on the roof—the symbol of the hated occupation. Radwan Kasmiya, lead developer at Afkar, says, "We [Muslims] are the terrorist, the enemy, in these [American] games. . . . Our games are not propaganda. Our games are a reflection of our history—past or present. The fact is, most movies, most TV shows, most video games, put Muslims in a bad light, so we have to try to tell our side of the story."[39]

While *Under Siege* shares many gameplay conventions with its American counterparts, it features an important innovation in weaving virtual combat into a virtual social fabric. The fighting swirls around a single Palestinian family, whose members personify different perspectives of the conflict. Ahmad is a young jihadi. Kahled cooperates with the Israelis in order to protect his family. Mary represents the suffering of Muslim women. Mann is a boy whose school has been closed by the Israelis. And Abu Himam, a veteran of the struggle, embodies the commitment to Palestinian nationalism. Galloway calls for a similar social engagement in American videogames and videogame criticism. He writes, "I suggest that game studies should . . . turn not to a theory of realism in gaming as mere realistic representation, but define realist games as those games that reflect critically on the minutia of everyday life, replete as it is with struggle, personal drama and injustice."[40]

We should be wary of Afkar's truth claims, however, just as we are wary of the U.S. Army's. Although they promote *Under Siege* as a dramatization of real events documented by the United Nations and claim that its characters represent a "pure reflection of the Palestinian Society," the game does not represent civilian casualties or suicide attacks. In the interest of Afkar's creed of "justice, acceptance, and love," the game abruptly ends if we turn our weapons on civilians. Both *America's Army* and *Under Siege* claim to be realistic depictions of the current global conflict, but they both neglect its most troubling realities. As critical thinkers and players, we should resist uncritical, emotional responses that propaganda compels, subjecting these games equally to the rhetorical analysis of what they say and, more significantly perhaps, what they do not. Now that armies and terrorist militias have got their hands on videogames, we can no longer dismiss them as mere entertainment. When we are talking about videogames, after all, we are really talking about war.

The Rhetoric of Interactivity

The law no longer draws a distinction between videogames and other forms of creative expression; all are entitled to constitutional protection. As a form of rhetoric, however, videogames fundamentally differ from other media. Their method of persuasion is not strictly verbal, like that of a speech or an essay; nor is it strictly visual, like that of a propaganda poster or a sculpture; nor is it strictly performative, like that of a play or a demonstration. Like film, videogames synthesize words, images, and drama, but they differ from film in their capability to create empathy and to construct arguments by demonstrating causal relations between player action and the changing conditions of the game world. Interactivity itself constitutes a distinct rhetoric.

During the congressional hearings convened to assess videogame violence, even those with little experience of the medium recognized that the nature of interactivity poses a unique threat. In 1994, the American Medical Association submitted a statement urging Congress to consider that the "role-modeling capacity" of videogames makes them more dangerous than music or film as potential inducements to violent behavior.[41] In 2000 Sam Brownback likewise cited their use of "role-playing" as a means of tempting children to violence, and John Kerry described his "intense" experiences playing *Pac-Man,* which left him "churned up" and "sweating." Kerry then posed the question: "Is it the interactivity that is so different, that really does something to the mind?" David Walsh, president of the National Institute of Media and the Family, explained, simply, "When I am watching a movie, I am in the role of observer. . . . When I am playing one of these games, I am in the role of participant, and so the entire psychological position is different, and so it is my actions that are causing the reaction, which makes it much more engaging." Craig Anderson of Iowa State University agreed that "active participation increases learning. The violent video game player is a much more active participant than is the violent TV show watcher. . . . Active participation is a more effective teaching tool in part because it because it requires attention to the material being taught."[42] If, as Walsh and Anderson argue, interactive entertainment has unique pedagogical potential, then videogames demand the close attention of educators. If the key to this potential lies in videogames' capability to induce a state of heightened identification between players and characters on screen, then we must consider that games, if they can teach aggression, can also teach empathy, one of core ideals of liberal education.

In fact, some developers have adopted empathy as a design principle in games meant to provoke political action. Bogost suggests, "We must not be afraid of putting people in the shoes of groups or people or individuals that are not comfortable, that we don't like, or think we don't like."[43] *Darfur Is Dying,* for instance, places us in the role of the refugees, emphasizing the vital importance of water in the context of the crisis. Without it, we cannot plant or make mud bricks for homes. We leave the village again and again to fetch the vital resource, placing our character, ourselves, in mortal danger each time. Even the most basic necessities of life, the game suggests, have been threatened by the crisis in Darfur.

At the same time, virtual death in *Darfur Is Dying* does not perpetuate the illusion of invulnerability, as in *America's Army* or *Under Siege.* If we are captured by the Janjaweed, the game asks, "As someone at a far off computer, and not a child or adult in the Sudan, would you like the chance to try again?" The illusion is dispelled, and we are ejected to reality with our empathy, but not our disbelief, intact. This simple message, perhaps, represents the game's subtlest and most effective rhetorical device. *Darfur Is Dying* places us, in Walsh's words, in a unique "psychological position," where we identify with the refugees through playing the game without seeing their struggle as merely a game.

In any videogame, our action results in a reaction and a reordering of the game world defined by the code. Working within the interactive medium, game developers construct arguments not with the enthymemes and exempla of classical rhetoric, but with integrated systems of rules that form the phenomenology of the game world: a web of causes and effects that determines everything that happens in the game. Videogame rhetoric is not logical but ludic, and the more complex the web, the more realistic the game. The encoded rules of cause and effect simulate social as well as physical reality, governing our interaction with characters in the game world, generating dialogue, and determining our allies and enemies. In complex game worlds with an extensive cast of nonplayer characters, these rules of socialization not only reinforce behavior, as Walsh and Anderson argue, but also convey ideologies. Their rhetoric is more effective because it disguises itself as simple causality, as truth inevitable as gravity.

Bogost has defined this method of constructing arguments through the simulation of causality as "procedural rhetoric," emphasizing its potential to convey complex sociopolitical ideas interactively, by programming reactions to player action and, reflexively, exercising control over player action.[44] This process emerges most clearly in a game's victory condition, the simple rule that defines the actions we must take to win the game. If we accept this condition, our in-game action becomes a reaction to conditions defined by the code, which compels our participation as a good argument compels our thinking.

In 2005, Red Storm released *Ghost Recon: Advanced Warfighter,* the most convincing and technically ambitious combat simulation available in the market. The game depicts an attempted coup in Mexico City, where we stalk terrorists through streets choked with smoke and litter, in the shadow of Chapultepec Castle and the spire of Angel Plaza. Reviewers marvel at the exquisitely detailed rendering of the urban battlefield. One writes:

> The first thing you'll notice . . . is how breathtakingly massive and believable the city looks. You take several helicopter rides throughout the campaign, and the city is literally sprawled out all the way to the horizon with buildings and streets. Fires and smoke curl up into the sky from patches of fighting or factories. As you land, you find yourself engulfed by the metropolis and plying your way through the maze of buildings, streets, and alleys.[45]

Like so many other games, *Advanced Warfighter* impresses us with its persuasive imitation of physical reality. But this realism only calls attention to a curious flaw. The reviewer continues:

> Our only major complaint about the graphics is that for a city that looks so believable, it's as empty as a ghost town. Apparently, all 9 million residents of Mexico City either vanished or are hiding indoors with all the unrest going on. Still, it's a little eerie to see no cars moving around the streets and highways or people trying to go about their daily business.[46]

Another review likewise observes that "you won't see a single civilian the entire game, which is extremely unrealistic. . . . I would have expected a *Black Hawk Down* situation, where you needed to be wary of the occasional straggling civilians mixed in with the bad guys."[47]

These casual observations illustrate a significant paradox in war games: the more realistic they become, the more they accentuate the unreality of virtual warfare. Through the conspicuous absence of civilians on the virtual battle-fields of *America's Army* and *Advanced Warfighter* a subtle rhetoric emerges. In Herman and Chomsky's terms, the games present "a dichotomized world" defined by the struggle between our ideology and its antithesis, us and them. Those who do not belong in either camp, who hold neither extreme beliefs nor the weapons to assert them, simply do not register. Civilians so rarely appear in our war games because they so rarely seem like the enemy, and in their effort to "go about their daily business," they too often seem like us. Clearly, *America's Army* and *Under Siege* occupy opposite ideological positions. Depending on our point of view, one of them represents a legitimate use of media to prosecute a just and necessary war, and the other represents a perfidious trick to spread a murderous dogma. Nevertheless, they share a common procedural rhetoric that forces us to take one of two sides and remain blind to everyone caught in the middle.

Other games present a different perspective on the troubling issue of collateral damage, almost always denied by commercial war games. Frasca created *September 12th: A Toy World* to call attention to the consequences of making war against an enemy concealed within a civilian population. The game begins with a pointed message: "This is not a game. You can't win and you can't lose. This is a simulation. It has no ending. It has already begun. The rules are deadly simple. You can shoot. Or not. This is a simple model you can use to explore some aspects of the War on Terror." We then enter an isometric aerial view of a Middle Eastern city, with a large population scuttling along the streets. Some of them, the terrorists, carry guns. The majority, however, are civilians—men, women, and children going about their daily business.

We control a large crosshairs that sweeps the city, and with a click of our mouse we may send a rocket into the streets. The implied victory condition is the same as that of the war itself: destroy the terrorists without destroying innocent civilians. As we launch rockets into the city, we find that our weapons do not strike with the same precision as those in commercial wargames. For every terrorist killed, inevitably, several civilians are also killed. Even worse, a group of mourners gather around each dead civilian, some transforming from civilians into terrorists. The more we bomb, the more terrorists we create. What was at the beginning of the game a city of mostly peaceful civilians and relatively few terrorists has become, after a few minutes of play, a devastated ruin swarming with terrorists. When we realize what is happening and stop bombing, some of the buildings are rebuilt and some of the terrorists change back to civilians. The procedural rhetoric of *September 12th* is clear: we will eliminate terrorists not by bombing but by ceasing to bomb.

Conscientiously designed and critiqued, videogames, especially the first-person and role-playing games that have drawn so much negative scrutiny, may teach us to see the world differently and to understand global conflict from new perspectives. If they can train us to become detached from others and to kill, as an army of doctors claim, then they can also train us to empathize with others and to connect with them. In the swirl of arguments surrounding videogames, educators need not feel befuddled by ideology or conflicting data. If we would teach our students to think critically, we need only to remember that games, like any rhetorical device, are neither inherently destructive nor inherently redeeming. Only Scrooge, if he had seen an Xbox, would think the former; only Candide the latter; and only Rip Van Winkle, awakening in dim amusement to a nation changed beyond his recognition, would miss the potential for videogames to shape students' thinking about gravely important issues like democracy, violence, and war.

❖ *5* ❖

The Ethics of Videogames

In one of the most notorious passages of *The Republic,* Plato banishes poetry from his ideal state. Save for hymns praising gods and heroes, Plato argues, poetry feeds selfish, destructive passions inimical to orderly society. Dramatic art, in particular, holds the power to infect audiences with the immoral or irrational feelings portrayed on stage. When we indulge in laughter or pity, we give reign to instincts that our reason normally restrains. Such irresponsible forms of entertainment, Plato concludes, sustain our desires "when they ought to be left to wither, and makes them control us when we ought, in the interest of our greater welfare and happiness, to control them."[1]

In 1516, almost 2 millennia after Plato's death, Thomas More completed *Utopia,* a sketch of an imaginary island where perfect order and happiness rule. Like his philosophical forebear, More strictly limits entertainment because it promotes not destructive passions, but idleness. When they finish their work, citizens of Utopia may attend public lectures to further their knowledge or play a game designed to foster ethical reasoning. The game, More writes, is "rather like chess," representing a "pitched battle between virtues and vices. . . . It also shows which vices are opposed to which virtues, how much strength vices can muster for a direct assault . . . what help virtues need to overcome vices, what are the best methods for evading their attacks, and what ultimately determines the victory of one side or the other."[2] While Plato warns against the antisocial effects of entertainment, More recognizes some potential for some forms of entertainment, games in particular, to serve as a tool for moral instruction.

Plato's and More's visions of the perfect society provide historical analogues for the controversies surrounding the effects of videogames in our own society. As we have seen in previous chapters, critics argue that the violence simulated on screen causes the children who play these videogames to become desensitized to violence or, worse, to become violent. Just as Plato would cautiously limit the forms of poetry and drama in his republic, our own legislators would restrict the content and distribution of videogames, based on their perceived antisocial effects. Others, like More, seek the social utility in gaming, bending its purpose toward educational and moral improvement. This chapter considers the claims that videogames, like More's imagined game of virtue and vice, might serve as a platform for moral instruction; that they offer a new means of investigating social relations between human beings; and, in the highest sense, that their interactive capabilities allow them to act as mirrors for self-examination.

As we have seen, games are no longer just the focus of debates concerning child welfare, violence, and censorship. They have become a medium for public discourse, capable of changing our minds about a range of issues, including presidential campaigns, military recruitment, and humanitarian crises. A growing number of game designers and critics suggest that games, just as they mediate political debate, can also mediate ethical inquiry through the simulation of moral choice. Miguel Sicart of the University of Copenhagen proposes that games are "moral objects . . . with values embedded in their design . . . that convey, via design, values and moral statements."[3]

This concept of games as "moral objects" capable of modeling values or simulating moral choice has motivated a search for ethical criteria that might guide the design and analysis of videogames. In 1992, games journalist Sara Reeder, writing in the popular computer magazine *Compute!* asked, "What cultural values do computer games communicate to their users?"[4] Reeder's question is simple but significant; prior to the early 1990s, when games like *Mortal Kombat* prompted the first major congressional hearings on videogame violence, few had thought games complex enough to communicate any "cultural values." More recently, Gordana Dodig-Crnkovic and Thomas Larsson, writing in the *International Review of Information Ethics,* express the need for new ethical standards to govern the new medium. In videogames, they observe, we "encounter new situations in which good and bad, right and wrong, are not defined by the experience of previous generations."[5]

I do not propose to establish firm categorical distinctions, like those of the Entertainment Software Ratings Board (ESRB), which will help us judge the moral content of videogames. Rather, I will consider in this chapter the more fundamental observation, expressed by More and more recently by Sicart, that games can be didactic. How do videogames promote ethical positions? Can they enhance our ethical sensibility, as some game designers and critics argue, by simulating moral choice and consequence? Should simulated experience reinforce the ethical principles of real experience, or should it, as play, be allowed to transgress them? Interactivity complicates these questions by collapsing subjective and objective experience. In other words, an action, moral or immoral, represented in a film and an action simulated by one's own hand affect one differently and require different modes of critique. Rather than banishing games as a menace to society, as Plato and some of our legislators would, I want to begin this critique.

Games and Ethical Reinforcement

In 1790 an English printer realized More's hypothetical notion of a game of moral education with *The New Game of Human Life,* an adaptation of the popular board game *Snakes and Ladders,* in which players, spinning a numbered totum, race to complete a spiraling path across the board. Inspired by John Bunyan's 1678 allegory *Pilgrim's Progress* and Samuel Johnson's 1759 essay "Voyage of Life," *The New Game of Human Life* recreates *Snakes and Ladders* in moral terms; the course itself represents the course of human life from infancy to immortality. Each of the 84 spaces on the course represents one year of life, marked with a personification of virtue and quick advance, or with a personification of vice and backsliding. Landing on the Duelist at the impetuous age of 22, for example, sends us back to age three for acting like a child, while landing on the Married Man at 34 speeds us forward to the Good Father at 56. Landing on the Romance Writer at 40 or the Dramatist at 44 also sends us backwards for practicing childish arts, but landing on the Tragic Author at 45, with his incomparable insight into the human condition, sends us onward triumphantly to the Immortal Man at 84. The game's instructions declare its "utility and moral tendency" and encourages parents to play with their children and "request their attention to a few moral and judicious observations explanatory of each character as they proceed and contrast the happiness of a virtuous and well-spent life with the fatal consequences arriving from vicious and immoral pursuits." Jill Lepore describes the game's central Christian allegory: "Life is a voyage that begins at birth and ends at death, God is at the helm, fate is cruel, and your reward lies beyond the grave."[6]

In *The New Game of Human Life,* only chance, the spinning totum, controls our fate. Winners and losers, like anguished Puritans, tumble helplessly toward predestined salvation or damnation. In 1860, the American lithographer Milton Bradley created *The Checkered Game of Life,* significantly revising *The New Game of Human Life* by balancing chance with choice. Bradley's game is more secular, inspired more by Horatio Alger than by John Bunyan. It allegorizes life's journey not as a spiraling course toward death, but as a checkerboard with squares alternately representing decisions and strokes of fate. As in *The New Game of Human Life,* we begin at Infancy, but we strive for Happy Old Age rather than immortality, collecting points, awarded by certain squares, along the way. In his application for the game's patent, Bradley declared his intention to "forcibly impress upon the minds of youth the great moral principles of virtue and vice."[7] Squares marked with virtues and vices help and hinder our progress, as they do in *The New Game of Human Life:* Industry leads to Wealth, Intemperance to Poverty, and Honesty to Happiness. Ambition leads to Fame, but Fame lies perilously close to Prison and Suicide. A seat in Congress is only a short leap from either Honor or Crime.

Although Bradley's lessons owe less to the Gospel than to Yankee good sense, both *The Checkered Game of Life* and *The New Game of Human Life,* like More's utopian game of virtue and vice, conceive of gameplay not simply as a diversion, but as a means to improve character and even to elevate the soul. A similar impulse motivates the serious games movement. As we have seen in the previous chapter, game designers like Gonzalo Frasca, creator of *September 12: A Toy World,* and Susana Ruiz, creator of *Darfur Is Dying,* see their work as a means of raising political awareness and encouraging a sense of ethical responsibility. What distinguishes More and Bradley from Frasca and Ruiz, however, is their sense that games might transform the whole person rather than simply changing our minds about a pressing issue. Games, in other words, might convey much more than a political idea—they might promote an entire system of normative ethics, a proscription for living.

In March 2006, Thailand's Department of Religious Affairs produced *The Ethics Game,* a collection of short, relatively simple games framed by a narrative in which a Buddhist monk guides three young player characters on the path to Enlightenment. Like anime incarnations of the Malignant Boy, the Thoughtless Boy, or the Negligent Boy in *The New Game of Human Life,* each character represents a form of youthful self-indulgence: the first carries a skateboard, the second a slingshot and a can of pop, and the third a guitar. Guided by the monk's words of wisdom, they take part in series of challenges, learning moral precepts such as compassion, honesty, fidelity, temperance, and kindness to animals. In one of these challenges, our character navigates a city street plagued by vice: a boy steals a pair of shoes; a man clutches what appear to be two prostitutes; and a drunk vomits in the street. By matching numbers to each of these characters, we properly identify the vice and, in doing so, gain the knowledge to avoid it.

Most commercially produced games do not risk alienating their mass audience with such obvious didacticism, but they are not ethically neutral. Rather, they are subtler in the ways they reinforce ethical positions. Adapting Ian Bogost's notion of procedural rhetoric—political argument expressed through rules of gameplay—Sicart suggests that code "ultimately regulates the architecture of the game, and therefore where the ethics of computer games start."[8] He observes that every game contains rules, embedded in the code, that distinguish between successful and unsuccessful players, and that the criteria for success or failure encoded in the game often carry moral weight. From a game designer's perspective, Valve Software's Gabe Newell, creator of *Half-Life 2,* discusses the development of "reinforcement schedules," a system of programmed rewards and punishments designed to encourage players to behave in proscribed ways:

> In *Half-Life 2,* if you shoot a civilian there's a cost associated with that. And we basically don't want you to do that. The rewards in *Half-Life* are getting to see new monsters, the plot . . . moving forward, getting to have a fun new weapon. . . . Those are the reinforcement schedules. And you want to make sure that throughout the course of the game that [players] are getting rewards.[9]

Craig Lindley agrees, arguing that the Aristotelian narrative structure of many games, which we have surveyed in Chapter 1, likewise conveys ethical meaning. The three-part plot structure, Lindley explains, includes "a conflict involving a dilemma of normative morality, a second act propelled by the hero's false resolution of this dilemma, and a third act in which the dilemma is resolved once and for all by an act that reaffirms normative morality."[10]

In videogames, ethical positions—encoded in fundamental rules, reinforcement schedules, or plot structure—often stand in contrast to the extensive freedom that many games claim to offer. In other words, interactive potential comes into conflict with ethics; the more a game allows us to do, the more likely we are to behave badly. In *The Sims,* for example, Will Wright took special care in representing domestic violence. He explains:

> When the characters get upset, they can slap each other. . . . There's one slap where they rear their arm back and then whack, and it's as if they're breaking their jaw. And there's another one that's kind of an insulting British Army slap. Whenever you have people of the same gender slapping, they use the really hard slap. . . . But whenever you have a man slapping a woman or a woman slapping a man, they use the polite slap. Because before, when we had the strong-arm slap, and you had a husband slapping his wife, it rubbed a lot of people the wrong way.[11]

Wright says that "there were certain things we decided we would leave out," such as murder and pedophilia, and "certain things we wanted to get in," such as the possibility for homosexual relationships: "We wanted to give people a reasonably . . . open-ended way to construct whatever family they came from or could imagine or wanted to play with."[12] In allowing some simulated behaviors and prohibiting others, the game encodes ethical proscriptions for domestic life. While it prohibits violence against spouses and children, it allows some violence against others. It upholds the standard of consent, prohibiting intimacy with children but allowing intimacy between heterosexual or homosexual adults.

Games that simulate crime likewise enforce a virtual social contract. Even in the fantasy world of Bethesda's *The Elder Scrolls IV: Oblivion,* acts of petty theft, breaking and entering, and unprovoked violence will quickly draw the attention of the town guards, who impose a fine, a loss of hard-earned gold, or throw us into jail, incurring a loss of valuable skill points. The *Grand Theft Auto* series is more complex, not because it frames violence within a contemporary urban context, but because the ethical norms encoded in the game come into direct conflict with the interactive freedom the game offers. While almost every mission in *Grand Theft Auto: San Andreas* demands that we commit some crime in order to succeed—including bribing, beating, murdering, bombing, and disposing of bodies—these acts, as in *Oblivion,* draw a swift and equally violent response from law enforcement. *Oblivion* features analogous quest sequences in which we ascend the ranks of criminal organizations by committing robberies and assassinations, but these quests are not necessary to complete the game. *San Andreas,* on the other hand, both necessitates and punishes crime, sending a mixed message that lies at the root of the public controversies surrounding the game.

War games likewise promote battlefield ethics. As we have seen, combat simulations like Ubisoft's *Ghost Recon* series, while boasting the most advanced graphics and artificial intelligence, remove the potential for collateral damage. Civilians who may wander in our line of fire do not appear on these virtual battlefields. In more morally vexed games depicting the Vietnam War, a conflict in which soldiers often struggled to distinguish the enemy from innocent civilians, the clarity of identifying and killing the enemy is imaginary but morally necessary. In 2015 Studios' *Men of Valor,* designer John Whitmore, like Will Wright, treads an ethical boundary. In his Vietnam, characters use profanity but not racial slurs. They bleed to death, but they are not dismembered by booby traps. We can wax Charlie, but, as in *The Sims,* we cannot kill children, nor can we solicit prostitutes. Neither side performs torture or executions.

Some critics argue that games such as *Men of Valor, San Andreas,* or even *The Sims* are patently unethical in the way they obscure the realities of battlefield, urban, and domestic violence. From another point of view, however, each game, though distinct in design, promotes a relatively consistent and socially constructive ethical position that prohibits violence against women, children, and innocent bystanders, as well as particularly sadistic forms of violence against enemies. Although we may, in *San Andreas,* kill women and innocent bystanders, the game metes out exaggerated punishment; cops shoot first, shoot often, and do not bother to ask questions. In general, videogames prohibit aggression by the strong against the weak, promoting an ethic of vigilantism or violence by justification. Our enemies are always clearly marked, always out to kill us first, and so they always deserve to be annihilated.

Games of Choice and Consequence

Although it involves the familiar tasks of raiding dungeons, slaying monsters, and collecting loot, Origin Systems' 1985 *Ultima IV: Quest of the Avatar*, created by Richard Garriott, anticipates current morally inflected adventure games such as Bioware's *Star Wars: Knights of the Old Republic* and Lionhead Studios' *Fable*. The game centers on eight virtues: compassion, honesty, honor, humility, justice, sacrifice, spirituality, and valor. Unlike the vast majority of role-playing games, including *Knights of the Old Republic* and *Fable, Ultima IV* has no big boss waiting for us at the end of the game, no ultimate evil that we must destroy. Rather, the evil is within us. Any action we perform within the game—running from monsters or standing our ground, pilfering gold from the treasury or giving it to the poor, boasting of our heroism or humbly concealing it—gains or loses a measure of virtue. In the game world, each virtue has its corresponding town and dungeon, where we recruit allies and discover artifacts corresponding to the eight virtues. As in *The Ethics Game*, we must demonstrate a thorough understanding of virtue and vice by performing numerous good deeds. Only when we have mastered all the virtues can we gain the Codex of Ultimate Wisdom and become the Avatar, the messianic embodiment of virtue itself.

While *Ultima IV* compels us to follow a hodgepodge of Christian, chivalric, and Buddhist precepts in the quest for spiritual ascendance, it begins, at least, with problematic choices. Before we enter the game world, we create our character not by allocating points for attributes and skills as we do in most other role-playing games, but rather by meeting a fortuneteller who poses a series of questions, each measuring one virtue against another. Matching honesty against compassion, for example, she asks us: "Entrusted to deliver an uncounted purse of gold, thou dost meet a poor beggar. Dost thou deliver the gold, knowing the trust in thee was well-placed, or show compassion, giving the beggar a coin, knowing it won't be missed?" Matching honor against spirituality, she asks us: "In thy youth thou pledged to marry thy sweetheart. Now thou art on a sacred quest in distant lands. Thy sweetheart asks thee to keep thy vow. Dost thou honor thy pledge to wed or follow thy spiritual crusade?" The questions test our moral priorities until one virtue wins out over the others. Our character class and attributes depend on the virtue we value most: a mage for honesty, for instance, or a fighter for valor, or a bard for compassion.

Like *Ultima IV, Fable,* and *Knights of the Old Republic* feature a kind of moral scorecard that tallies our good and bad acts and bends narrative and gameplay in response to our decisions. In *Knights of the Old Republic,* for instance, certain actions gain "light side" and "dark side" points, and throughout the game we face a number of choices that simulate ethical difficulties. Early in the game, when we arrive at a refugee camp below the city of Taris, we encounter Hendar, a man fleeing a pack of diseased, subhuman rakghouls in the no-man's-land beyond the camp wall. The guards, though horrified at the fate of their comrade, resolve not to open the gates, lest the rakghouls slip through the breech and infect the entire camp. We may force the guards to open the gate and rush to Hendar's rescue, thus jeopardizing the entire group, including our companions, or we may maintain their safety and watch Hendar die. We must choose either to save the one by risking the many or to save the many by sacrificing the one. Later, when we have discovered the serum to cure the rakghoul disease, we face further choices. We may immediately cure the refugees infected with the disease, aid an infected Republic soldier lost in the no-man's-land, give the serum to a doctor maintaining a hospital in the city, or sell it to a crime boss for a large profit. What finally distinguishes *Knights of the Old Republic* and *Fable* from *Ultima IV* is the degree of moral choice the games offer. Although *Ultima IV* opens with a dialogue that forces us to examine our ethical priorities, we can win the game only by being virtuous. In both *Fable* and *Knights of the Old Republic,* we can win by being virtuous or vicious. Giving the serum to the refugees or the hospital yields "light side" points, and selling it to the crime boss yields "dark side" points, but both options offer tangible benefits that contribute to our progress in the game. Good is not our only path.

If we can win by being good or evil, then what ultimately motivates our choices in the game? Does the way we play the game tell us something about who we are? While designers like Newell and Frasca have explored the ways that games can compel us to think or to behave in certain ways, others, led by Lionhead Studio's Peter Molyneux, creator of both *Fable* and *Black & White,* have sought to create games that foster self-examination through the simulation of moral choices. Molyneux's innovations follow Milton Bradley's modification of *The New Game of Human Life,* which hedged fate with the potential for players to choose their own path through life's checkerboard course. The belief that decisions rather than dicta promote a more acute ethical awareness underlie Bradley's and Molyneux's design philosophies. Molyneux has said that one of his goals in designing *Black & White* was to create a world that took shape in response to the actions of the player; he wanted the game to illustrate ethical consequences.[13]

This ambitious design principle has divided critics, who dispute the capacity for videogames to simulate the deep complexity of ethical conflicts, decisions, and consequences. Some argue that interactive games are a particularly useful tool for ethical inquiry because they may actualize the consequences of player decisions: if we choose to protect the besieged camp in Taris, we watch Hendar die a hideous death; if we save Hendar, we must aid the refugees in fighting the rakghouls that invade the camp. Greg Smith writes, "One of the many ideas implicit in the concept of 'interactivity' is this more complex notion of moral judgment that is no longer as externalizable as it is in film."[14] In other words, we remain morally detached watching characters on film. We may pass our judgment on their actions, concluding what we would or would not do in their place. A videogame allows no such detachment. Our decisions are our own, and so our ethical sensibility comes to bear not on external characters but on ourselves. For this reason, Henry Jenkins concludes that "games are the only medium where you could feel guilt. . . . When I am playing a game and . . . I choose to do something really nasty, then at some point, the game ought to have the ability to force me to reflect on that choice. . . . [Games] introduce the notion of choice and consequences."[15]

Others argue that our choices in videogames are simplistic, that the consequences of these choices are misleading, and that any moral reflection prompted by these consequences is shallow. Educational technology researcher Susan Smith Nash believes that such games are, in fact, "fraudulent and harmful" when the consequences they simulate are not faithful to "real-life situations." Combat simulators like Pandemic Studios' *Full Spectrum Warrior,* Nash writes, create a "cognitive disconnect" by neglecting the viscerally unpleasant experiences of warfare, such as "thirst, hunger, nausea, pain, dizziness, shock, or other conditions under which a fighter must work in the real world." Of course, no medium could accurately reproduce these experiences, and so no game could rightly claim to simulate the real ethical choices presented by something as complex and traumatic as war. On these grounds, Nash challenges the ethical relevance of any videogame. True ethical simulations require an unprecedented and perhaps impossible degree of realism.[16]

In his ethical evaluation of *Grand Theft Auto III,* technology writer Ren Reynolds agrees, citing the "Hooker Cheat," one of the most notorious aspects of the game. At any point in the game, we may solicit a prostitute and have sex with her, an activity that increases the health of our character. To do so, however, costs money. We may either pay the prostitute, exchanging money for health, or kill the prostitute after having sex with her, boosting our health for free. As Reynolds observes, the game's ridiculous assumption that having sex with hookers is "healthy" completely undermines any serious consideration of the choices and consequences attendant on the criminal actions the game simulates. The "Hooker Cheat" does not present any moral dilemma, only a tawdry, violent fantasy.[17] Sicart concludes more generally, "Morality is not algorithmical. Ethics cannot be evaluated with a fuzzy numeric quantification hardwired in the code. . . . These game designs ignore the depth and importance of moral decision making."[18]

Molyneux's *Black & White* makes no claim to realism. As a cartoonish moral allegory, the game serves as a more useful parallel to Bradley's *The Checkered Game of Life* and Bunyan's *Pilgrim's Progress*. In the game, we play an omnipotent intelligence that regulates the existence of a vital little community of cute, human-like creatures, controlling everything from rainfall, crop yield, and building projects to population growth, cultural expansion, and the ultimate destiny of their civilization. Our presence is manifested in their island world by a towering temple that serves as the focus of their worship and by a giant creature that acts as our agent among the people, performing deeds of benevolence or malice on our behalf. We also control a disembodied, ethereal hand that hovers over the landscape, emanating life-giving miracles or spectacular catastrophes. As a god, we demand faith, and we may gain faith both by inspiring love and by striking fear in our followers. Eventually, we may send our followers out to convert and conquer those who follow other deities, generating more faith and becoming more powerful, until we are the only god in the pantheon.

To what extent, then, does *Black & White* achieve Molyneux's purpose of designing a game that simulates ethical consequence and enhances our moral self-consciousness? Early in the game, evil acts seem to get faster results. Carefully managing supplies of food and building materials garners faith much more slowly than wreaking havoc with fireballs and lightning bolts. Efficient gameplay nudges us toward evil, even though, in real life, we may be kind to our ant farm, our hamsters, or our children, whose lives likewise depend upon our goodwill. In this sense, the game does not reveal our ethical fiber as much as our desire to reach the end of the game. At the same time, the game, as a whole, confronts us with the fundamental ethical dilemma expressed variously by the Gospels, Machiavelli, and Master Yoda. The path of evil, we find, is wide and easy, while the path of righteousness is narrow and difficult, but ultimately more rewarding. Which path do we take?

Like *The Sims,* the *Grand Theft Auto* series, and other games that promise considerable freedom within the game world, *Black & White* employs a subtle didacticism, visible in the graphical transformations of the game world that occur as we make decisions. If we love our villagers, send them rain, maintain their resources, and occasionally perform benevolent miracles, the sun is bright, the world is soft and green, and our temple grows into a shimmering, glorious tower. The game makes good look good. If we frighten our villagers, the sky darkens, the world becomes scorched and desolate, and our temple becomes an imposing, malicious citadel. In some ways, moreover, the game makes it more difficult to win the game as an evil god. In the short term, we can scare our followers into believing in us, but in the long term, production slows, our followers starve or defect to more benevolent deities, and our civilization falls. In these ways, *Black & White* reinforces rather than probes normative morality. Molyneux's design offers some choice, but that choice is manipulated by rules that subtly enforce a traditionally altruistic morality. While evil might be expedient, good is beautiful and ultimately triumphant.

The simple ethical dualism of games like *Black & White, Fable,* and *Knights of the Old Republic* seems to undermine Molyneux's claim that *Black & White* and videogames in general might provide models for real ethical dilemmas. Real dilemmas, after all, never manifest themselves as a choice between good and evil, but always as a choice between more complex alternatives, where right and wrong are never clearly marked. *Black & White* is unrealistic, not because the villagers look cartoonish, but because, unlike real life, trying to do the right thing in the game never has unexpectedly destructive consequences. Good and evil never masquerade as their opposite, nor do they partake of one another. One moment in the game where Molyneux nearly approaches this ethical realism is the plague, when the player is forced to destroy the food supply of the village, ostensibly committing an evil act to ensure a greater good. Molyneux momentarily encourages us to think about ends and means, to measure short-term sacrifice against long-term survival. These are not simple questions, though the game does not often match this level of intellectual complexity, nor do other games.

We might imagine a game that would force players to make more difficult decisions, not so much by displaying more realistic suffering, as Nash suggests, but by encouraging choices based on compromise and reconciliation rather than the direct opposition of incompatible ideals. There remains, however, a certain appeal in god games like *Black & White* that transcends their value as moral objects. They are not quite like having an ant farm, a hamster, or a child. God games, in fact, are more elemental. They stipulate rules, but they also simulate creation and destruction to a degree unknown to us in the real world. Although the game ostensibly forces us to choose between good and evil, we take pleasure, strangely, in both killing and healing. Videogames, in the end, awaken what Nietzsche called our "will to power." In *Black & White,* as in Nietzsche's moral philosophy, the key categorical difference is not between good and evil but between strength and weakness. It is not a game for the Calvinist sensibilities of the eighteenth century or the utilitarian sensibilities of the nineteenth century—it is a game for the modern world. God is dead, and Molyneux has put us in his place.

Fantasy and Ethical Evasion

In Valve's *Half-Life 2,* we battle the Combine, an alien force that has conquered Earth, depleted its natural resources, and introduced predatory alien life forms as a means of biological warfare. An army of "transhuman" cyborgs, born of human DNA and Combine technology, oversee the occupation, brutalizing the dwindling human population and battling resistance fighters. In a decisive move to exterminate the human race once and for all, the Combine has installed an invisible energy field that suppresses the enzymes necessary for reproduction. Like the dystopian London in the P.D. James novel *The Children of Men, Half-Life 2*'s City 17 is inhabited by a sterile, aging, and hopeless population. After two decades of Combine occupation, we meet no one under the age of twenty.

At one point in the game, we emerge from a zombie-infested tunnel into a rail yard, where we glimpse a graffiti picture of a transhuman soldier clutching a baby to his chest. The image, which has the look of propaganda, suggests a terrible irony. The Combine, having eliminated children from the planet, represents itself as our protector and nurturer. Earlier in the game, Dr. Breen, the city administrator who collaborates with the Combine, reinforces this message in a public service announcement. While instinct, the urge to reproduce, "was our mother when we were an infant species," we have evolved and now look toward the stars and immortality rather than our primitive "unreasoning impulses." Oddly, Dr. Breen sounds a little like Plato. In this new stage of human development, Breen says, we should not view the Combine as our oppressor but rather as our "benefactor," our new "mother" who holds the human race in a loving embrace, like the soldier holding the baby.

The childless world of *Half-Life 2* reveals a fundamental ethical imperative of videogame design. While the game carries an ESRB rating of "M" (Mature) for "Blood and Gore" and "Intense Violence," and allows us to blast our enemies with a shotgun, skewer them with a crossbow, bisect them with a saw blade, ignite them with gasoline, or simply crush their skulls with a crowbar, the children, mercifully, are spared. As one member of the resistance grimly remarks, "I'm glad there's no kids around to see this." In fact, the absence of children is a design feature of almost all violent videogames, including the maligned *Grand Theft Auto* series, combat simulators like the *Ghost Recon* and *Full Spectrum Warrior* series, and ethically freighted fantasy games like *Knights of the Old Republic* and *Fable.* When critics speak about videogame violence, in fact, they most often speak about fantasy violence. Violent videogames, including *Half-Life 2* and gory predecessors like *Quake, Doom,* and *Wolfenstein 3D,* reserve the worst mayhem for robots, cyborgs, aliens, zombies, and demons; the targets of "Intense Violence" are dehumanized by fantasy. Violent military games accomplish this maneuver more subtly: their human targets—terrorists and Nazis—are made monstrous by their ambitions to unleash weapons of mass destruction or to conquer the world.

If, as Susan Smith Nash argues, a high degree of realism is necessary to simulate ethical problems, then it seems that videogames have embraced unreality as a means of skirting the ethical dilemmas that arise with graphic representations of violence. The creators of *Half-Life 2* have discovered an ingenious way of concealing this ethical evasion within the narrative fabric of the game. By crafting a story in which the Combine have stunted human procreation, the designers have invented a legitimate reason to eliminate children from the otherwise exquisitely detailed battlefields. In other words, they have made a narrative virtue from an ethical necessity, using the absence of children as a realistic feature of the game world.

More generally, violent games like *Half-Life 2* reinforce the ethical notion that not all forms of violence are equal. Like *The Sims,* which strictly limits the potential for domestic violence and eliminates pedophilia from its simulated domestic reality, these games suggest that assaults on women and children are worse than assaults on men. They tell us that women and children are a protected class. As a potential criterion for game design, Dodig-Crnkovic and Larsson cite the United Nations Convention on the Rights of the Child, one of our highest and most articulate statements of normative ethics, which resolves "to protect the child from all forms of physical or mental violence."[19] A broad interpretation of this resolution suggests not only that the game industry should carefully regulate the distribution of violent games to children, as many legislators have argued, but also that game designers themselves should eliminate the depiction of violence against children in videogames, as, in fact, they have.

Violence against children represents an almost inviolable ethical dividing line that separates commercially viable games from those that are morally abhorrent or merely sick jokes. In 1976, Exidy released *Death Race,* a controversial arcade game based on Roger Corman's 1975 film *Death Race 2000.* In the dystopian future imagined in the film, competitors in a cross-country race win points for running down pedestrians, including women and children. More recent Flash games available online have stirred similar controversy. In *The Suicide Bombing Game,* we run along a busy sidewalk with a bomb strapped to our bodies, positioning ourselves to inflict maximum civilian casualties. In *Border Patrol,* we shoot at Mexican families, "breeders" drawn in racist cartoon stereotypes, dashing across the border. Both games award points for killing children.

The *Grand Theft Auto* series and other crime games have become targets of regulatory legislation because they flirt with the ethical boundary that

The Suicide Bomber Game and *Border Patrol* cross. Although children are conspicuously absent in the streets of Liberty City and San Andreas, we may freely inflict unprovoked brutality on innocent bystanders, including women. LucasArts, in contrast, is more cautious in its eponymous adaptation of the film *Star Wars: Episode III: Revenge of the Sith*. The only *Star Wars* movie to receive a PG-13 rating, the film includes two scenes of child violence. After Anakin Skywalker turns to the dark side and resolves to destroy the Jedi Knights, he enters their academy and meets a pack of cute, prepubescent padawans, his lightsaber drawn and a dastardly glint in his eye. Later, another Jedi student, older but still below the age of consent, briefly puts up a fight before he is cut down by a firing squad of clone troopers. Although potentially troubling to children in the audience who had cheered for Anakin through *Episodes I* and *II*, George Lucas includes the scenes to illustrate the depth of Anakin's moral descent. In the game, however, these scenes are not included in the cut scenes copiously lifted from the film. Moreover, the game significantly revises the purging of the Jedi temple as the film represents it, replacing the defenseless tots slaughtered by Anakin with a contingent of lightsaber-wielding grown-ups.

LucasArts' curious adaptation reflects a general pattern of evasion in videogames, which ethically neutralizes troubling forms of violence by recasting them as justifiable violence or outright fantasy. Ren Reynolds suggests that "blasting a space invader is hardly transgressive," but he also argues that fantasy violence does not obviate the ethical problems of representing violence in videogames.[20] He cites Michael Crichton's 1973 film *Westworld,* a story of androids run amok, to illustrate his view that "there is a moral reality" to killing "what looked and felt like other humans." Isaac Asimov's 1950 collection, *I, Robot* and Philip K. Dick's 1968 novel *Do Androids Dream of Electric Sheep?* offer better examples. These works pose a superficial moral dilemma: Do the almost human deserve the same treatment as the human? But as they blur the distinction between these two categories, the books become more subtle allegories of human rights, calling into question ideologies that define and delimit the "human," and undermining the intellectual evasions we employ to justify oppression and violence against certain groups.

Videogames have not yet demonstrated the keen awareness of Asimov and Dick, who use fantasy as means to allegorize and to study ethical questions rather than to evade them. As we have seen, however, Gonzalo Frasca's *September 12* gestures to such awareness, using videogame violence itself to dispel the fantasies that innocents never get hurt and that our enemy never has a human face. As we attempt to drop bombs on the terrorists scuttling along the streets of a Middle Eastern city, we clumsily and inevitably annihilate civilians, including women, with every attack. Suddenly our heroic efforts turn murderous. Frasca reverses the ideological polarity of the videogame industry, causing us to pause and question what we do when we compulsively click the "fire" button.

For all the criticism that violent videogames receive, however, the great majority, except for aberrations like *The Suicide Bombing Game* and *Border Patrol,* reinforce well-established humanitarian principles. The facelessness or hideousness of the enemies we compulsively destroy reflects the underlying belief that there is something essentially wrong with blasting, skewering, bisecting, igniting, or crushing other human beings—and with representing all of this on screen. Part of the escapist appeal of videogames, perhaps, is their utopian evocation of a world in which our ethical choices are always clear and never muddled, as they are in life, by confusion and guilt.

Ethics in the Magic Circle

On November 29, 2005, the Santa Clara University Markkula Center for Applied Ethics sponsored a panel discussion that sought to identify the major ethical issues in videogame design, marketing, and gameplay. The participants included professors of communication and computer engineering, a technology journalist, a professional game designer, and an undergraduate videogame enthusiast. The most energetic and single-minded speaker, however, was California State assemblyman Leland Yee (elected state senator in 2006), who had successfully sponsored a state bill to prohibit the sale of "ultraviolent" videogames to children under the age of eighteen. Yee, who holds a doctorate in child psychology, repeated the familiar claim that videogames "teach children, you know, how to hurt, how to stalk, how to hurt and maim," but he also entertained the argument that neither the state nor the videogame industry has the responsibility of mandating children's cultural diet, that his legislation, in fact, denies the responsibility of parents.[21]

This question about the location of ethical responsibility reaches back to Plato's *Republic* and examines the fundamental relation between art and normative ethics: Does the artist, in any sense, have a moral obligation to society? Does the game designer have an obligation to create games that Leland Yee, Socrates, the Buddha, or Jesus would endorse? Currently, most game designers and critics agree that the industry needs to consider the values that games convey, if games would take their place beside more established and respected art forms. At the "Computer and Video Games Come of Age" conference at MIT in 2000, Jenkins argued, "There has to be discourse about social and ethical responsibility. Not a defensive one that responds to every media effects study . . . but one that simply lays out . . . the place of games in American culture."[22] Molyneux, who has done the most to integrate game design with ethical sensibility, says that "anyone who does something for a mass market has a responsibility. You tread carefully on the lessons you teach. That line, 'if a game is fun, it's okay'—that sounds trivial."[23]

Jill Lepore arrives at a similar conclusion in her discussion of Milton Bradley's *The Checkered Game of Life,* one of earliest forerunners of videogames like *Black & White* and *The Sims.* In 1960, the Milton Bradley Company redesigned its founder's original game to commemorate its centennial. Just as Bradley adapted *The New Game of Human Life* to the newly industrial United States, emphasizing hard work and perseverance over humility and patience, Reuben Klamer, in Lepore's words, reinvented Bradley's game as "a lesson in Cold War consumerist conformity." In Klamer's *The Game of Life,* we drive a tiny automobile along a meandering road collecting paychecks and paying bills. As Lepore notes, "the game lacks any sense of life as a battle between vice and virtue. . . . You count your cash, not your good deeds." It seems a grotesque misinterpretation of Bradley's original invention. In *The Checkered Game of Life,* landing on Wealth gains us 10 points, but we arrive there by way of School, Industry, or Perseverance. While Bradley recognized wealth as a just reward for a life a virtue, Klamer represents wealth itself as a virtue. *The Game of Life,* Lepore writes, is "relentlessly amoral."[24]

At the same time, ludologists recognize a philosophical tradition that views play as something outside the province of moral reasoning, neither moral nor amoral. In 1938, the Dutch sociologist Johan Huizinga argued in *Homo Ludens* that play has a central role in the development of civilization. Like a game, civilization itself contrives rules of order for human action. Play underlies law, war, philosophy, poetry, and art. What sets the playful apart from the serious, Huizinga suggests, is the demarcation of a "magic circle" or sacred space in which play occurs:

> All play moves and has its being within a playground marked off beforehand either materially or ideally. . . . The arena, the card-table, the magic circle, the temple, the stage, the screen, the tennis court . . . are all in form and function playgrounds, i.e., forbidden spots, isolated, hedged round, hallowed, within which special rules obtain. All are temporary worlds within the ordinary world, dedicated to the performance of an act apart.[25]

Like the arena, the temple, and the stage, the virtual space of a videogame serves as a "magic circle" where ethical norms are suspended or subordinated to the rules of the game, which might freely transgress the norms of the "ordinary world."

The French philosopher Roger Caillois, who refines and expands Huizinga's theory of play in his 1958 book *Man, Play, and Games,* likewise emphasizes the importance of "make-believe" in play, "a special awareness of a second reality or of a free unreality, as against real life."[26] Huizinga and Caillois would likely regard *Grand Theft Auto III* simply as a digitized, expressionistic form of cops and robbers, which has distracted critics with a graphic manifestation of violence that remains merely imagined in old-fashioned games of make-believe. In other words, critics violate the magic circle in applying the ethical norms of the ordinary world to the game world. Whether we cheat a hooker, run down a pedestrian, or kill a cop, we perform "an act apart," "against real life," and insulated from the ethical judgments that apply outside the magic circle. In the panel discussion on videogame ethics, Assemblyman Yee makes a slight verbal error that illustrates this tendency to misplace critical judgment. Explaining the unique threat of interactive entertainment, he says, "When you are pushing a button you are literally then killing and hurting, maiming an individual."[27] Of course, we are not literally killing people when we play a game; we are literally pushing buttons. For both Huizinga and Caillois, play ceases to be play not when it simulates an immoral action but only when the magic circle, the boundary between make-believe and real life, dissolves; play turns serious when it assumes meaning beyond itself. As Huizinga explains, war is a game in that it is governed by rules and set apart on a battlefield, but it becomes serious when it is fought for a greater moral purpose, "for the aggressed, the persecuted, those who fight for their rights and liberty."[28]

We would be naïve to think that violent videogames "literally" teach us to be criminals, but we would be equally naïve to think that videogames do not have the potential to influence thoughts and actions. Plato recognized no make-believe world magically set apart from the ethical responsibilities of the individual and the state. Would he sit beside Hillary Clinton and Leland Yee, shaking his finger at irresponsible game designers, or would he join More, Bradley, and Molyneux in their more constructive efforts to use games as a tool for ethical education? Long considered the province of children, videogames have matured with the generation who discovered their appeal more than three decades ago, and they have inherited persistent philosophical questions concerning art, society, and morality. To quote a noted first-century ethicist: "Suffer the little children to come unto me, and forbid them not: for of such is the kingdom of God."[29] We can no longer neglect the children and their toys.

❖ 6 ❖

Religion and Myth in
Videogames

In the early hours of September 9, 2006, 15-year-old Jessie James was shot to death in the Moss Side neighborhood of Manchester, England. At first, police called the shooting an execution—Moss Side is notorious for its drug trade and gang violence. When they learned, however, that Jessie, a diligent student at Manchester Academy preparatory school, did not belong to a gang, they said the boy's death was probably a case of mistaken identity. Detective Tony Cook said, "Jessie was in the wrong place at the wrong time."[1] James's murder remains unsolved, a sign of what police call the rising "gun culture" in Manchester.

On November 11, two months after James's death, Sony unveiled PlayStation 3 and Insomniac Games' *Resistance: Fall of Man,* the new console's most highly anticipated launch title. The game imagines an alternate history of the twentieth century, in which an alien race invades central Asia shortly after World War II and overtakes Europe by 1951. The player leads an American strike force dispatched to England to mount a resistance, and the ensuing battle rages from York to London. In Manchester, we find ourselves in a wild shootout in the nave of the city's thirteenth-century Gothic cathedral, slaughtering hundreds of aliens before escaping through a hole blasted in the cathedral wall.

When the game came to the attention of Anglican leaders in June 2007 (PlayStation 3 was released in Europe in March 2007), Reverend Rogers Govender, Dean of Manchester Cathedral, declared it a desecration of the church. "We are shocked to see a place of learning, prayer, and heritage being presented to the youth market as a location where guns can be fired," Govender said.[2] Nigel McCulloch, Anglican Bishop of Manchester, agreed: "It is well known that Manchester has a gun crime problem. For a global manufacturer to re-create one of our great cathedrals with photorealistic quality and then encourage people to have gun battles in the building is beyond belief and highly irresponsible."[3] Govender and McCulloch claimed that Sony did not seek permission to represent the cathedral in the game and demanded an apology from the corporation as well as a substantial donation to support the church's work with families victimized by gun violence. They also asked that Sony pull the game from shelves and remove the level containing the cathedral battle. Sony did not pull the game, but offered a reluctant letter of apology:

> We do not accept that there is any connection between contemporary issues of twenty-first century Manchester and a work of science fiction in which a fictitious 1950s Britain is under attack by aliens. It is not our intention to cause offence by using a representation of Manchester Cathedral in chapter eight of the work. If we have done so we sincerely apologise.[4]

In the wake of the controversy, gamers scoffed at Govender's and McCulloch's statements, accusing the Church of England of censorship, self-promotion, and simple ignorance, just as they have responded to legislators' attempts to restrict the content of violent videogames in the United States. On GamePolitics.com, a popular discussion forum, one contributor writes, "The Church of England wants to get their name in the paper to cash in on the current 'blame video game' fad." Another says, "We value free expression over excessively whiny dogma." And another concludes, "This is blatant opportunism, using a silly issue like this to try and drum up support and . . . money for their church, in a time when the church is less and less relevant in people's lives."[5]

The Manchester controversy, however, does not represent just another protest by cultural conservatives against videogame violence. The Church of England specifically charged Sony with the portrayal of gun violence in a sacred setting, something new in videogame criticism. Govender and McCulloch are not so uninformed that they mistake science fiction for simulated murder, as many gamers believed, and as Sony implies in their condescending letter of apology. Rather, they object to a specific visual juxtaposition of assault weaponry in a place of worship—with good reason, perhaps. Every year, Manchester Cathedral holds a candlelight vigil in memory of the city's victims of gun violence. For those families who attend these services and mourn children like Jessie James, the jarring image of an American supersoldier spraying their church with bullets may indeed seem less like a meaningless violation of "whiny dogma" than a sick joke.

The fundamental question raised by the controversy is not whether Govender and McCulloch have irrationally confused an imaginary alien invasion with real gun violence, or whether videogame publishers require permission to render recognizable public spaces, but whether a virtual desecration is tantamount to a real desecration. Govender and McCulloch speak interchangeably of the actual and the virtual cathedrals, as if Sony, like latter-day moneylenders, has set up shop in the temple and profaned it with their business. What does it mean that church authorities have, in this case, held a sacred space and a virtual rendering of that space in equal regard?

This chapter considers the relation between religious faith, ritual, and videogames. In the most obvious sense, games, like other secular art forms, may promote values in conflict with religious or moral precepts. Likewise, they may be used as an evangelical platform, just as they are used to promote political or ethical ideals. In another sense, *Resistance* and other videogames point to a new intersection between sacred space and virtual space, between spirituality and virtuality. The Manchester controversy, however ridiculous to Sony and the videogame community, demonstrates a growing awareness, even among the severest critics of videogames, of their social and spiritual relevance. If games have the power to profane sacred spaces, do they also have the power to consecrate them? Can the virtual world serve as a symbolic expression of the spiritual world? Can games, more generally, manifest religious consciousness and express profound notions about creation, providence, revelation, truth, or the afterlife? Can gameplay be a form of spiritual transcendence and transformation?

Play and Prayer

In his 1938 book *Homo Ludens,* the Dutch sociologist Johan Huizinga recalls that Plato's idea of religion consists of "play consecrated to the Deity"—that play, in other words, is a form of prayer.[6] Plato writes in *Laws* that "a man should spend his whole life at 'play'—sacrificing, singing, dancing—so that he can win the favor of the gods and protect himself from his enemies." For Plato, play, art, and worship come together on the Greek stage. In singing and dancing we find the origin of the rites of Dionysus and Greek drama, given to us by the gods so that we may find temporary relief from our inevitable suffering. In spontaneous expression or the more ordered forms of theater, Plato concludes, play is a divine gift, given to human beings to please the gods.[7]

Augustine, on the other hand, traces the first sins of his youth, his disobedience to parents and teachers, to his "love of games," his attraction to athletics, gambling, and the theater. In his *Confessions,* Augustine writes, "I liked to score a fine win at sport or to have my ears tickled by the make-believe of the stage, which only made them itch the more." He resents his hypocritical teachers, who punish him for his indulgence in games even as they indulge in games themselves, and he finds that most adults engage each other in children's games that merely pass for "business." He begs God to free his mind from the folly of these delusions, so that his thoughts may approach the divine.[8]

Later, as a young professor of rhetoric at Carthage, Augustine senses a chance to make reparations for his youthful disobedience by rescuing a favorite student, Alypius, from his obsession with gladiatorial blood sport. From his academic podium, Augustine mocks the games and temporarily convinces Alypius to shun the amphitheater, but he despairs when Alypius, goaded by friends, succumbs to familiar temptations. He describes Alypius's backsliding in lurid terms:

> When he saw the blood, it was as though he drunk a deep draught of savage passion. Instead of turning away he fixed his eyed upon the scene and drank in all its frenzy, unaware of what he was doing. He reveled in the wickedness of the fighting and was drunk with the fascination of bloodshed. . . . Need I say more? He watched and cheered and grew hot with excitement, and when he left the arena, he carried away with him a diseased mind which would leave him no peace.[9]

We may easily imagine Augustine the child distracted by the folly of games like *Doom, Grand Theft Auto III,* and *Resistance: Fall of Man;* and we may likewise imagine Augustine the concerned intellectual joining the chorus of parents and lawmakers who caution us against the "fascination of bloodshed." Where Alypius, Eric Harris, and Dylan Klebold go, there, but for the grace of God, go I.

Plato's and Augustine's divergent views on play and prayer anticipate current debates about videogames. While cultural watchdogs, like Augustine, see videogames as a diversion from more worthy pursuits or, worse, an invitation to spiritual corruption, Huizinga, like Plato, sees gameplay as a potentially sacred act, a pathway to the divine. Huizinga argues that the fundamental act of make-believe, central to both gameplay and religion, challenges the "absolute determinism of the cosmos." The transportation of oneself into the "magic circle," the space in which make-believe replaces reality, is not simply an act of imagination—it is an act of creation, of raising our world to the "domain of the spirit." Huizinga writes, "Formally speaking, there is no distinction whatever between marking out a space for a sacred purpose and marking it out for the purposes of sheer play. The turf, the tennis court, the chess board, and the pavement hopscotch cannot formally be distinguished from the temple or magic circle."[10]

Huizinga further argues, like Plato, that play is inherently spiritual, "bound up with the sacred emotion of the sacramental act." In play as in the ecstasy of devotion, we are seized, thrilled, or enraptured. He hypothesizes a primitive ritual dance in which a "savage" enacts a "mystic unity" between himself and a kangaroo. To the rational observer, the savage is merely playing the kangaroo. To the savage, he and the kangaroo are one. The difference is only in our expression and vantage point. More familiar rituals, such as a sacrificial rite performed by a priest, work in a similar way; while Catholics see the Eucharist as a mystical transformation of bread and wine to Christ's body and blood, other Christians recognize only symbolism. In both cases, the ceremonial performance represents a cosmic event and "compels the gods to effect that event . . . by 'playing' it."[11] Man becomes kangaroo; bread becomes body. Make-belief becomes belief.

We can pose the same questions about videogames that Plato and Huizinga pose more generally about singing, dancing, and the theater. In what sense do they reflect a consciousness of the sacred? Can games, like language or art, serve as a medium for insight about creation and our place within it?

Evangelical Games

A growing number of game designers have adopted videogame technology as a platform for Christian evangelism, much as political campaigns and activist organizations have successfully exploited the unique rhetorical potential of new media. Until recently, however, designers and publishers have shunned games with explicitly religious themes. Todd Hollenshead of id Software, creators of the *Doom* series, questions the viability of religious games in the market; a denominational identification, after all, alienates a large number of potential buyers. Conventional wisdom, moreover, holds that gamers do not want games that preach to them—they want games that entertain them.[12]

With these concerns in mind, Troy Lyndon of Left Behind Games suggests that successful evangelical games must have an ecumenical focus, appealing broadly to the core beliefs of all Christians. Lyndon wants the emerging Christian videogames industry to follow the precedents of Christian rock and Christian fiction, two successful enterprises that demonstrate to Lyndon and others the compatibility of mass entertainment and the missionary ideal. Lyndon sees his games as a venue for spreading the Gospel message, a "means to reach the lost," but he also recognizes that the means for spreading this message is the entertainment market.[13] On its Web site, Left Behind Games declares:

> We expect gamers will find themselves "having a great time" while "thinking and talking" about matters of eternal importance. . . . Christian music has experienced tremendous growth, as have Christian themed movies including *The Passion of the Christ* and *The Chronicles of Narnia*. As high-quality Christian themed video games come to the market, the same American buying audience is expected to continue to be interested in inspirational entertainment.[14]

The aggressive marketing of evangelical games has become an explicit industry objective. A promotional leaflet circulated at the Christian Game Developers Conference in 2003 states: "The game is a smart vehicle. It satisfies a game player's expectations while subtly (and effectively) delivering God's message."[15]

This consciousness of "a game player's expectations" among Christian game designers reflects a recent shift in the design model for evangelical games, illustrated by the efforts of those like Lyndon who mean to create more sophisticated games within proven genres like real-time strategy and first-person shooters. For nearly two decades, both Christian and Jewish designers have been creating animated quiz games that focus mainly on teaching scriptural exegesis, such as Lifeline Studios' *Charlie Church Mouse Bible Adventures* series, Torah Educational Software's *Mitzvah Man*, Third Day Games' *Gospel Champions*, and Davka's *Ehud's Courage: The Cunning Blade*. In the more commercially conscious model developed by Lyndon and others, games more closely resemble popular titles. With a combined budget of $2.5 million, N'Lightning Software Development has created *Catechumen* and *Ominous Horizons: A Paladin's Calling*, two games that signal the crossover of Christian games into the mass market. In *Catechumen*, a first-person shooter set in pagan Rome, we play a Christian warrior dispatched to the catacombs to save our persecuted brethren and smite demons. Scrolls scattered throughout the tunnels present inspirational Bible verses to us, but they do not interfere with exploration or combat. In *Ominous Horizons*, we journey through time battling faithless Druids and Mayans in search of the original Gutenberg Bible, pilfered by Lucifer and hidden somewhere in time. In *Eternal War: Shadow of Light*, developed by Two Guys Software, we play a guardian angel sent by God to deliver a troubled teen from his personal demons, hacking and slashing our way though a metaphysical dungeon created with the Quake engine.

As game critic Jeremy Lemer writes, games such as *Catechumen, Ominous Horizons*, and *Eternal War* show us "what Christianity might have looked like if it hadn't turned the other cheek."[16] Indeed, the most persistent ethical problem confronted by Christian game designers has been the apparent incompatibility of the Christian message with the violent gameplay required to make Christian games competitive in the entertainment market. Sometimes the attempt to reconcile this conflict surfaces within the games. Near the outset of *Catechumen*, for example, an armor-clad guardian angel warns us, "Confrontation is often best avoided." We find that the bolt of divine power that issues from the Sword of the Spirit, given to us by the angel, not only smites demons but also converts pagan Roman soldiers to the true faith, bathing them in golden light and gracing them with a chorus of "Alleluia!" Lyndon, for his part, recognizes no conflict. He tells us, "Jesus did not say you have to let yourself be a punching bag or a murder victim."[17] Left Behind Games' Web site likewise explains, "Christians are quite clearly taught to turn the other cheek and to love their enemies. It is equally true that no one should forfeit their lives to an aggressor who is bent on inflicting death. Forgiveness does not require absolute defenselessness."[18]

Lyndon's own real-time strategy game, *Left Behind: Eternal Forces,* released in 2006, adapts Tim LaHaye and Jerry B. Jenkins's popular *Left Behind* book series, which dramatizes the events prophesied in the Book of Revelation, including the Rapture, the advent of the Antichrist, and the second coming of Jesus. In the game, we play as a band of Christian warriors, the Tribulation Force, against the Global Community Peacekeepers, a proxy United Nations controlled by the European Antichrist, Nicolae Carpathia. We control a variety of specialized units, including Christian rock singers, recruiters, missionaries, healers, and powerful "spirit warriors." Our enemies include heavy metal rock stars, college-educated "secularists," cult leaders, gang bosses, and the Antichrist's elite hell-spawned demons. Unlike the majority of real-time strategy games, *Left Behind* does not demand that we simply conquer new territory, gather resources, and wipe out opposing factions. Rather, we must use the special abilities of our units to convert neutral units into "friends," whom we may send to training facilities to create more specialized units. We do so by raising and maintaining the "spirit level" of friendly and neutral units. While rock stars and secularists, for example, negatively influence spirit levels, our own musicians and recruiters, spreading the good news of Jesus, draw people back into the fold. As our friends become more numerous, we develop an economic infrastructure and eventually meet the Global Community Peacekeepers in direct conflict with our soldiers, tanks, and attack helicopters. Evangelization, we find, "does not require absolute defenselessness."

Critics of the game have called attention to this apparent contradiction between Christian ideology and gameplay objectives relying on violent conquest. Progressive activist Frederick Clarkson, for example, argues that the game is dominionist and promotes an ideology of intolerance. "It's about religious warfare," he writes. "The way to win is to convert or kill. . . . Anybody who is not a follower of Jesus is the enemy." The message, Clarkson argues, is the "dehumanization of the feared other—Catholics, Jews, Muslims, the wrong kind of Protestant, people deemed to be sinners."[19] Other critics object to the distribution of the game by Christian megachurches, a strategy that seems to promote a Crusader ethic in the real world. Media analyst Evan Derkacz claims that the game "rewards children for how effectively they role play the killing of those who resist becoming a born again Christian."[20] Christian conservatives have also attacked the game. Attorney Jack Thompson, one of the most vigorous opponents of videogame violence, writes in an open letter to the conservative political action group Focus on the Family, "This [game] is the worst example I have ever seen of how pop culture has conformed the Church to its image, rather than the Body of Christ serving as light . . . in the world."[21]

Some of these criticisms, however, neglect the subtler and more unconventional aspects of the game. *Left Behind,* for instance, takes a more complex view of violence than most games. Although killing an enemy unit is the quickest way to spread our influence over the city, doing so reduces the morale, or "spirit level" of friendly units, hampering our long-term efforts to build the ranks of the Tribulation Force. The game suggests that trying to save a lost soul is better than sending it promptly to hell. Clarkson's claim, moreover, that "anybody who is not a follower of Jesus is the enemy" is misleading. At the outset of the campaign, the majority of units are not enemies but neutral bystanders, potential resources for either the Tribulation Force or the Global Peacekeepers. The game does not allow us to attack these neutral units—we may only proselytize them—and we may only attack enemy units in self-defense, after they have attacked us. As the game proceeds, however, it implies that every person faces a choice for good or evil. The game's Web site explains that neutral units cannot, in fact, remain neutral for long: "Their choice is to either join the Antichrist . . . or they may join the Tribulation Force—which seeks to expose the truth and defend themselves against the forces of the Antichrist."[22] The game also features a prayer function, by which we may raise the spirit level of any friendly unit simply by pushing a "prayer" button. Critics such as Clive Thompson, however, suggest that the integration of Christian ideology into gameplay is merely superficial. He writes, "I'd click the prayer button so instinctually that I pretty much forgot I was, well, praying."[23]

Left Behind is, nevertheless, a unique amalgamation of a conventional strategy game involving production and conquest and a novel critique of these conventions integrated directly into gameplay. Its creators seem divided by commercial ambition and Christian conscience. In this sense, the game illustrates the broader ideological problem faced by digital evangelizers as they attempt to bring the Gospel into the mainstream videogames market. Clive Thompson notes an unintentional, somewhat awkward irony in the game's adaptation of the more radically apocalyptic message of the *Left Behind* novels, in which Jesus, at the end of the Tribulation period, comes in glory "to slaughter all unbelievers, dissolving their tongues and bursting their bodies like overstuffed sausages." The Jews, finally, pay for their rejection of Jesus, as the earth itself becomes soaked with their blood. In their mindfulness of the public concerns about videogame violence and the need to appeal to a wider market with a more moderate message, Lyndon and the designers of *Left Behind* leave these grotesque fantasies out of the game. Thompson writes,

106

"*Left Behind* fans are apparently more worried about simulated violence in video games than about believing an actual prophecy . . . endorsed by their spiritual leaders."[24] At the same time, the "fire-eyed Jesus" of LaHaye and Jenkins's novels seems well suited to videogame evangelizers, who have taken to spreading the good news at the point of a sword and the muzzle of an assault rifle, albeit very peacefully.

Magic, Mythopoesis, and Messianism

In his critique of *Left Behind*, Clive Thompson casually observes a parallel between the world envisioned by millennialist Christianity and the virtual world evoked by fantasy role-playing games. "In both cases," Thompson writes, "the world is controlled by magical, invisible forces that only poten- tates can understand."[25] The Catholic Church, on the other hand, emphasizes the difference between miracles performed by God and occult magic. The *Catechism of the Catholic Church* states:

> All practices of magic or sorcery, by which one attempts to tame occult powers, so as to place them at one's service and have a supernatural power over others— even if this were for the sake of restoring their health—are gravely contrary to the virtue of religion. These practices are even more to be condemned when accompanied by the intention of harming someone, or when they have recourse to the intervention of demons.[26]

Although critics like Thompson may find the Church's doctrinal distinction irrelevant, it has, in fact, shaped public discourse about role-playing games and videogames. For two decades, advocates have claimed that games promote occultist ritual and demonology. In 1980, James Dallas Egbert III, a Michigan State University student and avid *Dungeons & Dragons* player, committed suicide after dropping out of school and going into hiding for more than a year. In 1982, sixteen-year-old Irving Pulling committed suicide after a curse, alleg- edly, had been placed on his *Dungeons & Dragons* character. Patricia Pulling, Irving's mother, attributed both Egbert's and her son's deaths to *Dungeons & Dragons* and founded the advocacy group Bothered About Dungeons and Dragons (BADD). Pulling described the game as a digest of deviltry:

> A fantasy role-playing game which uses demonology, witchcraft, voodoo, murder, rape, blasphemy, suicide, assassination, insanity, sex perversion, homo- sexuality, prostitution, satanic type rituals, gambling, barbarism, cannibalism, sadism, desecration, demon summoning, necromantics, divination and other teachings. There have been a number of deaths nationwide where games like *Dungeons and Dragons* were either the decisive factor in adolescent suicide and murder, or played a major factor in the violent behavior of such tragedies.[27]

Pulling's grief made her a zealot, but the popular identification of role-playing games with "occult powers" has some foundation in virtual worlds, which often come furnished with their own gods and imagined religions. *The Elder Scrolls* series, for instance, features an elaborate pantheon. The Nine Divines, the official cult supported by the emperors of Tamriel, include gods of time, life and death, wisdom, mercy, and commerce, as well as goddesses of love, beauty, and the air. The ninth Divine, a demigod, represents the ascent of Tamriel's first emperor to immortality. A competing demonic pantheon, the Daedric princes, includes lords of twilight, destruction, treachery, predation, rape, pestilence, thievery, ugliness, and madness. Over the course of the four *Elder Scrolls* games, the mythology of these beings unfolds as the player gathers tomes and magical artifacts that reveal the gods' histories and channel their powers. We gain magical abilities by praying at shrines dedicated to these spirits located throughout the game world. In *The Elder Scrolls IV: Oblivion,* each of the major cities of the empire hosts a temple dedicated to one of the Divines, and within these temples, a cult of worshippers offers healing and instruction in particular schools of magic. In the wilderness beyond the cities, infidel cults gather at hidden Daedric shrines, where we may undertake quests for the powerful relics of these princes of darkness.

In the *Forgotten Realms* series, based on *Dungeons & Dragons,* a large pantheon includes divine patrons of humans, elves, dwarves, gnomes, orcs, and halflings; gods of nature, the sun, death, and magic; gods of secrets, revelry, wealth, and wayfarers; and, finally, the twin gods of justice and tyranny, Heironeous and Hextor, eternally at war with each other for dominion of the world. In Obsidian's *Neverwinter Nights 2,* we choose one of these deities as our personal patron. Although our choice has no bearing on the game narrative, it is partly constrained by our character's race and moral alignment; a dwarf, for example, cannot worship the god of the orcs, nor can a righteous paladin pay homage to the evil god Hextor. If we choose to be a Cleric, one of many character classes available to us, our magical powers, in part, depend on the divine "realm" we serve. We may also play as a "planetouched" character, one descended from a union between a human and a celestial being—or an infernal one. Like Clerics, these semi-divines gain special powers depending on their spiritual identification.

Game critics have praised the ways in which these role-playing games integrate complex mythologies in order to enhance our sense of immersion within their virtual worlds. Ioan Sambeteanu, for instance, calls *The Elder Scrolls* "one of the richest unwritten fantasy universes ever created" and maintains that "the strongpoint of *Oblivion* [is] the huge world and its rich historical, religious and social background."[28] Fantasy games have simulated a cultural milieu more successfully than real-time strategy games such as the

Civilization and *Total War* series, notwithstanding the critical accolades these games receive. *Medieval II: Total War,* for instance, allows us to dispatch emissaries of Christianity and Islam to convert enemy lands or to build glorious cathedrals and mosques to impress our subjects, but our missionaries and monuments to the faith simply serve the cynical calculations of government. These games express a fundamentally atheistic sensibility. Like low taxes, ostentatious public entertainments, or a military garrison, religion is just another means to pacify conquered territories. Fantasy games, on the other hand, aim to simulate spiritual consciousness as well as the social relations arising among religious groups.

Unlike *Catechumen* and *Eternal War, Oblivion* and *Neverwinter Nights 2* do not proselytize familiar beliefs. Although the architecture of the temples dedicated to the Nine Divines closely resembles that of Romanesque churches, we find nowhere in these game worlds references to scripture or recognizable Christian iconography. Instead of the virtual missionary field envisioned by Troy Lyndon in *Left Behind,* fantasy games represent a new form of mythopoesis, the intricate construction of an imaginary belief system that shapes the fictional world and motivates the narrative. Inventing a religion rather than invoking the deeply held beliefs of real people insulates publishers from the sort of controversy that has buffeted *Resistance* and *Left Behind.* At the same time, the fundamental characteristics of these invented faiths subtly adapt Judeo-Christian beliefs and transform them for the realms of digital entertainment. While particular games invent particular gods, and the adaptation of both pagan and Judeo-Christian mythology varies wildly from one game to another, emerging patterns of videogame mythopoesis offer insight into the ways that computer games have assimilated the religious traditions of the wider culture. While media critics commonly observe that the most commercially successful games have, by necessity, eschewed religion, we find instead that they merely appropriate it in ways that are difficult to recognize.

Most significantly, a range of fantasy role-playing games feature a messianic narrative, more spiritually inflected than the "save the world" narrative most common in videogames. Here we fulfill an ancient prophecy of deliverance from a power that threatens to destroy the world. Fulfillment comes either by embodying a divine being or aiding a divine being in the quest to vanquish a rival deity and its hidden cult. In this way, fantasy games share more with *Left Behind* than the notion, in Thompson's terms, of "a world controlled by magical, invisible forces." In fantasy games, as in *Left Behind* and in the Book of Revelation itself, the world tilts on the brink of apocalypse awaiting its divine deliverer. In one of the earliest expressions of videogame messianism, the *Ultima* series portrays the ascent of the Avatar, the embodiment of virtue who leads the realm of Brittania, long plagued by diabolic tyrants, from the

Age of Darkness into the Age of Enlightenment. In *Ultima IV: Quest of the Avatar,* released in 1985, our transfiguration culminates with a symbolic death and resurrection, as we descend into a dungeon named "The Stygian Abyss" and emerge triumphantly with an artifact granting us "Ultimate Wisdom."

In the popular *Myst* series, we play an unnamed stranger in the service of Atrus, a bookish demiurge who, as a descendent of the ancient D'Ni civilization, holds the divine power to create or destroy entire worlds by writing about them in sacred, closely guarded books. Although the game portrays Atrus as a scholar rather than a deity, he spins worlds into being with his words, just as the God of Genesis does. In *Riven,* the second game in the series, we encounter a primitive society that worships the D'Ni as gods. Empowered by Atrus to travel between worlds using "linking books," we act as his agent, defending his creations against usurpers who mean to sow chaos and undo his work.

In *The Elder Scrolls III: Morrowind,* we travel to the island province of Vvardenfell, home of the Dunmer, or Dark Elves, who await a messiah to defeat a demonic overlord who inhabits a volcano and spreads disease and choking ash storms throughout the land. In the course of our adventures, we learn that we are indeed the prophesied savior, the reincarnation of an ancient Dunmer hero vanquished in the distant past by jealous, rival deities. In *Oblivion,* the assassination of the emperor of Tamriel by evil cultists reveals an imminent invasion of the realm by an army of demons led by the Daedric prince of destruction, Mehrunes Dagon. In our quest to close the gates that allow the demons to enter the mortal plane, we befriend Martin Septim, the long lost son of the slain emperor, help him to ascend the throne, and witness the fulfillment of an ancient prophecy. Martin is more than heir to Tamriel—he is the incarnation of the just god Akatosh, who ultimately transforms himself into a giant, luminous dragon, banishes Mehrunes Dagon forever, and ascends in glory to the heavenly plane. In *Knights of the Nine,* an *Oblivion* expansion module, we play the messiah, gathering sacred weapons and armor that transform us into the "Divine Crusader," a hero who, on behalf of the Nine Divines, destroys an undead heresiarch. Our crusade demands a pilgrimage to holy shrines as well as moral purity. As in *Ultima IV,* committing a crime, such as pilfering gold or killing an innocent person, negates our progress and forces us to begin the quest again.

While it appears that the religions imagined in these games are neatly removed from actual belief systems to polytheistic fantasy worlds, Judeo-Christian visions of apocalypse and messianic deliverance emerge within them. *Ultima IV, Neverwinter Nights,* and *Morrowind* do not grace us with scriptural passages as do *Catechumen, Charlie Church Mouse,* and *Left Behind,* but they do draw from the same wells as myth and religion, manifesting our fear of chaos, destruction, and oblivion, as well as our wish for order, deliverance, and immortality.

The predominance of messianic narratives in these games reflects deeply rooted Judeo-Christian beliefs shot through the lenses of commercial fantasy. Virtual messiahs are particularly at home in interactive media. More than pulp novels and film, videogames empower us within an imagined world, allowing us to indulge our fantasies of power. The player-messiah represents the fullest fictive expression of the virtual will to power, drawing the entire game world into orbit around us and making it utterly dependent on us, as players, for its salvation. Videogames actualize what religions only promise: not only the grand gifts of immortality and cosmic coherence, but also the more immediate certainty that the existence of the individual person means something. In this sense, videogames might appeal to us in ways that transcend their cultural novelty and technical dazzle. They might, in fact, speak to the deepest psychological or spiritual needs that only religion and the most sublime art can satisfy. We might claim for digital fantasy what the historian and art critic Simon Schama claims of Vincent Van Gogh, whose art, Schama says, "would reclaim what had once belonged to religion—consolation for our mortality through the relish of the gift of life."[29]

Virtuality and Spirituality

The potential for virtual reality to nurture a kind of spiritual consciousness has drawn together diverse camps of game designers: the missionaries and the myth-poets. The emergence and rapid growth of the online community *Second Life* since 2003 has given these two groups a common forum. In *Second Life,* players create customizable avatars and roam freely over a vast world of contiguous islands, on foot, in flight, or by teleportation. For a fee, we may purchase our own island, where we can build a virtual home for our avatar. Using an accessible modeling tool, we can design and create our own clothing, furniture, toys, animal familiars, and works of art, and we may sell these things for currency in the game world or the real world.

As in other massively multiplayer online (MMO) games, we communicate with other players through chat and instant messages, but *Second Life* is less a game than a social platform, a graphical chat room. It does not compel us to complete quests, engage in combat, collect treasure, garner experience, and ascend from one level to the next. Its founders at Linden Lab envisioned an online utopia free from the competition, acquisitiveness, and hierarchy that characterize other online game worlds. With its egalitarian ethos, its accessibility to users beyond the videogame subculture, and its free membership, *Second Life* has become a virtual commons for business, education, politics, and religion, where organizations of all persuasions can set up shop.

Bill Roper, head of the Christian development Studio Flagship Games, speculates that the most effective means of videogame evangelism would be a faith-based MMO: "It would be a great way to bring people in the Christian community together from all over the world. . . . You'd also get . . . outreach outside the Christian community."[30] In fact, *Second Life* has already realized Roper's vision, hosting a spectrum of faith communities, including Temple Beth Israel, the First Unitarian Universalist Church of Second Life, the interdenominational Life Church, and the Islamic Society, as well as mock churches such as the Avatars of Change, the Church of Burgertime, and the Church of Elvis. Journalist Cathy Lynn Grossman, a religion correspondent for *USA Today,* reports that "leaders of Christian, Jewish, and Muslim sites estimate about one thousand avatars teleport to churches, synagogues, or mosques on a regular basis. Hundreds more list themselves with Buddhist, pagan, Wiccan, and other groups."[31] Here we may participate in virtual religious services, complete with prayers, songs, scriptural readings, and meditations. Life Church, based in Oklahoma City, broadcasts its weekly service directly into *Second Life,* and the Islamic Society gathers in a virtual reconstruction of a tenth-century mosque in Cordoba, Spain.

Some question the authenticity of online worship. Are the *Second Life* faith communities, after all, using a new medium to express a deeply felt religious consciousness, or are they merely playacting? Francis Maier, chancellor of the Catholic Archdiocese of Denver, says that real worship is "not just going through mumbo-jumbo and dressing up. . . . [It means] submission to beliefs and practices revealed by God and passed down by generations of believers. You can't phone that in."[32] A member of the Buddhism Listening and Discussion group agrees: "I don't know anybody who meditates in front of a computer."[33] Noreen Herzfeld, a professor of theology at St. John's University in Minnesota, likewise argues that *Second Life* reflects only the "external face" of religion, the creeds and practices rather than the inwardly felt spiritual consciousness at the core of every faith. She concludes that virtual worlds are "more a diversion than a place to find God."[34]

For many others, however, *Second Life* fosters a real sense of religious community. In Sweden, isolated from large Muslim communities, Sten Muhammed Yusef Widhe has joined prayer groups at the *Second Life* Islamic Society. Widhe says, "I put my avatar in praying position and I pray at the same time. My prayer in my room is valid and my prayer online is symbolic."[35] Beth Brown, founder of Temple Beth Israel, holds holiday Seders for more than 200 members, including her mother, who lives in New York. She says, "Once people started coming, I felt deep down inside that this was an obligation to the Jewish people around the world. . . . I can't light Shabbat candles anywhere with my mother but *Second Life.*"[36] Others see *Second Life* as an ideal forum for interfaith communication. Yunus Yakoub Islam, a British Muslim, gathers with Sufi, Salafi, Sunni, and Shia Muslims in a *Second Life* mosque, and he has also attended evangelical Christian services. He says, "That would be a lot more difficult in real life. . . . I'd be a lot less comfortable doing it."[37]

Some, including conservative Christians, challenge Herzfeld's notion that *Second Life* does not foster the more deeply spiritual or "internal" experience of religion. For them, virtual reality is indeed a path to spiritual reality. As Shona Crabtree reminds us in her survey of online faith communities, the word "avatar," exchanged so freely by gamers and game scholars, derives from the Sanskrit word for the incarnation of a deity.[38] Julian Dibbell, a technology writer and former consultant at Linden Lab, claims that "virtual reality is in some ways an essentially spiritual experience."[39] George Byrd, who built the First Unitarian Universalist Church of Second Life, agrees: "The spiritual connection is in your brain and in your soul. It's the same either way [in *Second Life* or in real life]."[40] Larry Transue, a *Second Life* missionary, believes that in saving souls online he is saving souls nonetheless. "People think what they do in the virtual world is OK," Transue says, "because it's not real. But it is real, because your thoughts are real. Who you truly are will shine through eventually."[41] In this sense, virtual reality serves as an actualization of spiritual reality, and our avatar reflects our soul: roaming, dynamic, changeable, prone to both destruction and salvation. Transue's idea that sin and salvation in *Second Life* are real because *Second Life* reflects our thoughts, and our "thoughts are real," follows Huizinga's claim that the savage playing the kangaroo has, in his own mind, actually transformed and entered a spiritual world through the act of playing. Like the savage transfigured by the sacred dance, *Second Life* missionaries and mystics like Byrd, Dibbell, and Transue transcend the temporal world within the magic circle created by *Second Life.*

Others have been more radically transformed by gameplay. On August 5, 2005, Lee Seung Seop, a twenty-eight-year-old man from Taegu, South Korea, collapsed and died in an Internet café, following fifty uninterrupted hours playing *Starcraft* and *World of Warcraft* online. For two days and two nights Lee neglected to eat or sleep. Doctors concluded that he died of heart failure caused by dehydration and exhaustion, but the autopsy revealed only part of the story. Six weeks earlier, Lee had been fired from his job for missing work to play videogames, and his girlfriend dumped him. In the press, he became notorious as the first death explicitly attributed to videogame addiction.

Commentators, critics, and doctors continue to offer interpretations of Lee's death. Jennifer Veale, *Time* magazine's correspondent in Seoul, partly attributes it to the cultural climate of South Korea, where videogames are a national obsession. In Seoul, teams of professional gamers with corporate sponsorships compete in televised national tournaments, and videogame champions enjoy the same celebrity as world-class athletes and rock stars.

For South Koreans, gaming is not a waste of time or a potential addiction but a supreme test of mental and physical speed and acuity. As Veale says, the professional gamer needs "the focus of the Buddhist monk and the hand-eye coordination of a neurosurgeon."[42] In their grinding, frenetic efforts to sharpen their performance, millions of aspiring amateurs like Lee pack the cafés, log in, and abandon themselves, body and spirit, to the virtual proving grounds.

American doctors do not see Lee as a product of his game-crazy culture, but rather as the victim of a new kind of mental illness. In June 2007, a committee with the American Medical Association (AMA) proposed a revision of the Diagnostic and Statistical Manual of Mental Disorders (DSM-IV) that would classify videogame addition as a recognized disorder akin to alcoholism or drug addiction. The committee reports that 90 percent of American children and adolescents play videogames, and that 15 percent of these, more than 5 million, suffer from addiction. The symptoms, the report suggests, may include withdrawal from friends and family, threatening or manipulative behavior, and thoughts of suicide. One mother cited in the report compares her videogame-obsessed son, Michael, with her alcoholic father: "I saw exactly the same thing. . . . [Michael] would curse and call us every name imaginable. . . . It was as if he was possessed."[43]

The AMA report lends clinical support to media theorists' more vaguely expressed notion that virtual reality, in large doses, tends to unmoor us from the real world. Michael Heim has described Alternate World Disorder (AWD), a condition, he writes, that causes "images and expectations from an alternate world . . . [to] distort our functioning in the current world. . . . The virtual world obtrudes upon our activities in the primary world, and vice versa."[44] In the most extreme cases, the virtual world not only obtrudes on the primary world but replaces it entirely. In her book *Narrative as Virtual Reality: Immersion and Interactivity in Literature and Electronic Media,* Marie-Laure Ryan identifies the "loss of the capacity to distinguish textual worlds . . . from the actual world," as the deepest level of immersion in a fictional world, a condition she calls "Don Quixote Syndrome."[45] Ryan, Heim, and the AMA have sought to rationalize what Plato or Huizinga might recognize as an ineffable, essentially spiritual experience. What is religion, after all, but a chronic case of Alternate World Disorder? Lee's behavior, while disturbed and ultimately destructive by reasonable standards, mirrors that of the ascetic: a radical denial of the body leading to spiritual transport, ecstasy, and death in a luminous dream. From our perspective, he is a pathetic geek—from his own, he is the kangaroo.

❖ III ❖
PEDAGOGY

❖ 7 ❖

Videogames, History, and Education

A memorable 1993 episode of *The Simpsons* mocks the grand vision of educational technology. When the town of Springfield gains a financial windfall, Lisa Simpson imagines that the money might be spent on a virtual reality machine for Springfield Elementary School. Donning the high-tech helmet, she enters the world of Genghis Khan, who instructs her in the avuncular voice of Phil Hartman, "Hello, Lisa! I'm Genghis Khan. Today you'll go where I go. Defile what I defile. Eat who I eat."[1]

The reality of such experiments in "edutainment"—the marriage of education and entertainment—has been more modest, and creators of educational videogames, while exploiting their potential as entertainment, have been careful not to misrepresent the past simply to make history seem more fun. *The Oregon Trail,* one of the earliest and most successful attempts to use interactive entertainment to teach history, places us at the reigns of a wagon train migrating westward. We pass towns, trading posts, rivers, mountains, and deserts, learning about American geography. We purchase supplies for our journey, learning about nineteenth-century economy and material culture. Faced with threats of sickness, accident, or attack, moreover, we try to keep our virtual family alive, learning something of the human struggles of the past. If we perish before we reach Oregon, the game closes with an image of a tombstone bearing our name, cartoonish but vaguely disturbing.

The game does not require quick reflexes or particular cleverness at solving puzzles, nor does it feature dramatic cut scenes or surprising narrative twists. Its graphics are simple and mostly unanimated. Gameplay proceeds

117

through a series of menus and dialogue boxes confronting us with the daily decisions faced by the settlers themselves. How many spare axles should we buy before our journey? Should we move fast, risking damage to our wagons, or slow, risking a winter in the mountains? Should we ford a dangerous river or spend our diminishing funds on an expensive ferry ride? The game does not offer a clear path to victory. Every option bears its own risks, and even the wisest players can be undone by chance. Its structure, though uncomplicated compared to current historical simulations, illustrates a fundamental approach to thinking about the past, one that informs more advanced videogames as well as serious historical research: history is contingent upon decisions, and while some are more consequential than others, they all add up to what we know as history.

Counterfactual analysis seizes on the notion of contingency and seeks to understand the past by considering its alternative possibilities. What if the Allied invasion of Normandy failed? What if the South won the Civil War? What if the Chinese had settled the New World before the Europeans? Might the proverbial kingdom have been saved, in other words, if the horseshoe nail had not been wanted? By constructing a virtual past and granting the player agency within it, videogames have become the ideal medium for teaching the lesson of contingency, and history teachers have been quicker than those in other fields to experiment with this new medium. Students certainly find game-based learning more fun, but some historians question what students can really learn by playing videogames.

Counterfactual analysis, whether mediated in a videogame or a parlor game, is saddled with a paradox. How can we learn about what happened by studying what did not happen? Historical fiction, films, and videogames routinely inscribe imagined events into the historical record, but historians and educators have a more stringent obligation. In fact, some historians argue that counterfactual analysis constitutes an irresponsible form of revisionism. As Richard J. Evans, a historian with a moderate view, suggests, "It's hard enough finding out what was, let alone reaching any kind of tenable conclusions about what wasn't."[2] At the same time, others recognize an inherent value in the method. William H. McNeill says, "There is a serious intellectual kernel behind the game, for there are events . . . that did make quite an extraordinary difference in what followed. And by drawing attention to such occasions and wondering out loud how different the world would be, contingent, surprising, unpredictable aspects of the human past can become obvious to most readers."[3]

Videogames have compelled historians to scrutinize the fundamental methods underlying their discipline. While they carry, in Evans's view, "extremely severe" limitations as a means of representing the past, they also represent a powerful pedagogical innovation, in terms of their unique ability to evoke empathy and to consider events from multiple perspectives. In assessing the value of counterfactual history, Allan Megill draws a useful distinction between "exuberant" and "restrained" methods of inquiry. Like historical fiction, Megill suggests, exuberant counterfactual history freely rearranges chronology or intentionally ignores certain aspects of the past in the interest of telling a good story. Restrained counterfactual history, on the other hand, "involves an explicit canvassing of alternative possibilities that existed in a real past."[4]

Recently, videogame developers have taken a more restrained approach to simulating the past. This chapter considers the different ways commercial and pedagogical videogames have merged entertainment and education, attempting to resolve the counterfactual dilemma of representing what was by representing what was not. The essential difference, we will see, between playing a game based on the American Revolution and hearing a lesson on the American Revolution is that the game enables students to play the role of a historical persona or nation, making decisions and observing the consequences of their decisions on other personae or nations. Studying history interactively is not simply more fun—it invites students to consider a new range of issues, such as identity, perspective, agency, and causality.

Edutainment

Like the adoption of videogames by the military as training and recruiting devices, the emergence of videogames in American classrooms represents a major institutional appropriation of new media and has raised considerable controversy. Many regard edutainment as an aberration or a contradiction in terms. Seymour Papert, an educational technology researcher at MIT, believes that videogames foster cognitive development, but he remains skeptical about the use of games in an institutional context. The "mating of education and entertainment," Papert suggests, has resulted in "offspring that keep the bad features of each parent and lose the good ones." Curriculum designers, Papert argues, have adopted videogames for the same reason U.S. Army recruiters have: they believe that games are the best means of getting the attention of young people.[5] As a medium, however, games do not support institutionalized learning, which Papert regards as passive, abstracted, and unnaturally fragmented into separate disciplines. Games do not teach specific subjects. Rather, they teach students to teach themselves in more active, applied, and integrated ways. More recently, Steven Johnson has likewise argued that games teach children to solve complex problems faster and more creatively.[6] The nature of such learning, Papert argues, necessarily excludes it from institutional context. "Games are designed so that the learner can take charge of the process of learning," he writes, "thus making it very different [from] school learning, where the teacher . . . has made the important decisions and the 'learners' are expected to do what they are told."[7] Papert's critique of educational videogames, offered in the late 1990s, anticipates the efforts of more recent game developers, who have attempted to make the kind of independent, integrated learning Papert describes compatible with established pedagogies. In many ways, achieving this compatibility depends on the cooperation of the teacher, who may regard the game as a distraction, and the videogame, which obviates the authoritarian presence of the teacher—at least in Papert's view.

Some researchers promise that game-based learning will revolutionize educational institutions. Kurt Squire, an educational researcher at the University of Wisconsin, completed his doctoral work on teaching world history using *Civilization III*. Like Papert, Squire argues that games foster a way of learning that transcends traditional disciplinary boundaries and emphasizes integrated problem solving. "*Civilization III*," he writes, "represents world history not as a story of colonial domination or western expansion, but as an emergent process arising from overlapping, interrelated factors. . . . Successful students developed conceptual understandings across world history, geography, and politics." But Squire also suggests that videogames can complement traditional instruction, offering his own experiments as models for "integrating . . . [videogames] within classroom settings."[8]

For Squire and other researchers, multiplayer games especially encourage achievement through competition and reward both cooperation and teamwork. The learner takes the leading role in his or her own intellectual development, while the instructor becomes a facilitator who structures gameplay and guides inquiry, but does not exercise strict authority over what students learn or how they learn it. In this sense, teachers do not cede authority to computers, but rather to the students themselves. Beginning with *The Oregon Trail,* educational games privilege decision making and problem solving over memorization and repetition, teaching students to see historical problems from multiple points of view, and to understand the past as a complex reality where motives and actions are interrelated.

Educational videogame developer Muzzy Lane has incorporated these pedagogical ideals into its promotion of its *Making History* series. Their Web site explains:

> Interaction between students is often a missing component in a classroom. When students collaborate and compete, they are empowered to construct their own solutions to complex problems, and more fully explore and understand materials. Games encourage problem solving, team building and communication and foster complex decision-making skills. Our games provide players with variables

that simulate the often-unseen influences behind complex systems. In order to succeed, students learn that they must examine problems from various points of view. . . . When actively involved and when teaching others, students are more motivated to learn and more likely to retain what they learn.[9]

The obstacles to the widespread changes that Squire and the developers at Muzzy Lane promise are more practical than philosophical. Most public school districts cannot afford to license the most sophisticated educational software, much less fund the development of games specifically suited to their curricular needs. Even when budgets allow for games, strict state and district requirements further complicate their adoption in public schools. In the retail market, where they are forced to share shelf space with the newest entertainment titles, educational software has consistently failed. Creating educational games that could compete with popular historical simulator series—series that include *Civilization, Age of Empires,* and *Total War*—requires large production budgets and the sustained collaboration between educators and game designers.

So far, such collaboration has been limited to emerging commercial ventures like Muzzy Lane or to academic consortiums like the Education Arcade, a team of educators and game developers from MIT and the University of Wisconsin. Papert, however, errs in supposing that the difficult match between education and entertainment means that the two will never be married. Muzzy Lane and the Education Arcade present two distinct models that may represent the future of edutainment, one emerging from the corporate world and the other from the academic world.

Role-Playing Games and History

The most vehement critics as well as the most zealous defenders of videogames agree that the games' most compelling rhetorical appeal is in their ability to transform our perspective through role-playing. Worried legislators, researchers, and parents argue that role-playing games encourage children to identify with violent characters. In 2003, however, researchers from MIT and the University of Wisconsin, including Henry Jenkins, James Gee, and Kurt Squire, formed the Education Arcade, a partnership whose mission is exploring "social, cultural, and educational potentials of videogames by initiating new game development projects, coordinating interdisciplinary research efforts, and informing public conversations about the broader and sometimes unexpected uses of this emerging art form in education."[10] An outgrowth of the Games-to-Teach Project, an MIT-based, Microsoft-funded initiative with the purpose of developing game concepts that merge math, science, engineering, and humanities curricula with state-of-the-art gameplay, the Education Arcade promotes itself as a bridge between academic research and commercial product development. While they use commercial platforms and design tools to create their games, they also seek to integrate traditional pedagogy in their designs, supplementing their games with support materials for teachers.

One of their most ambitious projects has been *Revolution,* a multiplayer role-playing game set in Williamsburg, Virginia, in 1775, on the eve of the Revolution. Unlike Colonial Williamsburg, a living museum in which tourists and students may watch actors mime the daily life of eighteenth-century Virginia townsfolk, players themselves assume the role of the colonials, controlling their actions and observing their consequences. The game proposes to teach American history by giving students the "opportunity to experience the daily social, economic, and political lives of the town's inhabitants." We may play as one of seven distinct characters: Robert Carter Nicholas, a well-to-do lawyer and moderate patriot; Catherine Grimes, an independent tradeswoman with patriot sympathies; Hannah, a house slave; William Waddill, a silversmith loyal to the crown; Margaret Chadwell, a servant girl with loyalist sympathies; Dan, a field slave; and John Lamb, a carpenter and patriot.[11]

Although the characters are loosely based on historical residents of Williamsburg, we cannot influence momentous events or interact with recognizable historical figures, as we can in the *Civilization* and *Making History* series. Rather, we exist in a historical bubble, a dynamic, interactive, but self-enclosed virtual space in which we may react to events recorded by history but not participate in them, a design feature that effectively avoids the counterfactual problem. Instead of influencing world events, as we do in strategy games, we concentrate on personal and local dilemmas. Each character has a particular objective within the game. Committed patriots like Nicholas and Lamb must nudge the colony toward independence while remaining wary of impending violence; loyalists like Waddill must work to suppress insurrectionist activity; trades people and servants like Catherine and Margaret, regardless of their sympathies, must work to maintain their livelihood; and slaves like Hannah and Dan, indifferent to politics, struggle to reclaim families broken and scattered by the slave trade.

Like historical fiction, *Revolution* creates imaginary worlds within the world we know from history—a pocket of imaginary events that reflects and responds to the established historical narrative, but never intersects with it to create a counterfactual paradox. The game teaches history not by recounting the past, as textbooks do, nor by inviting students to rewrite the past, as strategy games do, but rather by constructing a simulacrum of the past, which brushes against history itself only lightly. We hear rumors of unrest in Boston, for instance, but we cannot orchestrate an assassination of Thomas Paine for publishing his inflammatory pamphlets, nor can we join the Continental Congress to stand among the Founders.

Revolution poses a clear solution to the problem faced by all historical games that propose to teach history: defining the limit between the imagined and the real, what happened and what did not. Different games negotiate this limit in different ways, and many regard it only casually. The cleverness of *Revolution* rests in its illusion of continuity between the game narrative and this historical narrative, which never collide. In *Revolution,* we think globally and act locally. As Catherine, a tailor, we may make disguises to aid patriots in their raid on a loyalist arsenal or to conceal a fugitive slave. As Nicholas, who seeks independence through peaceful negotiation, we inveigh against rioting against the British governor. As Waddill, we gather signatures for a petition to halt public intimidation of loyalist business owners. We achieve these purposes not through combat but through communication with other players, who likewise pursue their own goals in the game. The game fosters interaction between students and an understanding of the cross-purposes of revolutionary America. Our character's concerns, ideally, become our own, though they are not part of the grand narrative outlined in our textbooks.

The game simulates social context in a way that commercial role-playing games, propelled mostly by combat, individual character enhancements, and treasure hunting, do not. Our character's gender, race, class, and political affiliation directly impact the way we can interact with other players and nonplayer characters within the game. The Education Arcade describes the innovative "gossip mechanic" implemented in the game:

> Non-player characters . . . talk to one another about the events that are taking place within the world. What makes our implementation different from other games is that the gossiping that takes place is based upon the "memories" that a character possesses. A memory can be a memory another character gossiped, a "notable" action done by one of the players, or some pre-scripted memory that we want to happen in a particular scenario. For example, if a shopkeeper catches a player stealing something from a shop, the shopkeeper would shout out to the public that X had stolen something from Y, at which point the townsfolk that had heard the shout would begin to spread the memory by gossiping with other characters around them at regular intervals. Eventually, if the constable hears about this theft, he will arrest the culprit upon their next encounter.[12]

Further, the social interactions that govern the spread of such gossip are constrained by class difference. A patrician woman will avoid communication with servant or slave. Lower class nonplayer characters address higher class player characters with an honorific—"Mr. Nicholas"—while higher class characters address lower class characters by surname—"Waddill," "Lamb"—and women and slaves by their given name—"Cathy," "Maggie," "Hannah."

In spring 2005, the Education Arcade conducted tests to see what happens when students play *Revolution.* In a series of workshops at MIT's Teacher

Education Program lab, students adopted one of the personae and participated in multiplayer sessions, followed by guided discussion and a written exercise in which students related their character's experience in the form of a diary entry. The developers sought to answer three questions:

> How might students experience situated role-play within the Revolution environment? How might their experience of playing a character within the Revolution simulation impact on a student's ability to participate in discussion about aspects of social history? And what new opportunities for rich committed learning are created through this new kind of interactive multimodal educational resource?[13]

The tests revealed mixed results. Sometimes, students refused to play their assigned role, effectively nullifying the value of the game's complex "gossip mechanic." Often, students would use the game's instant message system for unrelated chat. In these cases, the role of the teacher as a guide for both gameplay and discussion became necessary. Contrary to Papert's claim that games might render teachers obsolete, the Education Arcade concludes that "the role of the teacher . . . seemed critical."[14] Students needed teachers not to dispense information, but rather to assist in the more complex task of interpretation and critical reflection:

> It is unclear to what degree students might reflect and form hypotheses about the significance of the interactions and events that they observed unless prompted to reflect by a question. . . . In this sense the teacher remains an essential part of the activity system and there remains a need to consider how devices and activities might be incorporated in the session to provoke critical reflection during gameplay.[15]

In other words, *Revolution* is not entirely revolutionary. It does not promise to replace traditional pedagogy, but rather reinforces the necessity of discussion guided by the teacher. Role-playing games place the teacher in a new role as facilitator in the students' process of collaborative learning. The machine handles the more mechanical tasks of distributing information, and the teacher handles the more intuitive tasks of interpretation and synthesis required for students to translate gameplay into historical understanding. The boldest conclusions, however, emphasize the insights students gain through identification with their characters and the intellectual versatility gained through the exploration of political and historical issues from multiple perspectives. Their summary observes:

> The game offers a fundamentally new kind of experience. The player is at once an actor within the virtual drama capable of influencing events and a spectator watching the drama unfold around their character. . . . The virtual avatar

positioned students in a particular role and encouraged them to experience the unfolding drama as an insider, empathizing with the distinctive concerns of their virtual persona as they attempted to achieve various personal goals. . . . At times, the multiplicity of perspectives stimulated a rich discussion as multiple students articulated their unique experience of a particular social theme and challenged each other's interpretation of events.[16]

Their findings support Papert's prediction that educational gaming will erode traditional disciplinary boundaries. They also seem to confirm the claims of education researcher James Paul Gee, who argues in *What Video Games Have to Teach Us About Learning and Literacy* that the pedagogical "power" of games resides in their potential to teach through the purposeful transformation of student identity. Gee explains:

If a player takes on . . . a projective identity vis-à-vis the virtual character he or she is playing in a game, this constitutes a form of identification with the virtual character's world, story, and perspectives that become a strong learning device at a number of different levels. This is so because, in taking on a projective identity, the player projects his or her own hopes, values, and fears onto the virtual character that he or she is co-creating with the video game's designers. Doing this allows the player to imagine a new identity born at the intersection of the player's real-world identities and the virtual identity of the character he or she is playing in the game. In turn, this projective identity helps speak to, and possibly transform, the player's hopes, values, and fears.[17]

"What is clear," the Education Arcade concludes, "is that virtual role play provides exciting and radically alternative modes for learning across the humanities. Indeed, when learning with *Revolution,* traditional barriers between academic disciplines such as history, sociology, geography, drama, art and media studies begin to break down."[18]

While we might imagine universities and schools without departments, we cannot imagine them without teachers, and so we justifiably question the educational value of commercial videogames that would teach us history removed from the guiding presence of the teacher. Gearbox's *Brothers in Arms* series, including *The Road to Hill 30* and *Earned in Blood,* represent the best attempt to deliver historical education in a commercial vehicle. The games are set in the weeks immediately following the Allied invasion of Normandy in June 1944. *The Road to Hill 30* casts us as Sergeant Matt Baker, a platoon commander in the 502nd Parachute Infantry Regiment of the U.S. Army's famed 101st Airborne Division. We parachute into France the night before D-Day and fight our way through a series of missions based on the actual combat operations of the 502nd between June 6 and June 14.

What distinguishes *The Road to Hill 30* and *Earned in Blood* from other popular World War II shooters is its measured narrative, which is faithfully drawn from actual "after-action reports" compiled by battlefield historians embedded with the paratroopers. *Earned in Blood* presents a frame narrative in which Sergeant Joe "Red" Hartsock, weary from two weeks campaigning in Normandy, relates his story to Colonel S.L.A. Marshall, one such historian. As Hartsock recounts each day's action, we assume his role as platoon commander, playing each mission as a flashback. The cut scenes between each mission return us to Hartsock's interview with Marshall, which gives *Earned in Blood* a self-consciously historical coherence lacking in most World War II shooters. In addition, the game emphasizes actual infantry tactics, as we repeatedly "find, fix, flank, and finish" the Germans, dug in between hedgerows and protected by machine gun nests and artillery emplacements.

As we finish each mission, we may unlock a variety of historical documents, including specifications of Allied and German weapons, photographs of battle sites from 1944 and the present, and facsimile excerpts of Marshall's reports on the actions of the 502nd. Gearbox refers to these documents scrupulously throughout their design; having seen a photograph of a bombed-out chateau in the French town of Baupte, we get the uncanny sense, as we approach the virtual chateau in the game, that we are replaying history in the role of Hartsock. Both *Brothers in Arms* games reward progress by unlocking additional documents, so that our historical understanding increases with our skill in the game. This careful integration of historical documents into game design makes *Brothers in Arms* more instructive than other commercial historical role-playing games and has attracted the attention of historians. In its review of *The Road to Hill 30,* the journal *Military History* praised the developers' extensive research and called the documentary supplements "illuminating."[19]

At the same time, an obvious historical glitch emerges when Baker's and Hartsock's squad mates, subject to our commands within the game, are killed during the missions, only to reappear, fully healthy and ready for action, in the next mission. Because the missions are drawn from Marshall's reports, the narrative quietly resurrects soldiers who die in the game but did not die in the actual battle for Normandy. In this case, *Brothers in Arms* resolves the counterfactual problem less gracefully than *Revolution* does. While *Revolution* constructs a narrative bubble, insulated from real events, *Brothers in Arms* allows us to enter the historical narrative presented in Marshall's reports, leading to inevitable contradictions between gameplay and history. Although the inclusion of historical documents responsibly clarifies these contradictions, the continual resurrection of dead comrades calls attention to the unreality of the simulation.

Strategy Games and History

Role-playing games like *Revolution* and *Brothers in Arms* present a bottom-up view the past, microhistorical narratives that offer a personal perspective of events. The Education Arcade defines this perspective: "Eschewing a 'master narrative' in which 'great men do great things,' the game teaches students an 'ordinary' experience of history that includes . . . economic frustration, political indifference, and the mundane of everyday life."[20] Founded on the presumption that players have their share of "the mundane" in the real world, strategy games— such as the *Civilization, Age of Empires,* and *Total War* series—allow players to engage history from the opposite, top-down perspective. In many ways, they appeal to us with fantasies of power, allowing us to shape world events, build global empires, and influence the course of human history. We do not experience history in the mud of the trenches or the town square but rather from the lofty position of a world leader, a master of war who defends or destroys nations in a single turn. Although some games, like the Creative Assembly's *Total War* series, have sought to balance these perspectives by including two distinct game modes—a strategic mode in which we oversee a campaign to build our empire and a tactical mode in which we control troop formations on the battlefield—our experience of history in these grand strategy games is necessarily more abstract than our experience in role-playing games.

Strategy games sacrifice the pedagogical advantages of experiencing history empathetically, as an "insider," which the Education Arcade finds crucial. But they offer greater insight into the larger patterns of causes and effects, illustrating the complex interrelations of economy, technology, politics, population, popular feeling, diplomacy, war, and chance. In this way, strategy games pose distinct advantages over role-playing games, emphasizing an interdisciplinary understanding of human events as well as the lesson of historical contingency, two of the greatest benefits that historians identify in counterfactual speculation.

Muzzy Lane's *Making History: The Calm and the Storm,* a strategy game—designed specifically for classroom use—that simulates international relations before, during, and after World War II, exploits these advantages by giving players the leadership of the United Kingdom, the United States, the Soviet Union, France, Italy, Germany, China, or Japan. *The Calm and the Storm* differs most clearly from commercial strategy games in its style of gameplay; its emphasis is not conquest but rather communication with other players. Like *Revolution,* it was designed primarily as a multiplayer game with a specific pedagogical principle in mind: collaboration among students fosters a more applied and independent style of learning. Lacking clear victory conditions, the educational games created by the Education Arcade and Muzzy Lane do not invite players to beat them. Instead, they serve as a medium of interaction between students, less like a book than a virtual playground activity that channels students' natural tendencies for cooperation and competition into the synthesis and application of course content.

Just as *Revolution* is more pedagogically adaptable than *Brothers in Arms, The Calm and the Storm* has been designed for teachers and students, in contrast to strategy games designed for the entertainment market, such as the *Total War* series. Muzzy Lane reinforces the role of the teacher by marketing the game with an array of classroom handouts and batteries of discussion questions corresponding to specific game scenarios. Unlike the documentation included in *Brothers in Arms,* which invites only our passive perusal, the materials accompanying *The Calm and the Storm* invite discussion, interpretation, and hypothesis.

The game is divided into six distinct scenarios, each one defined by specific dates reflecting key shifts in international relations between 1936 and 1945. Each scenario, in turn, is limited to between eight and sixteen turns. This modular structure, which effectively makes *The Calm and the Storm* a series of six interrelated though distinct strategy games, serves several purposes. Most generally, it exemplifies the "restrained" mode of counterfactual inquiry posited by Allan Megill. Each scenario is discrete; at the outset of a new scenario, the global order is realigned according to real historical conditions on the scenario's starting date, regardless of the outcome of previous scenarios. This structure limits the possibilities for "exuberant" counterfactual events such as an early Nazi victory over the Allies. The turn limit not only imposes a time limit on gameplay convenient for classroom sessions but also creates a more controlled exercise and discourages the free-for-all style of play that obstructed learning when students played *Revolution.*

Unlike commercial strategy games, *The Calm and the Storm* does not have a victory condition. While the *Civilization, Age of Empires,* and *Total War* series appeal to fantasies of conquest, each scenario in *The Calm and the Storm* tests a specific, well-defined problem in statecraft, diplomacy, or military action. For example, the second scenario, "The Politics of Appeasement," requires students to formulate a response to the German threat to invade Czechoslovakia in September 1938. As one of the Allies, students must decide to avoid war through diplomacy or to send forces to protect Czechoslovakia. As Germany, students must seek to expand their territory without provoking an overwhelming multinational retaliation from its neighbors.

The scenarios conclude by explaining the difference between the game result and the historical result, and the discussion questions prompt students to examine this difference. One of the questions for "The Politics of Appeasement" asks: "In the game, how did nations respond to German demands? What agreements were or were not reached? Why? Compare this to history—why did leaders choose appeasement? What domestic, international, or military pressures influenced game decisions and historical decisions?"[21] In order to answer these questions successfully, students must draw from their experiences in the game as well as from their understanding of actual history, synthesizing the two into a broader understanding of historical cause and effect.

This new understanding of contingency, identified by more conservative historians as the only significant advantage of counterfactual inquiry, does not obscure historical facts but animates them, illuminates their relations to one another, and provides students with a method for interpreting them. *The Calm and the Storm,* along with the discussion questions provided for teachers, not only clarifies the distinction between what happened in the game and "what really happened" but also exploits this distinction as a way to explore perspective and motive. Unlike *Revolution,* which avoids the counterfactual problem by separating the game narrative from the historical narrative; and *Brothers in Arms,* which nullifies the game narrative in favor of the historical narrative; *The Calm and the Storm* regards counterfactuals as a methodology rather than a narrative disruption.

The game also includes virtual "advisors," personifications of popular feeling and factional concerns within each nation that exert influence on the decisions of its leader. We might ignore our advisors, but by doing so we undermine our own leadership. In response to questions concerning the counterfactual dilemma, Muzzy Lane explains:

> Should students ignore their goals, or pick a path that is obviously unwise (deliberately attacking a close ally, for example) their advisors will immediately warn them about pursuing such a path. Should they continue, their popularity will plummet . . . and they could very well see coalitions forming against them. After enough foolish decisions, the player will more than likely lose power! The historically accurate goals in *Making History* scenarios will help them stay on track, and gain an accurate understanding of the historical era they are studying.[22]

In other words, Muzzy Lane has created a structure and a series of mechanisms to restrain counterfactual speculation, allowing the factual to inform the imaginary and not the reverse.

In general, *The Calm and the Storm* represents one of the most thoughtful attempts to merge interactive entertainment with traditional pedagogical models and to resolve the counterfactual dilemma in historical games. The game preserves and even enhances the role of the teacher by providing historical and pedagogical supplements. Most significantly, it seizes on counterfactuals as an opportunity for insight rather than concealing them in the interest of narrative coherence, translating gameplay into real historical understanding. In other words, the game allows for the coexistence of what was and what was not in a way that does not mislead the player.

In *The Calm and the Storm* and, to lesser extents, in *Revolution* and *Brothers in Arms,* we see the crucial difference between instructive historical games and those that set out to entertain us with only casual regard for the historical record. In these instructive games, the difference between what happens in the game and what happens in history is clarified and utilized rather than obscured or ignored, servicing a method of inquiry. The obscuring of this difference, which we find in many commercial games, justifies the concerns of historians that videogames, as vehicles of historical inquiry, do more harm than good.

The games in the Creative Assembly's *Total War* series are not divided into scenarios; instead, they present the player with a single campaign to build an empire that spans virtual centuries and may last hundreds of turns. As in *The Calm and the Storm,* the player chooses a faction. Although each faction has its own advantages and disadvantages, the goal of gameplay is the same for all: conquer territory to build wealth; build wealth to buy larger armies; buy larger armies to conquer more territory. If we sustain this cycle successfully, our empire may stretch from Ireland to Arabia, Morocco to Moscow.

The first four games in the series, *Shogun, Medieval, Rome,* and *Medieval II,* as well as several expansions, are ambitious productions, but they pose problems for teachers by favoring entertainment over education and obscuring or ignoring the counterfactual divide. The games have been widely praised by military historians and have been modified for use in television documentaries in the United States and the United Kingdom to illustrate the formations and troop movements in key historical battles, but even amateur historians have criticized the loose approach to history evident in the many accuracies and anachronisms. Throughout the games, for instance, event boxes appear noting the occurrence of a significant historical event, a feature that developers have incorporated to historicize gameplay more effectively. Mostly, the years in which these events occurred in history are the same as the years in which they occur in the game, but sometimes obvious differences emerge. In *Rome,* for instance, the military reforms of Gaius Marius, a particularly significant event in the game, which makes available stronger new military units, occurs between 220 B.C.E. and 180 B.C.E., a century or more before they actually occurred in 107 B.C.E.

Rome has been praised as "the very definition of an epic strategy game," but the depth, complexity, and playability has little to do with fidelity to the historical record.[23] Set between 270 B.C.E. and 14 C.E., the game plays loosely with the history of the period. At the start, Rome is still a republic dominated by its Senate, and we assume command of one of three families—the Brutii, the Julii, or the Scipii—with the goal of conquering territories, currying favor with politicians and the people, and, eventually, marching on Rome to overthrow the Senate and inaugurate our empire. Without the scenario structure of *The Calm and the Storm,* game results vary wildly from historical results. If players are aggressive, republic may give way to empire more than two centuries before it did in reality. Scrupulous critics note other flaws. The families represented in the game are imaginary, merely named for important historical figures. While other characters are named for actual historical figures, their roles do not correspond to those of their real-world counterparts. The style of armor and weaponry of the Egyptian faction matches that of the New Kingdom between 1570 and 1070 B.C.E., rather than that of the Ptolemaic period in which the game is set. Certain units—such as Saxon head hurlers, Celtic fighting Druids, and the Romano-British grail knights, all available in the *Barbarian Invasion* expansion—reflect a fantastic rather than a realistic perspective of the past and exemplify what Megill calls "exuberant" counterfactual history.

In the more recent, more technically impressive *Medieval II,* the historical inaccuracies are even more obvious. At the beginning of the campaign, in the year 1080, the game map contains a number of anachronisms. Stockholm, represented as the capital of Sweden, was not founded until the thirteenth century, and the city did not become Sweden's capital until 1634. Helsinki, which also appears on the game map, was not founded until 1550. Several other cities represented as factional capitals did not exist, or did not exist as capital cities, in 1080, including Caernarfon, Edinburgh, Oslo, Arhus, Krakow, and Bucharest. The political borders drawn on the campaign map are likewise inaccurate. Portugal, shown as a major power on the Iberian Peninsula, was not an independent kingdom until 1143. Milan, also shown as an independent faction, was part of the Holy Roman Empire until 1183. Significant European powers like Aragon, Sweden, and Bohemia appear only as minor "rebel" factions or not at all, while politically fractured regions like Ireland, Latvia, and Lithuania appear as unified territories. Major factional boundaries are also inaccurate: Venice did not control Crete until 1204; Sicily did not control Naples until 1091; and the Byzantines did not recapture Nicea from the Turks until 1097. The map of the New World is perhaps most distorted. The Aztec capital of Tenochtitlan is located near Guatemala, and Florida lies on the same lines of latitude as Ireland.

Although the Creative Assembly, like Gearbox, relies on careful historical research, they sacrifice accuracy for playability. Each of these geographical anachronisms contributes to a general balance of power and sense of competitiveness in the game, an incentive for players whose success relies less on the faction they choose than on the strategies they employ. They balance these concessions somewhat by including simulations of historical battles, entirely separate from the imperial campaign, which may serve as interactive reenactments of battlefield events. In this respect, the *Total War* series usefully illustrates not world events but tactics, troop types, and terrains of historical battlefields. Military historians and television documentarians, therefore, have embraced *Total War* more readily than history teachers. Bernard Dy, a software reviewer for *Military History,* writes that *Medieval* is "like a miniatures war game, but without the messy paints and preparation hassles."[24]

The *Medieval II* campaign, however, is not useless to economic and cultural historians, in spite of its distortions. In fact, the game appears distorted only when we wrongly consider it as a substitute for the historical record. *Medieval II* and other historical simulations are most valuable, in fact, when we consider them as allegories of historical contingency. In other words, videogames may not teach us what happened in the past, but they can teach us how things happen. *Medieval II* gets a lot wrong—the location of North America, for instance—but it offers legitimate insight into the larger patterns of causes and effects by illustrating the complex interrelations between individual personality, economy, technology, politics, population, popular feeling, diplomacy, war, and chance. In this sense, the game conveys the two major benefits that historians identify in counterfactual inquiry: an interdisciplinary understanding of human events as well as the lesson of historical contingency. As a whole, the series encourages the integrated, interdisciplinary style of learning that Seymour Papert, Kurt Squire, and others have identified as a primary advantage of game-based education.

The *Medieval II* campaign proves most relevant when it confronts us with practical problems of conquest, occupation, and governance. When we conquer a new city or fortress, for instance, we may occupy it, sack it, or exterminate the population. Each decision carries benefits and liabilities: occupation ensures the rapid economic development of our new territory but forces us to govern a large, hostile population; sacking the settlement provides an immediate economic boost but slows long-term growth; extermination stifles rebellion but destroys the economy of the region for years to come. If, as a Christian faction like England, we decide to act humanely and merely occupy a Muslim settlement like Jerusalem, we may quell the mob in a number of different ways: lowering taxes; increasing the garrison; building taverns, brothels, and tournament fields; or dispatching missionaries and building cathedrals to convert the infidels to the true faith.

In effect, we must reconstruct the settlement in our own likeness, but the cities that we construct, conquer, and reconstruct in *Medieval II* bear no resemblance to their historical counterparts. London lacks its Thames, Constantinople its Hagia Sofia, and Jerusalem its Dome of the Rock. In the game, the cities appear simply as collections of generic buildings distinguished only by the broadest cultural categories: "Northern European," "Southern European," "Eastern European," and "Middle Eastern." Like the campaign map, these architectural models tell us nothing about the history, politics, and geography of the medieval world. Instead they serve as symbolic representations of the more general interrelations between history, politics, and geography. In the game, the mosque pictured in Jerusalem does not correspond to the actual Dome of the Rock, nor does it serve as a place for virtual Muslims to say virtual prayers; it is simply a sophisticated icon that identifies Jerusalem as a "Muslim" settlement, which holds specific implications for gameplay. In fact, the "Settlement Details" scroll representing the constantly fluctuating levels of population, public order, income, and religious feeling in a city or castle reveals the underlying function of the simulation and its value as a pedagogical tool. Icons representing various counterbalancing conditions in our settlement rise and fall according to actions in the game. Lowering taxes will foster population growth; building a militia drill square, a cathedral, or a tavern will increase public order; and building a dockyard or paved roads will increase income. Our goal is to maintain control of our settlements and, by extension, our empire by keeping each of these scales tipped in our favor.

Alexander Galloway calls this type of calculated gameplay "playing the algorithm." When we play *Civilization IV* or *Medieval II,* we are not learning history. Instead, Galloway argues, we are "learning, internalizing, and becoming intimate with a massive, multipart, global algorithm. To play the game means to play the code of the game. To win means to know the system."[25] The game system serves as an allegory for the global system, for the processes of history. On its surface, *Medieval II* presents the kind of fantastic counterfactual hypotheses that foster anachronistic thinking and ultimately offends historians. What if England conquered all of Europe, subjugated the Vatican, secured the Holy Land, drove the Mongols back to the steppes, and discovered America—all before 1285? We may just as well ask: What if Leonardo da Vinci flew one of his mechanical whirligigs to the moon and discovered it was made of green cheese? More subtly, however, the game raises theoretical and practical questions relevant for any historical period: What makes war inevitable or profitable? What makes peace difficult? Can an occupied people be mollified with a military presence, an ambitious building program, government subsidies for businesses, or ostentatious public entertainments?

Developing a Counterfactual Pedagogy

Medieval II features a new engine that has allowed the Creative Assembly to represent the past in unprecedented graphic detail. On the battlefields, long blades of grass move gently in the breeze, and each soldier in the opposing armies, which may number more than 10,000, has a distinct physiognomy and equipage. History, in other words, has never looked so real, and by playing *Total War*, we may share something of Lisa's wonder when Genghis Khan promises her, "Today you'll go where I go!" The question for historians and teachers is whether or not this increasingly convincing simulation of the past actually contributes to historical understanding.

Although strategy games are merely symbolic and highly simplified models, limited or biased in their perspective and marred by inaccuracies and omissions, so too is a history textbook. As Megill suggests, however, using videogames to pose questions about the historical process does not free historians to neglect events, lest we treat history itself like a game. We should not dismantle the historical record, in other words, without knowing how to put it back together again, especially in our classrooms. At their worst, videogames may become vehicles for historical myopia or denial. *Medieval II* compels us to conquer and build an empire, suggesting that conquest is the necessary and inevitable purpose of civilization. We raze city after city in order to fill our coffers, hire mercenaries, and expand our rule over continents and oceans. While the game boasts an advanced diplomacy system in which we may forge military and economic partnerships with other factions, these alliances mostly serve as a way to delay warfare with one faction while we conquer three or four others. The game offers no alternative to constant warfare, nor does it illuminate the differences between the imagined past and the real past, nor does it teach very much about medieval civilization. England seems much like Egypt and Poland much like Portugal in terms of their political and cultural objectives: conquer as much as possible as quickly as possible. We should question these things with *Medieval II,* not accept them as given.

Videogames can never serve as a faithful representation of events as they occurred, and, in fact, should not attempt to do so. For historians like Niall Ferguson, who is currently collaborating with Muzzy Lane to create a real-time strategy game based on the War on Terror, their value rests not in their ability to simulate what happened but rather how things happen, the processes of history, and the contingency of events.[26] In this way, videogames complement textbooks, archives, lectures, discussion among students, and other established pedagogical methods, as Squire argues. Those like Papert who claim that videogames will obviate institutional learning are as limited in their view as authoritarian curriculum designers who would bar videogames from classrooms because they misrepresent historical events or because they distract students from more focused, productive exercises.

Like historical fiction, role-playing games address the counterfactual problem by constructing a fictional bubble within a larger historical reality, where players may witness or indirectly experience historical events without having any power to alter their course. The historical fidelity of the simulation often relies on its complete separation from history. When events in the game contradict actual events, as we see in the inexplicable resurrection of Joe Hartsock's men in *Earned in Blood,* they remind us of the irrelevance of the game to the past and undermine the usefulness of games as pedagogical tools. This pedagogy presents history from the bottom up, revealing the past through more personal, "mundane" experiences: microhistory. On the other hand, *The Calm and the Storm* consistently calls our attention to counterfactuals, frames them in opposition to factual events, and adopts the contrast as a pedagogical platform. It restrains our inquiry by penalizing ahistorical thinking, discouraging students from abandoning their roles, as some did playing *Revolution.* Moreover, its scenario structure limits the possibility for anachronism, closely tying gameplay to historical reality. Real-time strategy games present history from the top down, offering less insight into personal motivation or material culture and more into government, economy, and international relations: macrohistory.

Increasingly, many videogames—whether role-playing games or real-time strategy games, educational games or commercial games—have found new ways of synthesizing interactive narrative with historical narrative. Historical supplements now appear in many games, and through enterprises like the Education Arcade and Muzzy Lane, educators have begun to collaborate more closely with game developers, a partnership essential to the success of game-based learning. Videogames, they have found, need not replace teachers. In fact, they give teachers new importance as guides for counterfactual inquiry, helping students to examine their motives in making decisions and framing the contrast between game events and historical events as lessons in contingency.

Ideally, a deeper understanding of cause and effect, which games like *Medieval II* foster very well, will encourage students to assume a more critical view of the past as well as the present. We may see that things happen for reasons, that history is not inevitable, and develop a new method for investigating conditions, perspectives, motives, and decisions. Guided by established pedagogy, by tools as simple as well-crafted discussion questions, we may ensure that videogames and counterfactual inquiry need not become virtual Genghis Khans who overthrow traditional research and obliterate the past.

❖ 8 ❖

Identity and Community in Virtual Worlds

I entered Norrath near the bustling city of Freeport, a hub of trade and travel on the east coast of the continent of Antonica. I was a human, an aspiring paladin, and the city was my home. I hunted giant rats in the wilderness of the East Commonlands, just beyond the city walls, slowly gaining experience and wealth. I sometimes loitered at the edge of the impromptu bazaar convened near the gate, where dozens of other players gathered to exchange goods, form hunting parties, or chat. I was a newbie, still learning the basic mechanics and more subtle etiquette of communicating with other players, so I hesitated to join the ruckus and continued to make solitary forays outside the city, skinning rats with my broadsword.

One day, as I passed the Freeport Inn, a dark elf approached me and asked me to buy him food and drink at the inn. He was tired, hungry, and a long way from his home in Neriak, the shadowed city in the Nektulos Forest north of Freeport. His kind, I learned, was not welcome in the human settlements, and the innkeeper would not serve him. If I would buy him bread and ale, he would give me the cost of the provisions as well as ten gold pieces for my trouble. I bought the groceries and received my payment. The dark elf thanked me and was on his way.

I had completed my first modest transaction in the massively multiplayer online role-playing game (MMORPG), *EverQuest*, and it had given me an important insight about life in virtual worlds like Norrath: their design made it necessary and potentially profitable to communicate and transact with other players. The racial prejudice against dark elves in Freeport is part of the fiction

136

of Norrath, but it is also one of many ways that the game stimulates interaction and commerce between players. Because the innkeeper, a nonplayer character, would not deal with the dark elf, the dark elf had to deal with me, and we both benefited: he had provisions for another adventure, and I had gold fairly gained without having to smear my blade with another rat. The point, I learned, is not just to kill rats but also to talk to other players, even detestable dark elves.

Sociality represents the essential difference between single-player videogames, in which we interact with a program, and online games like *EverQuest*, in which we interact with thousands of other players through a program. Economists, sociologists, and lawyers have described these populous and expanding graphical worlds as communication platforms for emergent societies. MMORPGs, they argue, are not games at all but virtual worlds unto themselves. Edward Castronova, who closely studies the phenomena of online gaming and virtual worlds, writes in his book *Synthetic Worlds: The Business and Culture of Online Games:*

> These playgrounds of the imagination are becoming an important host of ordinary human affairs. There is much more than gaming going on there: conflict, governance, trade, and love. The number of people who could be said to "live" out there in cyberspace is already numbering in the millions; it is growing, and we are already beginning to see the subtle and not-so-subtle effects of this behavior at the societal level in real Earth countries.[1]

Castronova estimates that as many as 30 million people worldwide inhabit virtual worlds. In his survey of nearly 4,000 *EverQuest* players, he finds that 58 percent wish they could spend more of their time in Norrath; 22 percent wish they could spend all of their time in Norrath; and 20 percent said they "live" in Norrath and merely "travel" to the outside world. On eBay and other online markets, players trade virtual currencies against the dollar, and many of these virtual currencies trade at rates higher than those of real currencies. Players also exchange virtual goods acquired within the game—clothing, weapons, dwellings, or other items—for real money. "Gold farms" in China, India, and Mexico contract local laborers to play games and gather loot, which the companies trade for profit on eBay. Castronova suspects that online gamers and gold farmers, all told, trade more than $100 million annually in virtual goods and currencies.[2]

In her book, *Play Between Worlds: Exploring Online Game Culture*, games researcher T.L. Taylor claims that we can no longer speak of online life and offline life as separate spheres. Rather, virtual worlds sustain a "web of networks and relationships," particularly when friends, husbands and wives, and parents and children, play cooperatively:

> These situations . . . point to the ways families and friends bring social capital
> into the game space through preexisting relationships. . . . It is not at all unusual
> to find players helping newbies they know offline by giving them some money,
> items, or, just as important, crucial game advice and tips. . . . Out-of-game
> relationships give players an instant social network in the game.[3]

In their ethnography of *EverQuest* players, Florence Chee, Marcelo Vieta, and Richard Smith likewise conclude that Norrath is not a "closed world," isolated from real communities. Rather, it brings about "deep social involvements . . . committed to meaningful, mutual projects."[4] If videogames represent a digital-age "magic circle," Castronova suggests, then virtual worlds represent an "almost-magic circle," a porous boundary that allows for continual interchange between the real and the imaginary. He writes, "People are crossing it all the time in both directions, carrying their assumptions and attitudes with them. As a result, the valuation of things in cyberspace becomes enmeshed in the value of things outside cyberspace."[5]

This economic and social convergence of virtual life and real life raises significant questions for humanists as well as social scientists. What happens to the "human" at the frontier of real and the virtual? What makes millions of real people want to "live" in virtual worlds or claim to live there already? In fact, what is "life" in the virtual realm, beyond the sum of the economic and social relations described by Castronova and Taylor? More practically, how can online games serve as educational platforms, crucibles to study modes of identification and communication?

As Sherry Turkle demonstrats in her book *Life on the Screen: Identity in the Age of the Internet*, the fluidity of identity in virtual worlds, our capacity to adopt multiple personae and freely exchange these personae for others, undermines our conventional understanding of individual and social identity.[6] We must reconsider our assumptions about gender or race relations, for example, in an environment where these categories are freely exchanged rather than socially determined. At the same time, virtual worlds, like historical role-playing games, might teach new lessons about identity and social interaction by allowing us to assume different roles and experience a multiplicity of simulated perspectives while traveling, working, and living in an organic social world.

The Avatar and the Liquid Self

Games researcher Miroslaw Filiciak writes that virtual worlds are "the best argument against current views that perceive video games as a medium that alienates people. . . . On the contrary, the games make sense only when people are joined through it."[7] Filiciak assumes, however, that "people are joined" in open communication when, in fact, their communication is mediated through fantasy. As we assume the role of our avatar—a paladin, a dark elf, or an orc—our way of relating to others dramatically shifts. Because online games more closely resemble masquerade balls than open forums for communication, life in virtual worlds begins with the donning of a mask and the complex transformation from player to avatar.

The gorgeous, graphical avatars of current online games trace their genealogy, as we have seen, to Gary Gygax's 1974 *Dungeons & Dragons*, which conceived of the player as an individual character projected into a fictional world. Text adventure games beginning with Will Crowther's *Adventure*, created in 1976, transported player characters from tabletops to virtual space, and multiple-user dungeons (MUDs), such as Richard Bartle and Roy Trubshaw's *MUD1*, created in 1978, used network servers to bring multiple players together within a textually rendered game world. With the emergence of the first graphical online environments, Lucasfilm's 1986 *Habitat* and America Online's 1991 *Neverwinter Nights*—an online precursor to the single-player role-playing game, *Neverwinter Nights*, developed by Bioware in 2002—the player character, formerly a textual description and series of statistics, became visually incarnate—the avatar was born.

Later, 3DO Studios' 1996 *Meridian 59* and Origin Systems' 1997 *Ultima Online* dramatically enhanced our experience of virtual worlds. While *Habitat* and *Neverwinter Nights* rendered their graphical environments in two dimensions, *Meridian 59* introduced the first-person, three-dimensional perspective initially developed in first-person shooters, which now defines our interface with virtual worlds. Drawing the virtual landscape into focus around the player, the game conveyed presence, or the sense that we were not simply playing an online game but rather inhabiting an imaginary world. Although rendered in two-dimensional, isometric graphics, *Ultima Online* opened the breech between the virtual and real worlds that has come to interest researchers like Castronova and Taylor. Britannia was the first game world to host a complex economy, the first to generate currency and goods traded in the real world, and the first to witness a mass protest by players demanding "rights" for their avatars. For the first time, Taylor writes, *Ultima Online* confronted game designers with problems of "mass community management."[8] More recent successors such as *EverQuest*, *Star Wars: Galaxies*, *City of Heroes*, and *World of Warcraft* have established a standard design for online games, synthesizing the visual depth of *Meridian 59* with the economic and sociological depth of *Ultima Online*.

The relation between player identity and avatar is more difficult to trace. Many scholars and game designers interpret the avatar as a projection of the self into the virtual world. Although our identity and our modes of communication are mediated by the game, our avatar, at its core, virtually embodies our personality. In *Designing Virtual Worlds*, for instance, Bartle argues that avatars serve unconscious psychological desires manifested in four player archetypes: "Achievers" seek to achieve goals such as defeating monsters and acquiring treasure; "Socializers" seek to form social bonds by chatting or joining hunting parties and guilds; "Explorers" seek privileged knowledge through the exploration and mapping of the game world; and "Killers" seek to dominate other players by attacking them, robbing them, or impugning them.[9] Castronova agrees with Bartle, suggesting that we might profile players by reading the actions of their avatars. "How many people do I know," he asks, "who have a frustrated desire to go exploring in a new frontier? How many wish they could find a different social circle? How many find themselves dying on the vine of some corporate or academic achievement system? How many just want to exert their force on others but cannot?"[10] Filiciak also argues that character creation and gameplay express unconscious motivations. Although we have "unprecedented freedom" to exert conscious "control over our own image," he writes, we consistently "transfer" elements of our personality and emotions into the character: "Avatars are not an escape from our 'self,' they are, rather, a longed-for chance of expressing ourselves beyond our physical limitations."[11] In this sense, Castronova concludes, virtual worlds have transcended traditional role-playing games and evolved into a new forum for the "interaction of human minds."[12]

Castronova deliberates carefully before naming his wood elf in *EverQuest*. In Norrath, as in our own world, he explains, "Each person must have a name, and each name must be unique and unchanging." During the process of creating the elf, Castronova senses an "important moment" when he begins to think of the elf's attributes and possessions as his own. Later, he feels angry and vengeful when he believes that his avatar has been cheated by another. This emotional identification with the avatar, Castronova writes, "appears to be psychologically natural, because the avatar is just an extension of your body into a new space."[13] Taylor's *EverQuest* character, a gnome necromancer, expresses her "shadowed" and "nightowl-ish tendencies" as well as her ideological orientation; she will not adopt the outrageously oversexed appearance of a human or elvish woman. Like Castronova, Taylor carefully considers the choices she makes in creating her avatar, who represents her identity and her ideas in the virtual world. "How you choose to represent yourself," she writes, "has meaningful implications psychologically and socially."[14]

Others dispute the "meaningful implications" of the characters we choose to play. James Newman, for example, argues that the avatar is not a manifestation the "human mind," as Bartle and Castronova suggest, but simply an instrument for interacting with a computer program. Playable characters in a videogame, he says, do not compel our emotional identification, as characters in fiction and film do. Rather, they function as a "suite of characteristics or equipment utilized and embodied by the player."[15] The avatar is a tool, not an alter ego, and when he perishes, again and again, we feel no sadness or shock, only frustration that we have not manipulated him quickly or accurately enough to achieve our purpose.

While Castronova and Taylor report a sense of identification with their avatars from the moment of their creation, my own experience, at least at first, seems to support Newman's more instrumental view. While my human paladin in *EverQuest* probably reflects vague physical or moral ideals, I created him mainly to maximize my independence in the game. In Norrath, the human is the most versatile race, capable of quick advancement. The paladin, a warrior priest, is a hybrid class, combining the weapons skills and brute force of a fighter with the healing magic of a cleric. The paladin allowed me to roam the wilderness more freely, unhindered by the inconvenience of having to solicit myself to a hunting party. I wanted to travel alone and learn the game at my leisure. I could bash monsters and tend to my own wounds when necessary. In Newman's words, these abilities were part of my "suite of characteristics" that increased the time I could spend alone in the wilderness. These choices, I think, reflected my methods more than my identity. They were based on my understanding of the way the game works and my plan to pursue an independent style of play.

Bartle would argue, however, that my choices do reflect my personality, and that my solitary paladin plainly embodies the archetypal class of player he calls the Explorer. "Their joy is in discovery," he writes. "They seek out the new."[16] Castronova characterizes Explorers in further detail: "They are happiest with challenges that involve the gradual revelation of the world. They want the world to be very big, and filled with hidden beauty that can only be unlocked through persistence and creativity."[17] Maybe Bartle has me pegged—I doubt that I could express my own interest in videogames more succinctly. I do not play videogames to meet other people, to gain the next level, or to prove my skill against other players. I play games because their virtual worlds are rich in artistry and meaning. In this sense, my paladin, my solitary explorer, is indeed my other self.

Castronova's similar understanding of the avatar as "an extension of your body into a new space" provides a compelling reason that millions of people claim to "live" in virtual worlds. But how can we speak of the "body," or even its prosthetic "extension," in the ethereal realm of cyberspace? Are avatars embodied or disembodied? We speak of their muscles and their cleavage, their hair and skin tones. We calculate their strength, agility, and stamina. We wince when they are cleaved or immolated, and we smile when they emote and dance. Yet they may quest long hours, spend days and weeks in virtual wastelands without suffering, like so many players, from blurred vision, insomnia, backache, stiff joints, or malnourishment. They require no bathroom breaks. They are luminous, endlessly changeable, and slip into and out of being like a breath. We may trade them on eBay.

This vaguely Platonic notion of the avatar as a disembodied, ideal self inspires many scholars' belief in the potential for online games to revolutionize our concepts of identity and communication. Turkle writes, "When we step through the screen into virtual communities, we reconstruct our identities on the other side of the looking glass."[18] Media scholar Bob Rehak declares that videogames "offer the potential for profound redefinitions of body, mind, and spirit."[19] Filiciak likewise argues that "the objectivizing role of the body disappears" in virtual worlds, freeing our minds to commune without material encumbrance.[20] Castronova, perhaps, waxes most brightly about the potential for physical and social liberation in virtual worlds:

> Synthetic worlds may allow us to experience human social life in an environment in which many characteristics of the body are no longer fixed endowments but have become chosen attributes. People entering a synthetic world can have, in principle, any body they desire. At a stroke, this feature of synthetic worlds removes from the social calculus all the unfortunate effects that derive from the body. . . . Those who feel alone or discriminated against here may feel connected and accepted there. The social roles that we cannot have here may be possible there. Whatever you may not like about your body here, it can be undone in the building of a new body there.[21]

Before the advent of virtual worlds, Roger Caillois's 1958 study *Man, Play, and Games* anticipates this dream of physical and social liberation in his evocative account of the power of masks in aboriginal rituals:

> Masks . . . transform the officiants into gods, spirits, animal ancestors, and all types of terrifying and creative supernatural powers. . . . The use of masks is supposed to reinvigorate, renew, and recharge both nature and society. The eruption of phantoms and strange powers terrifies and captivates the individual. He temporarily reincarnates, mimics, and identifies with these frightful powers and soon, maddened and delirious, really believes that he is the god as whom he disguised himself. . . . It was sufficient for him merely to put on the mask that he himself made.[22]

These savage masks, full of significance and power, return to us as avatars. Like the religious rituals Caillois describes, virtual worlds temporarily draw scattered individuals together into a communal performance of "terrifying and creative supernatural powers," where masked players, wielding magic spells and epic weaponry, perform—though only temporarily—as a god.

But how can Castronova and Filiciak argue that the avatar represents both the extension of the self and the liberation of the self? Others remain wary of these promises of liberation and empowerment, claiming that virtual identity is not as fluid as it appears. Taylor writes, "While rhetoric of the fluidity of identity performance and meaning online has been dominant . . . avatars do not appear in the game world simply as blank objects that allow users to construct independent meaning systems on them."[23] Female players, especially, must reconcile with gender stereotypes imported into virtual worlds through sexualized images of female avatars. For many women, the buxom, bikini-clad barbarians and the lithe, little elf girls seem to fuel men's masturbatory fantasies rather than women's fantasies of empowerment. A female *EverQuest* player reflects:

> I don't have a problem with a 'sexy' character; I just don't want to play one where body parts are hanging out in the world (half-elves, dark elves). This did influence my choice of race, because the dwarven women are allowed to stand straight and keep themselves clothed in something that makes sense. Guess I have a gripe about representations of fantasy women; who would go into battle wearing a chain bikini? Really? OUCH! . . . [*EverQuest* developer] Verant probably did not consider women a viable market share of the game when they designed it.[24]

At the same time, virtual worlds might offer a solution to what many critics see as the deeply entrenched sexism of current videogame design. Mia Consalvo finds that most adventure games work with a "presumption of heterosexual interests," featuring "fairy-tale romances" that reinforce the ideas that "heterosexuality is natural and preferred, and romance between men and women . . . is expected, desired, and to be sought out."[25]

In virtual worlds, we are not bound by conventional romantic narratives, and we may choose our traveling companions, guild mates, and lovers freely from a teeming and diverse society. The choice to play as a male or a female is merely cosmetic; characters gain no statistical advantage and no special abilities based on sex. In this sense, female avatars reflect egalitarian fantasy as surely as erotic fantasy. Taylor observes that this aspect of virtual world design has profound psychological importance for female players:

> Women are afforded an experience they are not likely to have had offline. While both the landscape and its creatures might threaten the explorer, in the game space this threat is not based upon gender. Unlike the offline world in which gender often plays a significant role in not only the perception of safety but its actuality, in *EQ* [*EverQuest*] women may travel knowing they are no more threatened by the creatures of the world than their male counterparts are. . . . Because of this gender-neutral approach to threat and safety, there is a kind of freedom of movement that women often do not experience otherwise.[26]

Henry Jenkins further speculates that online games might help to instill confidence and ambition in young women: "Girls need to learn how to explore 'unsafe' and 'unfriendly' spaces. Girls need to experience the 'complete freedom of movement' promised by the boys' games, if not all the time, then at least some of the time, if they are going to develop the self confidence and competitiveness demanded of contemporary professional women."[27] Jenkins introduces a compelling idea: Virtual worlds, in fact, might be more than a vehicle for the expression or exploration of personal identity. They might, in fact, serve as a means for the transformation of social consciousness, a means of education.

Synthetic Education

For Jenkins, the liberation of virtual identity in virtual worlds shows the path to an egalitarian reconstruction of society on a larger scale. Others are more cautious. In his 1991 study, *The Saturated Self*, psychologist Kenneth J. Gergen argues that rapid technological change, particularly the development of communications technologies that extend the potential range of our relationships across the globe, leads to "social saturation" and the unmooring of personal identity. In the age of voice mail, e-mail, and cell phones, Gergen argues, our sense of truth, objectivity, or rationality erodes in a plurality of competing voices. "As these voices expand in power and presence," Gergen writes, "all that seemed proper, right-minded, and well-understood is subverted." Truth becomes relative, and we are left in "a world where anything goes that can be negotiated."[28] For research and pedagogy, these changes are "apocalyptic," calling into doubt our fundamental methods for knowing ourselves and the world:

> We come to be aware that each truth about ourselves is a construction of the moment, true only for a given time and within certain relationships. . . . Many now see science as a sea of social opinion, the tides of which are often governed by political and ideological forces. . . . And if scientific truth is the product of literary artifice, so too are truths about the self.[29]

Teachers, books, and even empirical observation are devalued, and the process of education comes under suspicion as an exercise in coercion. Ideology replaces knowledge.

The contention between those like Jenkins, who envision communications technology as a means for utopian transformation, and those like Gergen, who see it as a threat to Enlightenment ideals, drives the more practical debate concerning the educational potential for virtual worlds. Gergen argues that the fracturing of the self undermines the methodologies and philosophical premises of education, while Jenkins suggests that virtual worlds enable us to cast off the prejudices and narrow perspectives that limit our capacity to understand and sympathize with others. Does learning require a coherent sense of self, as Gergen argues? Does the potential to exchange identities freely within virtual worlds limit or enhance the educational potential of online games? What new pedagogical strategies will prove effective within virtual worlds?

Since the 1970s, several experiments have tested virtual world pedagogy. In 1978, the Minnesota Educational Computing Consortium (MECC) distributed Alan Klietz's *Milieu*, the first MUD designed specifically for educational use. *Milieu* allowed high school students throughout Minnesota to communicate with each other, but it fostered little more than disorganized chatting. The radically new teaching tool lacked the supporting classroom applications necessary to make it work effectively. Teachers simply did not know what to do with it, and in 1984, Klietz abandoned the project and adapted *Milieu* as a commercial fantasy MUD, *Scepter of Goth.*

More deliberate experiments created MUDs as a means to develop writing skills. Students could practice descriptive, dramatic, or persuasive writing, instantly distribute their work to readers, and receive editorial commentary in real time. In her 1995 article "MUDs in Education: New Environments, New Pedagogies," writing professor Tari Lin Fanderclai discusses the broad potential for these new "writing environments":

> Students could have contact with people from cultures and subcultures outside their own. They could construct their own spaces and try on new personae, new ways of thinking, new ways of interacting. They would get immediate responses to their ideas and to the text objects they created, experiencing dynamically the effects their words have on others.[30]

We should think of virtual space not as "an extension of the real life class-room" but rather as an "alternate learning environment" with its own peculiar capabilities and limitations. Because MUDs are designed for interaction, we would misuse them to deliver online lectures or to replicate established academic structures. Fanderclai writes:

> All too frequently I log onto an educational MUD to find myself in a virtual representation of a university campus. Separate buildings highlight the tradi-tional divisions among disciplines, and within these buildings are elaborately programmed classrooms. Teachers can lock students in and others out; they have tools for delivering lectures, for silencing one or all members of a class, and controlling who speaks when.[31]

Instead, Fanderclai argues, "MUDs could disrupt the hierarchy of the traditional classroom, giving students more power and responsibility and a chance to learn to use them wisely in order to accomplish their goals."[32] Unconfident or reticent students, she observes, lose social inhibitions and contribute more freely to class discussion. In the textual environment, students become more articulate in their writing and learn to apply new communications skills across the curriculum.

These early experiments have shown that adapting virtual worlds to education will require a clear pedagogical plan. The failure of *Milieu* demonstrates that we cannot rely on new tools to generate their own applications, or we will become tinkerers rather than teachers. At the same time, Fanderclai's use of MUDs in writing classrooms shows us that we cannot rely on conventional pedagogical practices that neglect the unique capabilities of virtual worlds, particularly those that enable us to adopt different personae and communicate instantaneously. The immersive graphical environments enabled by faster processors and Internet connections do not offer automatic solutions to the problems Fanderclai senses. Rather, they demand new approaches.

While the rapidly expanding island chains of *Second Life* now host a significant contingent of schools, colleges, and universities, many of these institutions have done little more than establish a virtual storefront, a new vehicle for publicity. Individual teachers, however, have adapted the unique features of the graphical world in the same way that Fanderclai has adapted textual MUDs to her writing classroom. Communications professor Aaron Delwiche says, "It's really difficult to understand new media or cyberculture or the ways the Internet is transforming our culture without actively participating in it. . . . The thing that's appealing about *Second Life* is that it's a shared virtual experience, and so it has that common element that the classroom brings."[33] Others have been more deliberate in their use of the graphical capabilities of virtual worlds, which allows users to design virtual objects, clothing, vehicles, or dwellings. Architecture professor Anne Beamish explains, "I use *Second Life* for students to explore ideas about public space and what makes a good public space. . . . Being in *Second Life* all of a sudden puts them in this different environment, which is similar but different, and it forces them to explore how they think about these things. . . . It makes them think more deeply about how one designs public spaces."[34] Delwiche, Beamish, and those teachers who follow them into *Second Life* will benefit from better administrative guidance than MECC could offer the first tentative users of *Milieu. Second Life* developer Linden Research has created online resources for educators and started Campus: Second Life, a program that invites teachers to work directly with *Second Life* designers to adapt courses to the virtual world.

Castronova speculates that the advancement systems of online role-playing games, which compel players to spend many hours in the game world working to build a strong and well-equipped avatar, might, with some retooling, motivate learning. He writes, "If we want society to value something, such as the plays of William Shakespeare, we would just build a synthetic world with exciting challenges, and make it so that a mastery of Shakespeare is required to meet them. A world built on that premise could produce hundreds of thousands of new Shakespeare cognoscenti in the course of a few years."[35] At Indiana University, Castronova's Synthetic Worlds Initiative (SWI) has put this idea into practice in *Arden: The World of William Shakespeare*, an online game that proposes to immerse us in a virtual world inspired by the history and lore of Shakespeare's plays—"*EverQuest* meets *Macbeth*."[36] Like commercial online games, *Arden* features quests, combat, crafting, trading, and guilds. Players progress, however, not by winning experience points but rather by discovering "Texts" containing passages from Shakespeare's plays. Different Texts give us different abilities, and certain combinations of Texts, such as series of soliloquies from the same play, further enhance these abilities. The game encourages us to learn passages from Shakespeare's works as well as their contexts, but SWI, like the educational game developer Muzzy Lane, emphasizes that the game should not serve as a substitute for reading the plays, seeing them on stage, or discussing them in the classroom "under the guidance of a trained mentor."[37]

Although these experiments have not proven that virtual worlds, at present, have the capacity to transform consciousness, they have demonstrated that teachers can successfully apply them to a range of classroom exercises. For Castronova, *Arden* is only the beginning. He imagines that virtual worlds will soon become an integral part of higher education:

> Research scholars now have in their hands, for the first time in history, a real social science laboratory tool. . . . Synthetic worlds could be a test bed for learning new practices for business, governance, and strategy. . . . Future generations of PhD students in anthropology, sociology, political science, and economics will work with paired versions of a world descended from *Ultima Online*, one experimental and the other control, tweaking social dynamics in specific ways and directly observing the results. . . . There are enough applications of this technology in the area of education and research to occupy several generations of teachers and researchers.[38]

Like Gergen, Castronova senses an apocalypse, but not the sort that will plunge us into epistemological vertigo. Virtual worlds signal a new millennium for law, the social sciences, and the humanities, in which familiar assumptions could be tested and revised under radically new conditions.

Law and the Synthetic Social Contract

As virtual worlds become integrated with the economic, social, and educational systems of the real world, legal scholars have begun to consider the special legislative and jurisdictional questions presented by online games communities. Who should control virtual worlds—governments, platform owners, or users? Should these groups, in some way, share power? If virtual goods trade for real currency, should they receive the same protection that private property does? Perhaps most fundamentally, are we now bound and protected by the social contract in the realms of Britannia, Norrath, or Azeroth?

In 1997, during an *Ultima Online* town meeting, a mischief-maker hurled a fireball at Lord British, Britannia's reigning monarch and the avatar of *Ultima* series creator Richard Garriott. Lord British perished in the blast, and Starr Long, another *Ultima Online* designer, dispersed the crowd by releasing a horde of demons. In the following days, players gathered to protest Long's wanton retaliation against the innocent bystanders. The incident marked the beginning of a tradition of player protest in virtual worlds. In 2001, Elizabeth Kolbert's article in the *New Yorker* magazine called wider attention to a later demonstration in Britannia, when players stormed Castle Britain and stripped naked to protest the inflation wrought by gold farmers. In November 2003, *EverQuest* players gathered to demand changes in the statistical configuration of warrior class characters and the mechanics of melee combat; more recently, *Star Wars: Galaxies* and *World of Warcraft* have witnessed similar demonstrations. Bemused by the "inadvertent and largely unsupervised experiment" in social relations that *Ultima Online* represents, Kolbert says that virtual worlds raise questions about "whether people can manage to coexist peacefully even when they don't really exist."[39]

Although these protests focus variously on codes of conduct, the socioeconomic conditions of the game world, or game design, all of them represent the more basic struggle for control between owners and users. Whose world is it? Jack Balkin, Yale Law School professor and editor of the 2006 collection *The State of Play: Law, Games, and Virtual Worlds*, believes that two fundamental values come into conflict: free speech and private property. On one hand, platform owners have the "right to design," to do what they will with the game, including the prohibition of gold farming and trading items on eBay, arbitrarily changing the conditions of the game, or shutting down the servers and ending the simulation if the enterprise becomes unprofitable. In this view, the game world is the intellectual property of the owners and gameplay a service provided to users. On the other hand, Balkin acknowledges that users have the "right to play," to demand protection for the property they have accumulated in the game world, which would vanish if owners decided to shut down servers. In this view, the game is a kind of marketplace and gameplay a form of free enterprise.[40]

Balkin positions himself against F. Gregory Lastowka and Dan Hunter, who argue in a 2004 *California Law Review* article that virtual worlds are "jurisdictions separate from our own, with their own distinctive community norms, laws, and rights." Lastowka and Hunter argue that virtual world inhabitants should develop their own norms and policies: "If these attempts by cyborg communities to formulate the laws of virtual worlds go well, there may be no need for real world courts to participate in this process."[41] Balkin, however, senses that the commodification of virtual worlds warrants the interest of the courts:

> Precisely because virtual worlds are fast becoming important parts of people's lives, and because they are likely to be used for more and more purposes in the future, legal regulation of virtual worlds is inevitable. . . . What happens in virtual worlds . . . has real-world effects both on players and non-players, and governments will have important interests in regulating those real-world effects.[42]

The Department of Homeland Security has already asserted these interests, issuing public warnings—circulated in online public service announcements like *Playing It Safe: Avoiding Gaming Risks*—about potential crimes connected to virtual worlds, such as the theft of virtual property, protection schemes within the games, and the exploitation of foreign labor by gold farmers.[43]

Balkin poses an important question: Do platform owners have the right to end the game, as amusement park owners have the right to close the gates to their fantasy land? In other words, is a virtual world a private holding of its creators or a commonwealth held in partnership with its users? As intellectual proprietor of the simulation, the owner may do with it what he chooses, but the virtual goods collectively generated in the game, traded for real currency on eBay, represent real investments by users. The law, Balkin ventures, will not tolerate destruction of such property. "If virtual items have real-world equivalent values," he argues, "the game designer may be destroying a considerable amount of value by turning off the game, and the more value that is destroyed, the less likely the law will stand for it."[44]

The debate between free speech and private property in virtual worlds has one of its first precedents in *Blacksnow Interactive v. Mythic Entertainment, Inc.*, a 2002 case asserting the right of Blacksnow, a gold farming business, to sell currency and items acquired in Mythic's *Dark Age of Camelot*. In his book *Play Money: Or, How I Quit My Day Job and Made Millions Selling Virtual Loot*, technology writer Julian Dibbell chronicles the "already legendary court battle." Blacksnow contracted low-wage laborers in Tijuana to mine gold, then sold the currency on eBay, in direct violation of Mythic's End User Licensing Agreement (EULA), which prohibits playing the game "for commercial, business, or income-seeking purposes." When Mythic informed eBay that Blacksnow had violated their intellectual property rights, eBay closed Blacksnow's auctions. Blacksnow sued Mythic for compensatory and punitive damages, citing "unfair business practices" and "interference with prospective economic advantage." The case remains unresolved. Shortly after filing suit, the Federal Trade Commission fined Blacksnow $10,000 for defrauding customers in a previous venture. Blacksnow defaulted on their legal fees and dropped the suit. [45]

Because Mythic prohibits the use of *Dark Age of Camelot* for "income-seeking purposes" in its licensing agreement, Blacksnow would have likely lost the case. Dibbell speculates that Blacksnow filed suit simply to confront the court with pressing questions about the political and economic constitution of virtual worlds. Who owns the wealth of virtual worlds—the companies that build them or the players who sustain them? Do players have rights to the time they spend in virtual worlds and the property they acquire there? As Blacksnow partner Lee Caldwell said in a press release, "What it comes down to is, does a MMORPG player have rights to his time, or does Mythic own that player's time?"[46]

Raphael "Raph" Koster, author of *A Theory of Fun for Game Design* and one of the original designers of both *Ultima Online* and *Star Wars: Galaxies*, has proposed some answers in a Declaration of the Rights of Avatars—a document closely modeled on the Declaration of the Rights of Man and of the Citizen, the manifesto drafted by France's National Assembly at the outset of the revolution in 1789. Koster offers two key premises for his proposal. First, virtual worlds represent a new "forum for interaction and society for the general public regardless of the intent of the creators." In other words, virtual worlds have become public spaces or commonwealths that exceed the sole proprietorship of the game companies that manage them. Koster asserts that "property is an inviolable and sacred right, and the virtual equivalent is integrity and persistence of data, no one shall be deprived thereof except where public necessity . . . shall clearly demand it." At a stroke, he decisively resolves Balkin's dilemma of "freedom to design" versus "freedom to play" in favor of players, who are no longer customers but now citizens. Second, Koster proposes that avatars are "the manifestation of actual people in an online medium, and that their utterances, actions, thoughts, and emotions should be considered to be as valid as the utterances, actions, thoughts, and emotions of people in any other forum, venue, location, or space." Koster argues that the "foremost" right of avatars is "the right to be treated as people and not as disembodied, meaningless, soulless puppets. Inherent in this right are therefore the natural and inalienable rights of man. These rights are liberty, property, security, and resistance to oppression."[47] At another stroke, he has settled the debate concerning the definition of the avatar: it is another self, not merely the instrument we use to interact with the program.

These two central assertions—virtual world as commonwealth and avatar as person—allow Koster to adapt the rights of citizens of a free society to the virtual realm, including free speech, free assembly, and private property. By playing the game, he reasons, we affirm our membership in this commonwealth and form a social contract with other players and administrators, a "code of conduct" prohibiting "those actions and utterances that are hurtful to society, inclusive of the harm that may be done to the fabric of the virtual space via hurt done to the hardware, software, or data." Administrators are equally bound by this new form of social contract. They may silence, disperse, or ban players only to preserve the continued existence and integrity of the commonwealth— the hardware, software, or data—and they must always provide a clear account of their policies and decisions. Administrative authority, ultimately, "must proceed from the community." At the same time, administrators' unique knowledge of the game world and their responsibility to maintain it grants them considerable discretion in exercising their power, much as "national security" grants real governments the power to act expediently.[48]

Koster acknowledges a list of objections raised by his fellow virtual world designers. Many do not accept, for instance, the document's fundamental premises. One critic asks: "Rights of *avatars?* Why not of 'chess pieces'? Maybe the players have rights, but avatars are just representations." There is no binding social contract, another suggests, when disgruntled players may simply close their account and emigrate to a game with more enlightened administrators.[49] Still, the document represents a significant leap in thinking about virtual worlds, a philosophical extrapolation of economists' and sociologists' claims that virtual communities are no longer separable from real communities. Koster reasons that we should apply the same political principles to both. Virtual worlds should be constituted as liberal democracies rather than tyrannies, and while the mechanism of online games mandates a functional division between administrators and players, administrative operations should be fair, transparent, and executed only by the consent of the players, as in any good government.

For now, Koster says, his document is merely a "hypothetical exercise," but he envisions a future when virtual worlds become so pervasive that users will demand the protections it offers. "Your avatar profile might be your credit record and your resume and your academic transcript, as well as your XP [experience points] earned," Koster writes. "On the day that happens, I bet we'll all wish we had a few more rights in the face of a very large . . . virtual world where it might be very, very *hard* to move to a different service provider."[50] From this perspective, Koster's Declaration of the Rights of Avatars manifests concerns about the rights and the definition of the person in the digital age. Like Gergen, Koster senses an apocalypse, a revolution, and he attempts to reaffirm Enlightenment notions of the self and natural human rights in an historical moment when these ideas appear to be threatened by technological change.

Cooperation, Diversity, and Consumerism

The Declaration of the Rights of Man and of the Citizen holds that "liberty consists in the freedom to do everything which injures no one else."[51] Koster, in turn, adopts this definition in his document. The statement suggests that our freedom is bounded only by our obligation to respect the freedom of others, but in a more modern sense it ignores the range of social and historical conditions that impose limits on our agency. What we can accomplish in life is determined, in part, by our sex, our race, our class, our nationality, our genes, and our historical moment. In online games, our liberty is likewise limited by much more than rights of other avatars. Most significantly, game design, a fixed mechanical code, determines what we can and cannot do. Game design itself reflects more than the arbitrary will of the designers; it emulates successful features of previous games and, less consciously, the ideologies of the global capitalist system that has, in the first place, nurtured the ascendance of virtual worlds and virtual economies. While virtual worlds promise unlimited agency, ideologies such as cooperation, diversity, and consumerism are hardwired as physical laws.

Players often complain about the strict hierarchies of virtual worlds, such as the social inequality between newbies and experienced players or the status conveyed by a particular epic weapon or guild membership. The rules encoded in virtual worlds, however, foster a cooperative approach to gameplay that emphasizes the need to work together and channel individual skills toward a common good. We may adopt any one of a gallery of classes—warrior, wizard, priest, thief, and many others—but even the most powerful avatars cannot succeed on their own. While the wizard decimates enemies with arcane firepower, she needs the hearty warrior to bear the brunt of the enemy counterattack. As he stands his ground, the warrior, in turn, needs the priest to heal his wounds and fortify his body. The thief, though he shuns combat, disarms the lethal trap and opens the secret door leading to the shared loot. Encoded in virtual worlds, these roles necessitate negotiation and cooperation with fellow players. We may quest alone for petty prizes, but we must join a party to bring down the big game and reap greater rewards, such as unique treasures, substantial experience points, and quicker leveling.

Learning the complex dynamics and etiquette of cooperative action represents one of first and most difficult tasks for new players, particularly those more accustomed to the egomaniacal aesthetic of single-player videogames.

The virtues that serve us well in single player games—cleverness, quickness, dogged persistence—amount to nothing in online games. Playing alone, we may not advance beyond a certain limit, nor may we travel too widely beyond the safety of the town. With sheer strength or numbers, the beasties overwhelm us, and each time our avatar dies we lose experience points, loot, and precious time. As a consequence, we learn to work with others, play our part, and divvy up the profits. In short, we learn to be cooperative and egalitarian.

Brad McQuaid, one of the original creators of *EverQuest*, emphasizes the importance of cooperative play in virtual world design:

> Without community, you simply have a bunch of independent players running around the same environment. Players won't be drawn in, and there won't be anything there to bind them. The key to creating community, therefore, is interdependence. In *EverQuest*, we forced interdependence in several ways, and although we've been criticized for it, I think it's one of a couple of reasons behind our success. . . . By creating a class-based system, players NEED each other. By creating an environment often too challenging for a solo player, people are compelled to group and even form large guilds and alliances. All this builds community.[52]

Guild membership, crucial to advancement in the game, relies heavily on our collegiality, our reputation for trust and responsibility, and our value as a team member. Taylor explains that antisocial or opportunistic players "can acquire a reputation that has serious effects on their ability to get groups, be invited into a guild, and by extension advance in the game." Persistently self-interested behavior, Taylor says, "carries significant costs and is typically weeded out."[53]

In learning to cooperate with other races and other classes of avatars, we also learn to value diversity. In the same way that each character class features skills that complement those of other classes, each race complements the others. In *EverQuest*, for example, we may play as one of fifteen different races—varieties of humans and elves, dwarves, halflings, gnomes, ogres, trolls, as well as anthropomorphic lizards, frogs, and tigers. Because each race has its favored classes, each party will likely include a variety of races and represent a microcosm of the multicultural game world. Often, racial tensions in the game world limit our exploration. In *EverQuest*, the "evil" races, such as dark elves, ogres, and trolls, will be attacked on sight in "good" cities like Freeport, Riverdale, and Kaladim. Likewise, humans, halflings, dwarves, and other "good" races will find no welcome in Neriak, Oggok, or Grobb. While the animus between certain races and alignments simulates intolerance and adds depth to Norrath's sociology, it also promotes cooperation between the seemingly hostile races. Just as the dark elf I met in Freeport paid me to buy his food and drink, I would have to engage a dark elf if I found myself in need of provisions in Neriak. For virtual world researchers, this programmed sociality is an integral dynamic of the emergent culture in virtual worlds and elevates them above other kinds of videogames. Online games, as various scholars have said, are not mere diversions but "new communications technologies," "forums," or entire "societies."

A pervasive consumerism, however, works against cooperative gameplay and generates an ideological tension in virtual worlds. While online games mandate that we work with other players, they also foster a monomaniacal drive for individual advancement. This tension fuels debates over gold farming, online trading, and virtual currency exchange. Players who defend the cooperative ethic, as well as game companies, view these practices as cheating, while other players view a quick purchase of an epic weapon or a high-level avatar as entrepreneurialism, an extension of the game.

While game designers claim to weave fantasy and produce mere entertainments not meant to serve "income-seeking purposes," they often stimulate and feed players' consumerist drives. To accommodate advanced players who have exhausted the resources of existing worlds, designers have regularly served expansions with more continents to be explored, claimed, and harvested by avaricious avatars. Dibbell relates his frantic participation in a virtual land rush in 2003, when *Ultima Online* designers opened a virgin continent, Malas, to relieve overcrowding and urban sprawl in Britannia:

> Malas was overrun with land-grabbers within seconds of its opening, and if I'd had to waste ten minutes deciding where to place the two houses my two user accounts entitled me to, I would have ended up with a couple of shack-sized plots out in the spawn-infested boondocks, if that. Instead, I was able to grab two ample sites inside the walls of Luna, a bright-lit, sandstone city that my gut told me was destined to be a prime real-estate location.[54]

Propelled by this kind conspicuous consumption and the compulsory drive for acquisition and advancement, virtual worlds, perhaps, have become too much like our own. Killing giant rats has become a rat race. What is left for us, after all, when we reach level 70, construct our elegant and impregnable stronghold, amass a warehouse of epic weapons, slay the biggest monsters, and command the most prestigious guild? All-too-human, the avatar, at the pinnacle of his ascent, confronts an existential crisis, a loss of purpose. Perhaps the subtlest achievement of online games is not their opening of brave new worlds for education and commerce, but rather their uncanny imitation of modernity in the guise of fantasy.

❖ 9 ❖

Modding, Education, and Art

In Gus Van Sant's 2003 film, *Elephant,* a stark fictionalization of the Columbine High School shooting, Eric, one of the lanky teenage killers, flops onto a bed, turns on a laptop, and begins playing a videogame. Pedestrians, identically sketched in black silhouette, wander aimlessly against a blank, white background, while the player character, switching between a submachine gun and a shotgun, runs among them, shooting them in the back, spattering their blood.

For the viewer, the scene brings a sense of foreboding. Its minimal graphic and narrative content is a projection of the killer's own view of the social world he inhabits, a featureless landscape populated with uniformly faceless and insensible shadows. For Eric, the experience is temporarily soothing, a way of playing out his revenge fantasies against the students in his chemistry class who, in an earlier scene, pelt him with gooey trash. At school, Eric bears the humiliation in silence, retreating to the restroom after class to scrub the stain from his jacket. In the game, though, Eric has absolute power, and watching his expression of bored determination as he plays, we know that he imagines the blank killing zone as the corridors of his school.

The scene rehearses the familiar charge that videogames lay at root of the nihilistic violence afflicting American youth, and it reminds us that Eric Harris, one of the two Columbine shooters and an avid *Doom* player, had created customized levels using the game's source code and distributed them on his Web site. More subtly, though, the scene illustrates the actualizing power of games, their potential to animate our interior desires. Games like Eric's, those modified to reflect the idiosyncratic sensibilities of their users, animate these desires most vividly. We will not find Eric's game on the shelves of EB Games. It has been created by an amateur developer from an existing game. It might be any first-person shooter stripped down to its barest elements, but it lacks something game-like. The human targets do not shoot back or run away, and for most viewers the violence is strangely unwholesome, as if Eric's private fantasy has infected our more commercial, more comfortable images of warfare against aliens or terrorists. Whether he has downloaded this modified shooter or created it himself, Eric has made the game his own, and although he seems monstrous, Eric represents what many gamers, developers, and critics find most exciting and most liberating about videogames today. He has obviated the intentions of the game's original creators and seized control within the simulated world.

Mods, modifications of computer game programming, are created by users to customize play experience, to make the games their own. By altering the code of the game program or, more frequently, by using editing utilities packaged with the game, users may create new maps, characters, or even entire narratives from the original game. While many games grant players godlike control within the game world or provide interactive spaces expansive enough to allow ways of playing that do not effect the conclusions scripted by the game's original developers, modding fosters an even deeper level of user control. As videogame theorist Alexander Galloway explains:

> A videogame can be modified in three basic ways: (1) at the level of its visual design, new level maps, new artwork, new character models, and so on; (2) at the level of the rules of the game, changing how gameplay unfolds—who wins, who loses, and what the repercussions of various gamic acts are; or (3) at the level of its software technology, changing character behavior, game physics, lighting techniques, and so on.[1]

Gamers like Eric may rewrite the rules that govern interaction within these spaces, removing enemies' capacity to hurt them, rendering walls permeable and gravity irrelevant, or enabling other users to enter their modified game universe so that they can play with them, talk to them, or kill them.

Mods may also reshape game spaces for purposes that need not be as narcissistic and destructive as Eric's. As we have seen, contemporary digital artists such as Anne-Marie Schleiner, Brody Condon, and Joan Leadre—creators of *Velvet-Strike*—and Cory Arcangel—creator of *NES Home Movies: 8-bit Landscape Studies*—have developed mods as a vehicle for protest or as a new form of pop art. Architects at Cambridge University have remodeled the infernal corridors of *Quake* as a three-dimensional model for a proposed building project.[2] The History Channel has adapted *Rome: Total War* in its documentary series *Decisive Battles* to digitally reenact ancient military conflicts. And while many institutions of higher education still regard videogames as inconsequential diversions or agents of student brain-rot, programs at MIT and the University of Arizona have developed elaborate pedagogical modifications of the fantasy role-playing game *Neverwinter Nights.*

Such unexpected applications of videogames beyond the dim lairs of disaffected students have gained the attention of media critics, who now routinely speak of modding as an intriguing innovation. In fact, mods have existed as long as videogames themselves have. Mark Brayfield writes, "The practice of modifying videogames has probably been around since the days of *Pong.*"[3] In 1972, a Federal District Court in California decided that *Pong* itself was a mod, compelling Atari founder and *Pong* designer Nolan Bushnell to pay royalties to Magnavox for his alleged use of a concept introduced by the Odyssey home game system. We may look back even further. In 1961, errant programmers at MIT created *Spacewar!* for the PDP-1, an open-source two-player space combat game adapted from a star-mapping program. Ceaselessly modified by other programmers for nearly two decades, *Spacewar!* finally went commercial in 1977, when Cinematronics built and copyrighted the coin-operated version, *Space Wars,* familiar in arcades and convenience stores in the 1980s.

Although mods themselves are not new inventions, users such at the architects at Cambridge, the documentarians at The History Channel, and the educators at MIT and Arizona have only recently discovered more inventive applications for them. Considering that mods have existed for the past four decades, then, we should not marvel that architects, documentarians, educators, and others now put them to constructive use, but rather that no one did so before. A brief look at the history of modding suggests that no one did so because no one—or rather very few—could.

This chapter considers the implication of the increasing availability of mod tools, particularly in terms of the creative potential they grant to educators and students with no technical knowledge of game design. What capabilities do currently available tools offer? How have educators made use of these tools, and what else might we accomplish with them? The recent incorporation of modding has complicated the conventional understanding of mods as user-controlled activities. What was once appropriated from the industry by users has now been reappropriated from users by the industry. But rather than simply dismissing the inevitable corporate mods and their creators as sellouts, as some users have, we find that the incorporation of modding into the game industry facilitates, rather than hinders, deeper and freer levels of interactivity. In recent years, partly as a cause and partly as a consequence of corporate modding, mods have proliferated within the videogame community, leading to a widespread change in the way users orient themselves to computer games. Through the proliferation of corporate mod tools such as map editors, casual gamers and educators—like hackers and amateur programmers—have now gained the ability to remake their game world, to transform themselves from player characters to player creators.

Mods and the Videogame Industry

Until recently, modding has remained an arcane discipline practiced by a clique of hackers adept in the same programming languages used by professional developers. In its underground domain, modding evolved as a subversive expression of the "hacker ethic" described by Steven Levy in 1984: "Access to computers should be unlimited and total. Always yield to the Hands-On Imperative. All information should be free. Mistrust authority—promote decentralization. . . . You can create art and beauty on a computer. Computers can change your life for the better."[4] Fashioning themselves as avatars of free expression, modders practiced art as cultural sabotage, appropriating and embellishing mass-marketed game software, circumventing commercial distribution networks, and sharing their creations for free on the Internet. Chris Rogiss, creator of the *Quake* mod *Urban Terror,* explains, "The whole point of making a mod is to be free and not have some company telling you what to do."[5]

For their own part, the game industry has sensed the threat posed by anticorporate mavericks such as Rogiss. In 2000, Doug Lowenstein, former president of the Entertainment Software Association (ESA), an organization dedicated to protecting the commercial and political interests of game companies, identified piracy as "the greatest challenge we face." Lowenstein explains, "This industry loses $3.2 billion a year . . . due to piracy. . . . Our industry's control over its intellectual property is at greater risk than it's ever been before. . . . Mod chips and other devices to circumvent console copy protections, counterfeit cartridges and CDs, it's endless."[6] While hacker-modders like Rogiss have certainly wrested some control of interactive experience from game companies and harried regulators like Lowenstein, they have shown little interest in exploring the wider usefulness of their activities and realizing Levy's promise that hacking could somehow foster the common good. In the past, those who might have been interested in pursuing the constructive possibilities of modding most likely lacked the technical skills to do so.

More recently, though, modding has become more widely practicable to those who seek not simply to undermine corporate authority but to "change life for the better" in more useful ways. The traditional antagonism between modders and game companies expressed from opposite perspectives by Rogiss and Lowenstein has evolved into a collaborative relationship, as developers share their tools with users and invite them to participate more actively in the creative process. Game companies now facilitate modding in a variety of ways. Many games include mapping, scripting, and animation utilities, more advanced and user-friendly versions of the mod tools originally pioneered by hackers. Expansion packs retail separately or with repackaged versions of the original games. Valve's *Half-Life,* for example, is packaged with the multi-player mods *Team Fortress Classic* and *Counter-Strike.* Likewise, Bioware's *Neverwinter Nights* is packaged with a collection of expansion modules, in addition to Bioware's Aurora toolkit, a utility that allows users to create their own modules and has served education research groups as a primary tool in their creation of pedagogical ones.

For the most part, profit rather than progressive attitudes motivates the new openness to modding within the game industry. Game producers, begin-ning perhaps with Cinematronics, which incorporated user modifications of *Spacewar!* into their arcade version as optional game modes, have recognized the commercial potential of modding and integrated it into their design and marketing strategies. Because mods cannot be created or used without the original game software, re-creations of old games increase the demand and shelf life of the original product by dramatically enhancing its replayability. In a move to create what might be the first purely commercial mod, Valve hired former modders to create *Team Fortress II,* a commercial sequel to the outdated *Team Fortress* mod for *Quake.* This trend of using modding as a marketing strategy has caused some hacker-modders to brand the creators of commercial mods like *Team Fortress II* as "sell-outs."[7] What was once ap-propriated from the game industry by hackers has been reappropriated from hackers by the game industry.

Surprisingly though, this "selling out," more accurately seen as a fruitful partnership between amateur and professional developers, has served Levy's vision of decentralization more effectively than the traditional friction between modders and game companies. The proliferation of mods among more users and their emerging uses in applied art and education suggest that the com-mercialization of modding has expanded rather than limited the possibilities for deeper and freer modes of interactivity. Control of interactive experience has not become more consolidated within game companies, but rather more diffused among a greater number and a greater variety of users. Widely available and user-friendly mod tools distributed by game companies have enabled users with no specialized coding skills to rewrite games and become amateur developers.

Counter-Strike, an online multiplayer mod of *Half-Life* that pits teams of terrorists and counterterrorists against each other in player-created combat maps, exemplifies the commercialization and consequent democratization of mods since the 1990s. Following Valve's release of *Half-Life,* amateur developer Minh Le created *Counter-Strike* and distributed it for free online.

As Cinematronics appropriated and retailed the privately created *Spacewar!* in 1977, Valve capitalized on the underground popularity of *Counter-Strike* by releasing a retail version of the mod in 2000. Valve's appropriation of the game, however, has not hindered users from downloading the original mod for free, but simply created another avenue for distribution, expanding accessibility and increasing the number of users, albeit at a profit. From their survey of 50 different *Counter-Strike* servers, researchers Talmadge Wright, Eric Boria, and Paul Breidenbach estimated that nearly 25,000 players were online at any given time playing *Counter-Strike* during the period of their study in 2002.[8]

Wright, Boria, and Breidenbach further note elements of map design and player behavior that "flaunt ordinary social conventions" and foster nonpreferred play. They recount an incident of simulated mass-suicide, when players took turns "jumping off the edge of the building . . . just so that they could hear the scream and the resultant thud of their virtual character. . . . [The] thought of professional counter-terrorist or terrorists jumping off tall buildings to a virtual death contradicts the mission of catching the 'bad guys' or killing the 'good guys.'" They describe game maps that appropriate images from popular culture and "speak more to art and ritual than to simply commercial interest." Players may strafe the aisles of Wal-Mart and tag the simulated combat zone with imported personal logos such as film icons, political slogans, or pornography. Following the attacks of September 11, 2001, while one player terrorist adopted the online name "Osama yo mama," another player counterterrorist tagged maps with a photograph of the devastation at Ground Zero.[9]

Game companies have not only embraced the sort of nonpreferred play that Wright, Boria, and Breidenbach observe, but have publicly encouraged users to devise play possibilities unimagined by the original developers or prohibited by the original programming. John Carmack, a former hacker and lead programmer for id Software's archetypal first-person shooter *Doom* watched with amusement when hackers replaced Nazis with purple Barneys in id's *Wolfenstein 3D* in 1992. Carmack says, "Ever since then . . . it's been one of my highest strategic decisions to make all of these things possible. Putting these games in the hands of users, the game becomes a new canvas for people." Hacker-modders no longer had to work so hard to get their hands on games; developers like Carmack were now handing them over. Disregarding the need for product protection Lowenstein would later emphasize, Carmack ceded a share of creative control to users, providing editing utilities that allowed them to restructure levels within the game. David Kushner views Carmack's sharing of *Doom*'s source code as a critical moment in the evolving relationship between game companies, games, and users. He writes, "This was a radical idea not only for games but, really, for any type of media. Although some level of editing programs had been released in the past, few programmers—let alone owners—of a company had released the guts of what made their products work. It was an ideological gesture that empowered players and, in turn, loosened the grip of game makers."[10]

Galloway explains that the increasing interdependence of the videogame industry and amateur designers, which began with Carmack's invitation to players to modify *Doom,* relies on the technical difference between the game engine, the core programming that governs game physics and basic rules of play, and the wide variety of individual games that designers might generate using the engine. Galloway writes, "The game engine is a type of abstract core technology that, while it may exert its own personality through telltale traces of its various abilities and features . . . is mostly unlinked from the gameplay layered within it. . . . Few new-media artists build their own game engines from the ground up, and practically none of them build their own computers." In other words, while modders may experiment freely with game design, engine design remains constant, providing the common code and design platform for amateur and commercial designers. This relative constancy of game engine design, Galloway claims, fosters a "symbiotic relationship between mod artists and the industry in a way not seen in previous avant-garde movements."[11] With engines and toolkits, the industry provides a creative platform, while users ensure the continuing viability of the engine by developing inventive applications, some of which the industry appropriates, as Valve has done with *Counter-Strike.* Still, while Carmack's utilities proved useful mainly to gamers with programming skill, the Doom Editor Utility, released soon afterward by hackers, offered an editing interface accessible even to the code-illiterate. Kushner writes, "The Doom Editor Utility was a watershed in the evolution of the participatory culture of mod making. Anyone with the interest could create a level of a complex game the equivalent of writing a new chapter into a book, and then, via the Internet, publishing that creation. . . . Mod tools turned game players into game makers."[12]

Since Carmack's radical "ideological gesture" to break down the wall between amateur and professional developers, game companies have sought to tap the creative reservoir of their users. Atari, Epic, and NVIDIA have established a contest that awards the license for Epic's Unreal Engine to the creator of the best *Unreal Tournament 2003* mod. Mark Brayfield explains, "The companies sponsoring the contest hope to discover new talent hidden in the ranks of casual gamers . . . like Hollywood's Project Greenlight for modders."[13] Electronic Arts' former Westwood Studios adopted an even more direct method for utilizing amateur developers, inviting unknown talents to produce a multiplayer mod for *Command and Conquer: Renegade* in 2002. Westwood not only provided users with complex editing tools for the game, as Carmack had done in 1993, but also convened a "Mod College" to more quickly familiarize users with them. In a 2002 interview, Louis Castle, cofounder of Westwood, explains:

> We flew a bunch of the people who had made some of the more successful mods out to Las Vegas. . . . The first product as a milestone was really *Counter-Strike.* That was a product that was built by the mod community. So rather than wait for them to do it, we flew them out to Las Vegas, took care of them for a week, sat them down with the development teams, gave them copies of all our tools, and showed them how to use them. . . . In fact, our hope is that out of this group of people come some really innovative ideas, and that we can publish those ideas in a future product.[14]

Castle reveals that the creators of *Renegade* envisioned potential mods even before they conceived the original game design: "As we were developing the tools for . . . *Renegade,*" he explains, "it became really clear from the beginning that it was really important to engage the mod community, because these folks have a great deal to do with why the game is successful three . . . or four months later. They're the ones creating new and interesting ideas and concepts."[15]

Scenarios such as those that Castle describes—a gathering of amateur and professional developers collaborating on a new game, and programmers writing palimpsest code that facilitates rather than resists successive rewritings—call for a new understanding of both mods and commercial games. Galloway writes, "Since hacking is generally unloved in other sectors (the music industry, the film industry), the fact that the gaming industry allows such activities is quite significant."[16] In fact, as Castle's work shows, the industry not only "allows" it, but also actively facilitates it. Less frequently born from the conflict between users and the game industry, mods now emerge from their cooperation. Commercial games, similarly, now serve as ready platforms for user modification, "living products," in the words of John Cook, one of the developers of *Team Fortress II.*[17] Certainly, corporate sponsorship of amateur developers has enabled the industry to regulate the way these developers modify games, to guard against the rampant, uncontrolled piracy that Lowenstein fears, and to cull profits from the creative work of unpaid talent. As Castle says, game companies may actively adopt the ideas of these amateur developers in expansion modules developed by their own in-house programmers or passively benefit from the enhanced replayability of the original games.

Mods in Education

The distribution of user-friendly mod tools, even as an exercise in self-interest, has also had the effect of facilitating unprecedented applications of videogames among the more casual or public-mined gamers excluded from Steven Levy's "revolution" by their technical illiteracy. Angela McFarlane, an education correspondent for the *Times* of London, considers a variety of game programming languages—Lisp, Smalltalk, Flash, Director, and Panda—"useful tools" in adapting games to education but concedes that "they require specialist knowledge." She claims, rather, that modding "can get you a long way without specialist programming" and concludes that development tools packaged with "games such as *Half-Life, Unreal, Baldur's Gate,* and many others" may foster a variety of classroom activities, particularly in creative writing.[18]

At the University of Edinburgh's Institute for Communicating and Collaborative Systems, Judy Robertson has designed *Ghostwriter,* a writing instruction tool modified from Epic's *Unreal.* Robertson and Peter Wiemer-Hastings explain, "*Ghostwriter* involves a 3D role-playing environment which puts the students in a stimulating situation and gives them something compelling to write about. . . . Role-play activities are used in classrooms to encourage children to explore the feelings of the characters in a story . . . [and] can give a story personal significance for each child." According to Robertson and Wiemer-Hastings, role-playing mods promote "feelings of social presence" as well as "self-presence," helping student writers to hone basic skills such as character development, dramatic conflict, and personal reflection.[19]

The Learning Games Initiative (LGI), a research group based at the University of Arizona, has developed *Aristotle's Assassins,* a role-playing mod of *Neverwinter Nights* constructed with Bioware's Aurora toolkit. Like Wiemer-Hastings and Robertson, LGI claims that the emotionally compelling and "sensorily rich" experience of immersive role-playing "engage[s] players powerfully enough to entangle historical and cultural learning with game play." Set in ancient Greece, the game casts the student-player in the role of Mellifluous, an apprentice musician who must discover and thwart a plot to kill Aristotle. In the course of the game, its developers explain, the player must "sneak along treacherous caravan roads; explore busy bazaars full of vendors, itinerant charlatans, sages, peasants, and thieves; infiltrate moonlit secret meetings in the desert; walk the peripatos and explore the mysterious Temple of the Nymphs; and search for a secret escape route through the imperial gardens of Alexander the Great." With its "deeply researched historical and cultural detail," LGI promises, *Aristotle's Assassins* "will sneak in a college-level humanities course's worth of knowledge about ancient Greece."[20]

As we have seen in Chapter 7, the Education Arcade, a research group affiliated with the University of Wisconsin and MIT, has created *Revolution,* an online multiplayer mod of *Neverwinter Nights.* Developed in consultation with Colonial Williamsburg historians and Boston-area social science teachers, *Revolution* is set in Virginia between 1773 and 1783. Like *Aristotle's Assassins,* the game seeks to convey cultural and historical information through immersive role-playing. *Revolution* offers student-players the option to assume a variety of roles: "a wealthy farmer whose loyalty to the crown is tested by a son who joins the rebels, . . . a slave who sees the coming chaos as a possible bid for freedom, . . . a politician struggling to protect the community through diplomacy, . . . a merchant seeking to exploit this war for personal gain." Having chosen a character, the Education Arcade developers explain, each student-player "navigates the space of the town, interacts with other players, and is given the opportunity to act in or react to events that in one way or another represent the coming of the war." The game is organized in chapters, each one playable within one class session and each one variable according to the character the student has chosen: "each chapter involves a historical circumstance or series of circumstances that each player has to negotiate to a lesser or greater degree depending on their role. . . . Ultimately, each smaller chapter will represent an overall narrative progression towards the outbreak of the war."[21] In order to "entangle," in LGI's words, "historical and cultural learning with game play," researchers at the Education Arcade propose to integrate the mod with more traditional classroom activities such as teacher-led discussions about the problems and decisions students confront within the game.

The Aurora toolkit, originally distributed for free online and later packaged and retailed with *Neverwinter Nights,* has allowed these educators to realize Levy's promise that what began as corporate sabotage could lead to a wider social benefit. Levy probably did not imagine, though, that such a benefit might be realized only when game companies co-opt and mass-market the tools of the saboteurs. From the galaxy of role-playing games on the shelves, *Neverwinter Nights* has emerged as a preferred platform for educational mods because its editing utility has proven most accessible for amateur developers. While specialist skills are necessary to model the historically specific architecture, characters, and objects in *Aristotle's Assassins* and *Revolution,* Aurora enables code-illiterate users to control the fundamental elements of game design such as mapping, event scripting, and dialogue. Developers of *Revolution* marvel that Aurora grants control of the artificial intelligence at the core of *Neverwinter Nights,* allowing them to create nonplayer characters "that are smart enough to converse and spread rumors, to maintain levels of friendship or enmity with player characters, to follow the roads in the town, to congregate when they hear of meetings, and to identify and arrest lawbreakers."[22]

Developers for the Education Arcade also explain that the core programming of *Neverwinter Nights,* like the palimpsest code developed for *Renegade,* facilitates rather than hinders their modifications, sometimes to stunning and unanticipated effect. They explain, "One of the great things about working with mods is that, occasionally, something that was preexisting in the game engine interacts with our own content in a particularly compelling way." While playtesting a chapter in which British soldiers suppress a riotous crowd of American patriots, they observed one such interaction as the redcoats assaulted the mob, employing a "knockdown" ability in *Neverwinter Nights* that allows characters to brutalize and subdue other characters without killing them. "Given that our game is extremely low violence when compared to other role-playing games," the developers write, "moments like these are pretty shocking when they happen."[23] Strangely, the violence manifested by the core programming of the fantasy role-playing game in an otherwise peaceable educational simulation proved unexpectedly instructive, as the creators of *Revolution* sought to illustrate the events leading to war with escalating emotional intensity. The "knockdown" serves as both a dramatic climax within the game and, within the classroom, a lesson in the way negotiation deteriorates to violence; historical learning becomes entangled with gameplay, the role of player entangled with the role of student.

Games designer Will Wright, creator of *SimCity* and *The Sims,* suggests that games that facilitate an active, creative engagement with the medium, including those that distribute mod tools, "break down the wall between producers and consumers," in the same way that Louis Castle's Mod College does. "By moving away from the idea that media is something developed by the few," Wright explains, "we open up a world of possibilities. Instead of leaving player creativity at the door, we are inviting it back to help build, design, and populate our digital worlds. More games now include features that let players invent some aspect of their virtual world. . . . And more games entice players to become creative partners in world building, letting them mod its overall look and feel. . . . For these players, games are not just entertainment but a vehicle for self-expression." According to Wright, they also foster a more critical, more creative kind of education. Students who use games as learning tools will "treat the world as a place for creation, not consumption."[24]

The frightening scene from *Elephant* where Eric's player character rampages murderously through blank space now seems only one of many possible demonstrations of the potential for mods to empower gamers in the way that Wright describes. With mods in the hands of educators as well sociopaths, they may be used not only to slaughter students but also to teach them. Utilities such as Aurora, moreover, remove the need for specialist training, or even for fully funded, fully staffed programs at major research universities such as LGI or the Education Arcade.

Using the Aurora Toolkit

In my own preparation for a course on medieval Ireland, I have used Aurora to develop Inisfallen, an interactive learning environment featuring a ninth-century monastery busy with monks, farmers, tradesmen, merchants, pilgrims, and beggars. While I am an experienced gamer, I lack the skill to modify games by rewriting programming. Aurora enables me to use *Neverwinter Nights* as a course tool by crossing the barrier between game development technology and pedagogy.

Like the creators of *Aristotle's Assassins* and *Revolution*, I sought to merge cultural and historical learning with gaming in an immersive role-playing experience. Although Aurora does allow me to create historically specific character and object models such as those in the more sophisticated *Neverwinter Nights* mods developed by LGI and the Education Arcade, its palette allows me to approximate a medieval Irish world by modifying existing game models. An ivy-covered mausoleum serves as a chapel, a wizard's tower serves as an Irish round tower, and priest's robes serve as the rough white cowls of the Celtic ascetics. The variety of hairstyles for character models even allows me to replicate the unique Irish tonsure, with the hair shorn in the front and grown long in the back. The distinctive Celtic high cross, a focal point of almost every Irish monastery, remains beyond the capability of Aurora, which offers a wide variety of paganish shrines but no explicitly religious object models.

Neverwinter Nights modules consist of a network of areas, interior and exterior spaces linked by area transitions. Aurora first prompts the user to generate a number of areas from a menu of tile sets, a variety of environments ranging from rural countryside to dungeon passageways. I began Inisfallen, a relatively simple module, by generating four rural exteriors, which serve as the monastery, an adjacent cemetery, and two outlying farms; and six interiors, which serve as the chapel, storehouse, round tower, scriptorium, refectory, and a small monk's dwelling. I can create the structural framework of the module, the game map, by marking the area transitions between the central monastery area and the nine other secondary areas. Aurora features a familiar interface with tool bars, menu bars, and viewing windows, so that the toolkit will not seem unfriendly to anyone who has used common word processing, web design, or spreadsheet applications. With my areas now defined and linked, I add details to the play environment: landscape elevations, terrain textures, buildings, a variety of miscellaneous objects that add graphic complexity to our simulated medieval world, sound effects, and, perhaps most importantly, the cohort of nonplayer characters with whom students will interact.

The structural complexity of play environments in *Quake* or other first-person shooters proves particularly useful for architectural models, and the panoramic perspective of *Rome: Total War* lends itself well to large-scale battle simulations. The interactions between player characters, other player characters, and nonplayer characters in *Neverwinter Nights* make the game a uniquely effective pedagogical tool. In general, role-playing and adventure games foster practices critical to learning: the confrontation of a problem, the investigation of possible solutions, and the collaboration with others in an effort to achieve these solutions. Generating the graphical environment of my monastery takes only a few hours with Aurora. The real work in creating the mod comes in scripting the interactions, between these nonplayer characters and the player. Without these interactions, Inisfallen is nothing more than a digital diorama, a visually rich but intellectually lifeless place. Aurora's primary usefulness to amateur developers such as us, then, lies in its facilitation of scripting these interactions.

Writing dialogue for games or other interactive role-playing exercises differs fundamentally from writing for a play or a film. In traditional dramatic genres, dialogue follows a single path determined by the writer. In a game, a player chooses from a menu of possible things to say or even writes his or her own part in the dialogue. Game developers must write branching dialogue, conceiving of multiple conversations the player characters and nonplayer characters might or might not pursue. Aurora offers no creative shortcuts for writing such dialogue; I must type each word that characters might say to each other. It does, however, provide a series of "wizards," step-by-step prompts that guide us through the complex processes of scripting nonplayer characters' conversations and actions and sketching the overall game narrative.

Unlike *Aristotle's Assassins, Revolution,* or most other role-playing games, Inisfallen, in its nascent form, does not compel players to participate in actions that drive the progress of the game; it lacks a narrative. My goal is simply to create a graphic-interactive environment for conveying historical information. Using Aurora, however, I might edit and expand in the game in any direction. With the script wizard, I can vary the reaction of nonplayer characters according to player character type, making our monks friendly to brother monks, generous to pilgrims, wary of merchants, and terrified of heathen Vikings. With the plot wizard, we can generate a participatory narrative like those in *Revolution,* one in which the player witnesses a raid on the monastery and sets out to recover a stolen relic. Finally, using the area wizard, I might expand Inisfallen to include distant, dangerous lands beyond the borders of the monastery, perhaps beyond the borders of Ireland itself, which the player must explore in search of the relic.

Skilled hacker-modders may rightly claim that Inisfallen is not really a mod, not a core alteration of the game itself, but rather a module, an assemblage of ready-made data files. I grant that I have not added new models, new sound effects, new animation, or new character actions. I have used only those elements provided by *Neverwinter Nights* and configured them using the toolkit included in the game. If we define modding more broadly as the use of commercial editing utilities to create unique configurations facilitating alternative, applied modes of play, then we may consider Inisfallen a rudimentary act of creative appropriation, a gesture toward liberation from a more deterministic interactive experience. Although unsophisticated compared to *Aristotle's Assassins* and *Revolution,* Inisfallen is nonetheless something not included in the software we purchased; it is something new.

Living Art

In talking about mods, media critics and game developers tend to draw comparisons to established art forms. Steven Levy declares, "You can create art and beauty on a computer," and John Carmack released *Doom*'s source code to hackers so that videogames might become a "new canvas" for users. Cook says that a mod is "living product," but more ideally, we might call modding a living art. In his opening address to MIT's "Computer and Videogames Come of Age" conference in 2000, Henry Jenkins of the MIT Program in Comparative Media Studies cited a book published in 1924 to assess the place of videogames in the larger culture. Gilbert Seldes's *The Seven Lively Arts,* Jenkins explained, calls attention to popular art forms such as comic strips, jazz, Broadway musicals, and cinema as "vital centers of American creative contribution to the twentieth century." Much like these "lively arts" of the 1920s, Jenkins claims, videogames are embedded in everyday life: "This is the art those citizens engage with. This is the art that everyday consumers are embracing; that speaks to them." Jenkins remains uncertain, however, about the future of videogames. He suggested they might follow the route of early cinema, graduate from the status of "parlor toy," and attain "social respectability, aesthetic complexity, and thematic maturity." On the other hand, they might follow the route of comic strips and remain marginalized as "a geek fan boy sort of phenomenon." Jenkins concluded that to sustain the cultural life of videogames, to expand their aesthetic and thematic limitations, "there has to be a space for innovation on the margins of the dominant industry. There has to be a space where the game equivalent of *The Blair Witch Project* gets made, and we have to worry collectively about how that space is going to emerge and what it is going to look like. It's not going to be a serious art form unless there is experimentation, innovation, some space with low barrier entries."[25]

Modding provides this "space for innovation on the margins of the dominant industry." Indeed, it has already begun to transform the dominant industry, to change the way professional developers make games and the way companies market them. The user-friendly mod tools distributed by companies now provide "low barrier entries" for amateur developers who might experiment, invent, and eventually produce the "game equivalent of *The Blair Witch Project*": a low-budget, clumsy, but stunningly original creation that forces us to reconsider the possibilities of the genre. Modding, in this sense, sustains videogames as a living art. In 2006, Obsidian released the Electron toolset with *Neverwinter Nights 2*. Electron represents the evolution of Aurora, allowing users to work with more sophisticated graphics and scripts, and also to import content developed with its predecessor, so that custom modules like Inisfallen may be updated and recreated for *Neverwinter Nights 2*. The partial compatibility of the two tools represents the continuing commitment of game companies to amateur developers as well as the potential for the creations of these amateurs to evolve with commercial videogames. Perhaps it also represents the beginning of the independent game design movement that theorists like Galloway and Jenkins eagerly anticipate, the growth of a hobby into an art form.

Citing the work of mod artists such as Anne-Marie Schleiner, Brody Condon, and Cory Arcangel, whose work I have surveyed previously, Galloway senses the growth of a "countergaming" movement that parallels the countercinema of French director Jean-Luc Godard. Film theorist Peter Wollen observes that Godard's films often break with "narrative transitivity" by disrupting "the emotional spell of the narrative and thus force the spectator . . . to reconcentrate and refocus his attention." Galloway argues that mods often foster this same kind of narrative and emotional disruption in games. "Indeed, artist-made game mods," he writes, "tend to conflict violently with the mainstream gaming industry's expectations for how games should be designed. They often defy the industry's design style point-for-point, with the goal of disrupting the intuitive flow of gameplay." Instead of mimesis, classically contoured narratives, and realistic graphics, the countergaming movement calls attention to the discontinuity between the game world and the real world with formal experimentation, nonrepresentational images, incoherent physics, and barriers between controller input and gameplay.[26]

Galloway believes that countergaming remains an "unrealized project," but he also suggests that it marks the beginning of a gaming movement controlled by individual users rather than design studios and producers.[27] In this sense, modding motivates a nascent independent gaming movement that will develop radically new design concepts and critical perspectives, just as independent film transformed classic Hollywood film. If games themselves have their precedent in the early cinema, as Jenkins suggests, then perhaps modding has it own precedent in another art form that emerged in the modernist era: the ready-made creations of the Dadaists and their heirs, the Surrealists and the Pop Artists, who appropriated, deconstructed, recombined, and subverted commercial images and objects. Marcel Duchamp, however, never received congratulations or sponsorship from the Mott Works plumbing company, whose urinal he introduced to perplexed gallery audiences; nor did James Rosenquist from *Life* magazine, whose glossy photographs he transformed into pointed mockeries of Cold War consumerism; nor did Andy Warhol from Campbell's Soup, whose product label he reproduced and multiplied on his canvas. As collaboration between commercial media and idiosyncratic self-expression, modding is unprecedented. It grants code-illiterate gamers the power to subvert culture like the first generation of modders, to disseminate culture like the developers at LGI and the Education Arcade, or to withdraw from culture altogether into our own narcissistic fantasies. The point is not that gamers should or should not do these things, but that they can.

❖ Notes ❖

Introduction

1. Dorie Turner, "Orangutans Play Video Games at Zoo Atlanta," *MSNBC,* April 11, 2007, www.msnbc.msn.com/id/18064686/.

2. Turner, "Orangutans Play Video Games at Zoo Atlanta."

3. Turner, "Orangutans Play Video Games at Zoo Atlanta."

4. Marc Prensky, *Digital Game-Based Learning* (New York: McGraw-Hill, 2001), 145, 147.

5. James Paul Gee, *What Video Games Have to Teach Us About Learning and Literacy* (New York: Palgrave Macmillan, 2003), 45, 205.

6. Steven Johnson, *Everything Bad Is Good for You: How Today's Popular Culture Is Actually Making Us Smarter* (New York: Riverhead, 2005), 45.

7. Johnson, *Everything Bad Is Good for You,* 24, 57–58.

8. Will Wright, "Dream Machines," *Wired* 14, April 2006, www.wired.com/wired/archive/14.04/wright.html.

9. Donna Haraway, "A Manifesto for Cyborgs: Science, Technology, and Socialist Feminism in the 1980s," in *The Norton Anthology of Theory and Criticism,* ed. Vincent B. Leitch, et al. (New York: Norton, 2001), 2270.

10. Haraway, "A Manifesto for Cyborgs: Science, Technology, and Socialist Feminism in the 1980s," 2270–2271.

11. Gee, *What Video Games Have to Teach Us About Learning and Literacy,* 199.

12. "Grand Theft Auto," *60 Minutes,* prod. Mitch Weitzner, narr. Ed Bradley, CBS, March 6, 2005.

13. Lindsey Tanner, "Is Video-Game Addiction a Mental Disorder?" *MSNBC,* June 22, 2007, www.msnbc.msn.com/id/19354827/.

14. Espen J. Aarseth, "The Dungeon and the Ivory Tower: Vive La Difference ou Liaison Dangereuse?" *Game Studies* 2, no. 1 (July 2002), www.gamestudies.org/0102/editorial.html.

Chapter 1

1. *The Poetic Edda*, trans. Carolyne Larrington (Oxford: Oxford University Press, 1996), 39–49.

2. Markku Eskelinen, "Towards Computer Game Studies," in *First Person: New Media as Story, Performance, and Game,* ed. Noah Wardrip-Fruin and Pat Harrigan (Cambridge: MIT Press, 2004), 36.

3. Henry Jenkins, "Game Design as Narrative Architecture," in *First Person: New Media as Story, Performance, and Game*, ed. Noah Wardrip-Fruin and Pat Harrigan (Cambridge: MIT Press, 2004), 119.

4. Steven Jacobs, "Writesizing," *Game Developer*, November 2004, 21.

5. Jacobs, "Writesizing," 33.

6. Nick Montfort, *Twisty Little Passages: An Approach to Interactive Fiction* (Cambridge: MIT Press, 2003), 4.

7. Gary Gygax, "On the Influence of J.R.R. Tolkien on the *D&D* and *AD&D* Games," *The Dragon* 95, March 1985, 12–13.

8. International Game Developers Association, *Foundations of Interactive Storytelling,* www.writing/InteractiveStorytelling.htm.

9. Aristotle, *Poetics,* trans. Malcolm Heath (New York: Penguin, 1996), 10–20.

10. John Gardner, *The Art of Fiction: Notes on Craft for Young Writers* (New York: Vintage, 1991), 56, 127–128.

11. Roland Barthes, "The Death of the Author," in *The Norton Anthology of Theory and Criticism,* ed. Vincent B. Leitch, et al. (New York: Norton, 2001), 1467–1468.

12. Espen J. Aarseth, *Cybertext: Perspectives on Ergodic Literature* (Baltimore: Johns Hopkins University Press, 1997), 1.

13. Aarseth, "Genre Trouble: Narrativism and the Art of Simulation," in *First Person: New Media as Story, Performance, and Game*, ed. Noah Wardrip-Fruin and Pat Harrigan (Cambridge: MIT Press, 2004), 51.

14. Gonzalo Frasca, "Simulation Versus Narrative: Introduction to Ludology," in *The Video Game Theory Reader,* ed. Mark J.P. Wolf and Bernard Perron (New York: Routledge, 2003), 232.

15. Frasca, "Simulation Versus Narrative," 230.

16. MIT Program in Comparative Media Studies, "The Future of Games," an unedited transcript from "Computer and Video Games Come of Age: A National Conference to Explore the Current State of an Emerging Entertainment Medium," February 11, 2000, http://web.mit.edu/cms/games/future.html.

17. Wonderland, "SXSW: Will Wright Keynote," South by Southwest Interactive Festival, 2007, Austin, TX, March 13, 2007, www.wonderlandblog.com/wonderland/2007/03/sxsw_will_wrigh.html.

18. Marie-Laure Ryan, *Narrative as Virtual Reality: Immersion and Interactivity in Literature and Electronic Media* (Baltimore: Johns Hopkins University Press, 2001), 12, 256.

19. International Game Developers Association, *Foundations of Interactive Storytelling.*

20. MIT Program in Comparative Media Studies, "Games as Interactive Storytelling," an unedited transcript from "Computer and Video Games Come of Age: A National Conference to Explore the Current State of an Emerging Entertainment Medium," February 11, 2000, http://web.mit.edu/cms/games/storytelling.html.

21. Ryan, *Narrative as Virtual Reality,* 246, 257.

22. Jenkins, "Game Design as Narrative Architecture," 128, 129.

23. Richard Bartle, *Designing Virtual Worlds* (Berkeley: New Riders, 2003), 269.

24. Janet H. Murray, *Hamlet on the Holodeck: The Future of Narrative in Cyberspace* (Cambridge: MIT Press, 1997), 83.

25. Aristotle, *Poetics,* 24.

26. Gardner, *The Art of Fiction,* 45, 46.

27. Steve Ince, *Writing for Video Games* (London: A.C. Black, 2006), 60, 62.

28. MIT Program in Comparative Media Studies, "Games as Interactive Storytelling."

29. Steve Theodore, "Uncanny Valley," *Game Developer*, December 2004, 43, 44.

30. MIT Program in Comparative Media Studies, "Games as Interactive Storytelling."

31. Montfort, *Twisty Little Passages,* 151.

32. Ince, *Writing for Video Games,* 64.

33. MIT Program in Comparative Media Studies, "The Future of Games."

34. Henry Jenkins, "Games, the New Lively Art," in *Handbook of Computer Game Studies,* ed. Jeffrey Goldstein and Joost Raessens (Cambridge: MIT Press, 2005), 175–192.

Chapter 2

1. Annenberg Media, "Modernist Portraits," *American Passages: A Literary Survey,* www.learner.org/amerpass/unit11/context_activ-4.html.

2. Virginia Woolf, "Mr. Bennett and Mrs. Brown," in *Collected Essays,* vol. 1 (New York: Harcourt, 1969), 320.

3. Bryan Ochalla, "Are Games Art? (Here We Go Again . . .)," *Gamasutra,* March 16, 2007, http://gamasutra.com/features/20070316/ochalla_01.shtml.

4. Jack Kroll, "'Emotional Engine'? I Don't Think So," *Newsweek,* March 6, 2000, 64.

5. Henry Jenkins, "Art Form for the Digital Age," *Technology Review,* September 2000, www.technologyreview.com/InfoTech/wtr_12189,294,p1.html.

6. Roger Ebert, "Why Did the Chicken Cross the Genders?" *rogerebert.com,* November 27, 2005, http://rogerebert.suntimes.com/apps/pbcs.dll/article?AID=/20051127/ANSWERMAN/511270302.

7. Roger Ebert, "Games vs. Art: Ebert vs. Barker," *rogerebert.com,* July 21, 2007, http://rogerebert.suntimes.com/apps/pbcs.dll/article?AID=/20070721/COMMENTARY/70721001.

8. Ebert, "Why Did the Chicken Cross the Genders?"

9. Ebert, "Why Did the Chicken Cross the Genders?"

10. Steven Poole, "Virtual Aesthetics," *Modern Painters* 14, no. 2 (2001): 76.

11. Henry Jenkins, "Games, the New Lively Art," in *Handbook of Computer Game Studies,* ed. Jeffrey Goldstein and Joost Raessens (Cambridge: MIT Press, 2005), 175.

12. Peter Lunenfeld, "Game Boy," *Art & Text* 68 (2000), 38.

13. Steven Poole, *Trigger Happy: Videogames and the Entertainment Revolution* (New York: Arcade, 2004), 11.

14. Mark J.P. Wolf, "Abstraction in the Video Game," in *The Video Game Theory Reader,* ed. Mark J.P. Wolf and Bernard Perron (New York: Routledge, 2003), 54.

15. Warren Robinett, "Foreword," in *The Video Game Theory Reader,* ed. Mark J.P. Wolf and Bernard Perron (New York: Routledge, 2003), xiii.

16. David Heyward, *Videogame Aesthetics: The Future!* http://modetwo.net/users/nachimir/vga/.

17. Aristotle, *Poetics,* trans. Malcolm Heath (New York: Penguin, 1996), 6.

18. Wolf, "Abstraction in the Video Game," 60.

19. Wolf, "Abstraction in the Video Game," 47.

20. Rochelle Slovin, "Hot Circuits: Reflections on the 1989 Video Game Exhibition of the American Museum of the Moving Image," in *The Medium of the Video Game,* ed. Mark J.P. Wolf (Austin: University of Texas Press, 2002), 139.

21. Alexander Galloway, *Gaming: Essays on Algorithmic Culture* (Minneapolis: University of Minnesota Press, 2006), 2.

22. Poole, "Virtual Aesthetics," 77.

23. Marie-Laure Ryan, *Narrative as Virtual Reality: Immersion and Interactivity in Literature and Electronic Media* (Baltimore: Johns Hopkins University Press, 2001), 3.

24. Janet H. Murray, *Hamlet on the Holodeck: The Future of Narrative in Cyberspace* (Cambridge: MIT Press, 1997), 97–98.

25. Ryan, *Narrative as Virtual Reality,* 67.

26. Ryan, *Narrative as Virtual Reality,* 21.

27. Poole, *Trigger Happy*, 121.

28. Alison McMahan, "Immersion, Engagement, and Presence: A Method for Analyzing 3-D Video Games," in *The Video Game Theory Reader*, ed. Mark J.P. Wolf and Bernard Perron (New York: Routledge, 2003), 71.

29. James Newman, *Videogames* (New York: Routledge, 2004), 108.

30. Poole, "Virtual Aesthetics," 76.

31. Henry Jenkins, "'Complete Freedom of Movement': Video Games as Gendered Play Spaces," in *From Barbie to Mortal Kombat: Gender and Computer Games,* ed. Justine Cassell and Henry Jenkins (Cambridge: MIT Press, 1998), 265.

32. Ryan, *Narrative as Virtual Reality*, 122.

33. Ryan, *Narrative as Virtual Reality*, 123.

34. Slovin, "Hot Circuits," 137.

35. Barbican Gallery, *Game On—Tour*, www.barbican.org.uk/artgallery/event-detail. asp?ID=4964.

36. William Martin, "Game On: Videogames, Popular Culture, and the New Aestheticism of Interactivity," *Art Criticism* 20, no. 1 (2005), 92.

37. Lunenfeld, "Game Boy," 38.

38. Martin, "Game On," 93.

39. Poole, "Virtual Aesthetics," 77.

40. Ellen Sandor and Janine Fron, "The Future of Video Games as an Art: On the Art of Playing with Shadows," *Playing by the Rules: The Cultural Policy Challenges of Video Games,* http://culturalpolicy.uchicago.edu/conf2001/papers/sandor.html.

41. Lunenfeld, "Game Boy," 37.

42. Robinett, "Foreword," viii–ix.

43. Jenkins, "Games, the New Lively Art," 186.

Chapter 3

1. Roger Ebert, "*E.T.: The Extra-Terrestrial,*" rogerebert.com, March 22, 2002, http://rogerebert. suntimes.com/apps/pbcs.dll/article?AID=/20020322/REVIEWS/203220304/1023.

2. Dan Levy, "Lucas' Presidio premiere," *San Francisco Chronicle*, June 26, 2005, www.sfgate.com/cgi-bin/article.cgi?f=/c/a/2005/06/26/BAGTQDF4RU1.DTL.

3. Lucasfilm, Ltd., "Letterman Digital Arts Center: A New Vision for the Digital Arts," June 24, 2005, www.lucasfilm.com/press/presidiopreview/index.html?page=2.

4. Eric-Jon Rössel Waugh, "Worlds Are Colliding!: The Convergence of Film and Games," *Gamasutra*, December 12, 2005, www.gamasutra.com/features/20051212/waugh_01.shtml.

5. Lucasfilm, Ltd. "Letterman Digital Arts Center: A New Vision for the Digital Arts."

6. George Lucas, "Future of Entertainment," *Hollywood Reporter*, September 13, 2005, www.hollywoodreporter.com/hr/search/article_display.jsp?vnu_content_id=1001096310.

7. WNYC New York Public Radio, "Joystick Nation," *On the Media*, December 19, 2003, www.onthemedia.org/yore/transcripts/transcripts_121903_joystick.html.

8. Bryan Ochalla, "Are Games Art? (Here We Go Again . . .), *Gamasutra*, March 16, 2007, http://gamasutra.com/features/20070316/ochalla_01.shtml.

9. "The New Force at Lucasfilm," *BusinessWeek*, March 27, 2006, www.businessweek. com/innovate/content/mar2006/id20060327_719255.htm.

10. "The New Force at Lucasfilm."

11. Lucas, "Future of Entertainment."

12. Lucas, "Future of Entertainment."

13. Henry Jenkins, *Convergence Culture: Where Old and New Media Collide* (New York: New York University Press, 2006), 94–96, 114.

14. Tom McNamara, "GDC 2004: Warren Spector Talks Game Narrative," *IGN.com*, March 26, 2004, http://pc.ign.com/articles/502/502382p1.html.

15. "The New Force at Lucasfilm."

16. Jenkins, *Convergence Culture,* 107.

17. Henry Jenkins, "Games, the New Lively Art," in *Handbook of Computer Game Studies,* ed. Jeffrey Goldstein and Joost Raessens (Cambridge: MIT Press, 2005), 175–192.

18. Graham Leggat, "Chip Off the Old Block," *Film Comment* 40 (2004), 29.

19. Ryan Davis, review of *The Movies, Gamespot,* November 8, 2005, www.gamespot.com/pc/strategy/movies/review.html?om_act=convert&om_clk=gssummary&tag=summary%3Breview&page=2.

20. Steve Ince, *Writing for Video Games* (London: A.C. Black, 2006), 54.

21. W. Haden Blackman, "Collaborative Connections: Teamwork Unleashed," May 1, 2007, www.lucasarts.com/games/theforceunleashed/#/diary/.

22. Leggat, "Chip Off the Old Block," 29.

23. Mark J.P. Wolf, "Inventing Space: Toward a Taxonomy of On- and Off-Screen Space in Video Games," *Film Quarterly* 51, no. 1 (1997), 11–12.

24. Wolf, "Inventing Space," 20.

25. Wolf, "Inventing Space," 22.

26. Alexander Galloway, *Gaming: Essays on Algorithmic Culture* (Minneapolis: University of Minnesota Press, 2006), 63–64.

27. MIT Program in Comparative and Media Studies, *Computer and Video Games Come of Age,* "The Future of Games," http://web.mit.edu/cms/games/future.html.

28. Galloway, *Gaming,* 40.

29. Galloway, *Gaming,* 56, 59, 63.

30. Laura M. Holson, "Out of Hollywood, Rising Fascination with Video Games," *New York Times,* April 10, 2004, www.nytimes.com/2004/04/10/technology/10GAME.html?ex=1396929600&en=871fe925a859ddc9&ei=5007&partner=USERLAND.

31. Galloway, *Gaming,* 67.

32. David Thomson, "Zap Happy: World War II Revisited," *Sight & Sound* 11, no. 7 (2001), 35.

33. Thomson, "Zap Happy," 35.

34. Steven Poole, *Trigger Happy: Videogames and the Entertainment Revolution* (New York: Arcade, 2004), 153.

35. Kate Stables, "Run Lara Run," *Sight & Sound* 11, no. 8 (2001), 19.

36. Anthony Lane, "Creating Monsters," *The New Yorker,* May 24, 2004, 97.

Chapter 4

1. Mary Beth Schneider, "Bayh vs. Video Game Violence," *The Indianapolis Star,* December 2, 2005, A1.

2. Gonzalo Frasca, "Videogames of the Oppressed: Critical Thinking, Education, Tolerance, and Other Trivial Issues," in *First Person: New Media as Story, Performance, and Game,* ed. Noah Wardrip-Fruin and Pat Harrigan (Cambridge: MIT Press, 2004), 85, 88.

3. David B. Goroff, "The First Amendment Side Effects of Curing Pac-Man Fever," *Columbia Law Review* 84, no. 3 (April 1984), 751, 753.

4. Goroff, "The First Amendment Side Effects of Curing Pac-Man Fever," 750.

5. United States House of Representatives, *Violence in Videogames: Hearing Before the Subcommittee on Telecommunications and Finance,* June 30, 1994 (Washington, DC: GPO, 1994), 2.

6. United States House of Representatives, *Violence in Videogames,* 14.

7. Cyn Shephed, "AOL User Profiles," *4-20: A Columbine Site,* www.acolumbinesite.com/profiles2.html.

8. United States Senate, *The Impact of Interactive Violence on Children: Hearing Before the Committee on Commerce, Science, and Transportation,* March 21, 2000 (Washington, DC: GPO, 2003), 33.

9. United States Senate, *The Impact of Interactive Violence on Children,* 13.

10. United States Senate, *Marketing Violence to Children: Hearing Before the Committee on Commerce, Science, and Transportation,* September 13, 2000 (Washington, DC: GPO, 2003), 30.

11. United States Senate, *Marketing Violence to Children,* 70.

12. Hillary Rodham Clinton, "Senators Clinton, Lieberman Announce Federal Legislation to Protect Children from Inappropriate Video Games," Statements & Releases, November 29, 2005, http://clinton.senate.gov/news/statements/details.cfm?id=249368&&.

13. GovTrack.us, Statements on Introduced Bills and Resolutions—The United States Senate, Section 60, December 16, 2005, www.govtrack.us/congress/record.xpd?id=109-s20051216-60&bill=s109-2126.

14. Plato, *Gorgias,* trans. Chris Emlyn-Jones and Walter Hamilton (New York: Penguin, 2004), 23.

15. Aristotle, *The Art of Rhetoric,* trans. Hugh Lawson-Tancred (New York: Penguin, 1991), 66–70.

16. United States Senate, *The Impact of Interactive Violence on Children,* 40.

17. Ian Bogost and Gonzalo Frasca, "Videogames Go to Washington: The Story Behind The Howard Dean for Iowa Game," in *Second Person: Role-Playing and Story in Games and Playable Media,* ed. Noah Wardrip-Fruin and Pat Harrigan (Cambridge: MIT Press, 2007), 237.

18. Steven Johnson, "SimCandidate: Videogames Simulate Sports, Business, and War. Why Not Politics?" *Slate,* December 16, 2003, http://slate.msn.com/id/2092688/.

19. Gregg Sparks, "Political Video Game Simulates 2004 Election," Wisconsin Technology Network, March 24, 2004, http://wistechnology.com/article.php?id=695.

20. Ian Bogost and Gerard LaFond, *Persuasive Games,* www.persuasivegames.com/.

21. Bogost and Frasca, "Videogames Go to Washington," 243.

22. Bogost and Frasca, "Videogames Go to Washington," 233.

23. Bogost and Frasca, "Videogames Go to Washington," 233.

24. Ian Bogost, "Frame and Metaphor in Political Games," Proceedings of the DiGRA 2005 Conference: *Changing Views—Worlds in Play,* www.digra.org/dl/db/06276.36533.pdf.

25. Michael Erard, "In These Games, the Points Are All Political," *New York Times,* July 1, 2004, http://query.nytimes.com/gst/fullpage.html?sec=technology&res=9C01E4DD1338F932A35754C0A9629C8B63.

26. Bogost and Frasca, "Videogames Go to Washington," 244.

27. Bogost and Frasca, "Videogames Go to Washington," 233.

28. Clark Boyd, "Darfur Activism Meets Video Gaming," *BBC News,* July 6, 2006, http://news.bbc.co.uk/2/hi/technology/5153694.stm.

29. Edward S. Herman and Noam Chomsky, *Manufacturing Consent: The Political Economy of the Mass Media* (New York: Pantheon, 1988), 2, 30–31.

30. Tim Lenoir and Henry Lowood, "Theaters of War: The Military-Entertainment Complex," www.stanford.edu/class/sts145/Library/Lenoir-Lowood_TheatersOfWar.pdf.

31. Lenoir and Lowood, "Theaters of War."

32. United States Army, *America's Army,* "Parents Info," www.americasarmy.com/support/faqs.php?t=9&z=59#59.

33. United States Army, *America's Army,* "Parents Info."

34. The White House, "President Reiterates Goal on Homeownership," June 18, 2002, www.whitehouse.gov/news/releases/2002/06/20020618-1.html.

35. Alexander Galloway, "Social Realism in Gaming," *Game Studies* 4, no. 1 (November 2004), www.gamestudies.org/0401/galloway/.

36. "Hezbollah's New Computer Game," *WorldNetDaily*, March 3, 2003, www.world-netdaily.com/news/article.asp?ARTICLE_ID=31323.

37. Jose Antonio Vargas, "Way Radical, Dude," *Washington Post*, October 9, 2006, www.washingtonpost.com/wp-dyn/content/article/2006/10/08/AR2006100800931.html.

38. Afkar Media, www.afkarmedia.com/en/index.htm.

39. Vargas, "Way Radical, Dude."

40. Galloway, "Social Realism in Gaming."

41. United States House of Representatives, *Violence in Videogames*, 24.

42. United States Senate, *The Impact of Interactive Violence on Children*, 2, 29, 37.

43. Boyd, "Darfur Activism Meets Video Gaming."

44. Ian Bogost, *Persuasive Games: The Expressive Power of Videogames* (Cambridge: MIT Press, 2007).

45. Bob Colayco, review of *Ghost Recon: Advanced Warfighter*, GameSpot, March 9, 2006, www.gamespot.com/xbox360/action/tomclancysghostrecon3/review.html?om_act=convert&om_clk=gssummary&tag=summary;review.

46. Bob Colayco, review of *Ghost Recon: Advanced Warfighter.*

47. Review of *Ghost Recon: Advanced Warfighter*, Groovalicious Games, June 22, 2006, www.groovgames.com/display.cfm?id=321.

Chapter 5

1. Plato, *The Republic,* trans. Desmond Lee (New York: Penguin, 1987), 375.

2. Thomas More, *Utopia,* trans. Paul Turner (New York: Penguin, 1965), 76.

3. Miguel Sicart, "The Ethics of Computer Game Design," *Proceedings of the DiGRA 2005 Conference: Changing Views—Worlds in Play,* www.digra.org/dl/db/06276.55524.pdf.

4. Sara Reeder, "Computer Game Ethics," *Compute!* 137, January 1992, 100.

5. Gordana Dodig-Crnkovic and Thomas Larsson, "Game Ethics—Homo Ludens as a Computer Game Designer and Consumer," *International Review of Information Ethics* 4 (2005), 19.

6. Jill Lepore, "The Meaning of Life," *New Yorker*, May 21, 2007, 40.

7. Lepore, "The Meaning of Life," 41.

8. Sicart, "The Ethics of Computer Game Design."

9. MIT Program in Comparative Media Studies, "Games as Interactive Storytelling," an unedited transcript from "Computer and Video Games Come of Age: A National Conference to Explore the Current State of an Emerging Entertainment Medium," February 11, 2000, http://web.mit.edu/cms/games/storytelling.html.

10. Craig A. Lindley, "The Semiotics of Time Structure in Ludic Space as a Foundation for Analysis and Design," *Game Studies* 5, no. 1 (2005), www.gamestudies.org/0501/lindley/.

11. Dean Takahashi, "The Ethics of Game Design," *Game Developer*, December 2004, 19.

12. Takahashi, "The Ethics of Game Design," 16, 19.

13. MIT Program in Comparative Media Studies, "The Future of Games," an unedited transcript from "Computer and Video Games Come of Age: A National Conference to Explore the Current State of an Emerging Entertainment Medium," February 11, 2000, http://web.mit.edu/cms/games/future.html.

14. Greg M. Smith, "Computer Games Have Words, Too: Dialogue Conventions in Final Fantasy VII," *Game Studies* 2, no. 2 (2002), www.gamestudies.org/0202/smith/.

15. "The Values in Video Games," *Religion and Ethics Newsweekly*, May 30, 2003, www.pbs.org/wnet/religionandethics/week639/cover.html.

16. Susan Smith Nash, "The Ethics of Video Game-Based Simulation," *E-Learning Queen*, August 25, 2004, http://elearnqueen.blogspot.com/2004_08_25_archive.html.

17. Ren Reynolds, "Playing a 'Good' Game: A Philosophical Approach to Understanding the Morality of Games," *International Game Developers Association*, www.igda.org/articles/rreynolds_ethics.php.

18. Sicart, "The Ethics of Computer Game Design."

19. Dodig-Crnkovic and Larsson, "Game Ethics," 22.

20. Reynolds, "Playing a 'Good' Game."

21. Markkula Center for Applied Ethics, "Video Gaming: Playing with Ethics?" November, 29, 2005, www.scu.edu/ethics/publications/submitted/video-game-panel.html.

22. MIT Program in Comparative Media Studies, "Opening Remarks," an unedited transcript from "Computer and Video Games Come of Age: A National Conference to Explore the Current State of an Emerging Entertainment Medium," February 11, 2000, http://web.mit.edu/cms/games/storytelling.html.

23. Takahashi, "The Ethics of Game Design," 16.

24. Lepore, "The Meaning of Life," 42.

25. Johan Huizinga, *Homo Ludens: A Study of the Play Element in Culture* (Boston: Beacon, 1955), 10.

26. Roger Caillois, *Man, Play, and Games*, trans. Meyer Barash (Urbana: University of Illinois Press, 2001), 10.

27. Markkula Center for Applied Ethics, "Video Gaming: Playing with Ethics?"

28. Huizinga, *Homo Ludens*, 210.

29. Luke 18:16, *The Bible* (King James Version).

Chapter 6

1. "Police Positive in Shooting Probe," *BBC News,* September 11, 2006, http://news.bbc.co.uk/2/hi/uk_news/england/manchester/5332918.stm.

2. "Cathedral Row over Video War Game," *BBC News,* June 9, 2007, http://news.bbc.co.uk/2/hi/uk_news/england/manchester/6736809.stm.

3. "Church Wants Cash for 'Sick' Game," *CNN.com,* June 11, 2007, www.cnn.com/2007/TECH/fun.games/06/11/sony.manchester/index.html.

4. "Sony Apologises over Violent Game," *BBC News,* June 15, 2007, http://news.bbc.co.uk/2/hi/uk_news/england/manchester/6758381.stm.

5. GamePolitics.com, "Church of England Condemns Sony over Cathedral Setting in *Resistance: Fall of Man*," http://gamepolitics.com/2007/06/10/coe-bashes-sony-over-manchester-cathedral-setting-in-resistance-fall-of-man/.

6. Johan Huizinga, *Homo Ludens: A Study of the Play Element in Culture* (Boston: Beacon, 1955), 18–27.

7. Plato, *Laws*, trans. Trevor J. Saunders (New York: Penguin, 2004), 43, 246.

8. Augustine, *Confessions,* trans. R.S. Pine-Coffin (New York: Penguin, 1961), 31.

9. Augustine, *Confessions,* 122–123.

10. Huizinga, *Homo Ludens,* 3, 4, 20.

11. Huizinga, *Homo Ludens,* 18, 16, 15.

12. Chris Morris, "The Greatest Story Never Played," *CNNMoney.com,* July 6,

2005, http://money.cnn.com/2005/07/06/commentary/game_over/column_gaming/index.htm.

13. Troy Lyndon, "The World Is Primed for Christian Video Games," *GameDaily BIZ,* November 28, 2006, http://biz.gamedaily.com/industry/myturn/?id=14572.

14. Left Behind Games, "About Left Behind: Eternal Forces, The PC Game—Mainstream Media FAQ," www.leftbehindgames.com/pages/faq.htm.

15. Tom Loftus, "God in the Console: Looking for Religion in Video Games," *MSNBC,* August 20, 2003, www.msnbc.msn.com/id/3078392/.

16. Jeremy Lemer, "Religion Goes Digital in Faith-Based Computer Games," *Columbia News Service,* March 1, 2005, http://jscms.jrn.columbia.edu/cns/2005-03-01/lemer-religiousgames/.

17. "Video Game Battles Satan," *WorldNetDaily,* June 15, 2006, http://worldnetdaily.com/news/article.asp?ARTICLE_ID=50658.

18. Left Behind Games, "About Left Behind: Eternal Forces, The PC Game—Mainstream Media FAQ."

19. Richard Allen Greene, "Christian Video Game Draws Anger," *BBC News,* December 14, 2006, http://news.bbc.co.uk/2/hi/technology/6178055.stm.

20. "Video Game Battles Satan."

21. "Video Game Battles Satan."

22. Left Behind Games, "About Left Behind: Eternal Forces, The PC Game—Mainstream Media FAQ."

23. Clive Thompson, "Going into Godmode in Left Behind," *Wired,* November 6, 2006, www.wired.com/gaming/gamingreviews/commentary/games/2006/11/72071.

24. Thompson, "Going into Godmode in Left Behind."

25. Thompson, "Going into Godmode in Left Behind."

26. *Catechism of the Catholic Church* (New York: Doubleday, 1995), 570.

27. David Waldron, "Role-Playing Games and the Christian Right: Community Formation in Response to a Moral Panic," *Journal of Religion and Popular Culture* 10 (Spring 2005): www.usask.ca/relst/jrpc/art9-roleplaying.html.

28. Ioan Sambeteanu, review of *Elder Scrolls IV: Oblivion, Softpedia,* April 14, 2006, www.softpedia.com/reviews/games/pc/The-Elder-Scrolls-IV-Oblivion-Review-21532.shtml.

29. BBC, *Simon Schama's Power of Art,* "Van Gogh," www.bbc.co.uk/arts/powerofart/vangogh.shtml.

30. Morris, "The Greatest Story Never Played."

31. Cathy Lynn Grossman, "Faithful Build a Second Life for Religion Online," *USA Today,* April 1, 2007, www.usatoday.com/tech/gaming/2007-04-01-second-life-religion_N.htm.

32. Grossman, "Faithful Build a Second Life for Religion Online."

33. Shona Crabtree, "Finding Religion in Second Life's Virtual Universe," *Washington Post.com,* June 16, 2007, www.washingtonpost.com/wp-dyn/content/article/2007/06/15/AR2007061501902.html.

34. Crabtree, "Finding Religion in Second Life's Virtual Universe."

35. Grossman, "Faithful Build a Second Life for Religion Online."

36. Crabtree, "Finding Religion in Second Life's Virtual Universe."

37. Crabtree, "Finding Religion in Second Life's Virtual Universe."

38. Crabtree, "Finding Religion in Second Life's Virtual Universe."

39. Grossman, "Faithful Build a Second Life for Religion Online."

40. Grossman, "Faithful Build a Second Life for Religion Online."

41. Grossman, "Faithful Build a Second Life for Religion Online."

42. Jennifer Veale, "Where Playing Video Games *Is* a Life," *Time,* May 14, 2007, www.time.com/time/world/article/0,8599,1620799,00.html.

43. Lindsey Tanner, "Is Video-Game Addiction a Mental Disorder?" *MSNBC,* June 22, 2007, www.msnbc.msn.com/id/19354827/.

44. Michael Heim, "Alternate World Disorder," *Mediamatic* 8, no. 4 (1996), 3.

45. Marie-Laure Ryan, *Narrative as Virtual Reality: Immersion and Interactivity in Literature and Electronic Media* (Baltimore: Johns Hopkins University Press, 2001), 99.

Chapter 7

1. "Marge vs. the Monorail," *The Simpsons.* Episode no. 71, Fox Network, January 14, 1993.

2. Richard J. Evans, "Telling It Like It Wasn't," *Historically Speaking: The Bulletin of the Historical Society* 5, no. 4 (March 2004), www.bu.edu/historic/hs/march04.htm.

3. William H. McNeill, "Counterfactuals and the Historical Imagination," *Historically Speaking: The Bulletin of the Historical Society* 5, no. 4 (March 2004), www.bu.edu/historic/hs/march04.htm.

4. Allan Megill, "The New Counterfactualists," *Historically Speaking: The Bulletin of the Historical Society* 5, no. 4 (March 2004), www.bu.edu/historic/hs/march04.htm.

5. Seymour Papert, "Does Easy Do It? Children, Games, and Learning," *Game Developer,* June 1998, 88.

6. Steven Johnson, *Everything Bad Is Good for You: How Today's Popular Culture Is Actually Making Us Smarter* (New York: Riverhead, 2005).

7. Papert, "Does Easy Do It? Children, Games, and Learning."

8. Kurt Squire, *Replaying History: Learning World History Through Playing Civilization III,* "Abstract," http://website.education.wisc.edu/kdsquire/dissertation.html.

9. Muzzy Lane, *Education,* "Why Games?" www.muzzylane.com/education/.

10. The Education Arcade, *About the Education Arcade,* www.educationarcade.org/about.

11. The Education Arcade, *Revolution,* www.educationarcade.org/revolution.

12. The Education Arcade, *Revolution,* "Mechanics," www.educationarcade.org/node/119.

13. The Education Arcade, *Revolution,* "Student Testing," www.educationarcade.org/revolution/testing.

14. The Education Arcade, *Revolution,* "Summary of Findings," www.educationarcade.org/revolution/testing/findings.

15. The Education Arcade, *Revolution,* "Summary of Findings."

16. The Education Arcade, *Revolution,* "Summary of Findings."

17. James Paul Gee, *What Video Games Have to Teach Us About Learning and Literacy* (New York: Palgrave Macmillan, 2003), 199.

18. The Education Arcade, *Revolution,* "Summary of Findings."

19. Bernard Dy, review of *Brothers in Arms: The Road to Hill 30, Military History,* October 2005, 69.

20. The Education Arcade, *Revolution.*

21. Muzzy Lane, *Making History: The Calm and the Storm,* "Assessment and Discussion Questions," www.making-history.com/downloads/Making_History/The_Calm_and_the_Storm/assess_discuss_questions.pdf

22. Muzzy Lane, *Making History: The Calm and the Storm,* "FAQ: The Calm and the Storm," www.making-history.com/content_packs/calm/faq.php#a5.

23. Jason Ocampo, review of *Rome: Total War, GameSpot,* September 23, 2004, www.gamespot.com/pc/strategy/rometotalwar/review.html.

24. Bernard Dy, review of *Medieval: Total War, Military History,* June 2003, 68.

25. Alexander Galloway, *Gaming: Essays on Algorithmic Culture* (Minneapolis: University of Minnesota Press, 2006), 90–91.

26. Clive Thompson, "Why a Famous Counterfactual Historian Loves Making History with Games." *Wired,* May 21, 2007, www.wired.com/gaming/virtualworlds/commentary/games/2007/05/gamefrontiers_0521.

Chapter 8

1. Edward Castronova, *Synthetic Worlds: The Business and Culture of Online Games* (Chicago: Chicago University Press, 2006), 2.

2. Castronova, *Synthetic Worlds,* 1–2, 55, 59.

3. T.L. Taylor, *Play Between Worlds: Exploring Online Game Culture* (Cambridge: MIT Press, 2006), 30–31, 53.

4. Florence Chee, Marcelo Vieta, and Richard Smith, "Online Gaming and the Interactional Self: Identity Interplay in Situated Practice," in *Gaming as Culture: Essays on Reality, Identity, and Experience in Fantasy Games,* ed. J. Patrick Williams, Sean Q. Hendricks, and W. Keith Winkler (Jefferson, NC: McFarland, 2006), 161, 169.

5. Castronova, *Synthetic Worlds,* 147.

6. Sherry Turkle, *Life on the Screen: Identity in the Age of the Internet* (New York: Simon and Schuster, 1995).

7. Miroslaw Filiciak, "Hyperidentities: Postmodern Identity Patterns in Massively-Multiplayer Online Role-Playing Games," in *The Video Game Theory Reader*, ed. Mark J.P. Wolf and Bernard Perron (New York: Routledge, 2003), 88.

8. Taylor, *Play Between Worlds,* 28.

9. Richard Bartle, *Designing Virtual Worlds* (Berkeley: New Riders, 2003), 130.

10. Castronova, *Synthetic Worlds,* 73.

11. Filiciak, "Hyperidentities," 90–91, 100.

12. Castronova, *Synthetic Worlds,* 48.

13. Castronova, *Synthetic Worlds,* 33, 45.

14. Taylor, *Play Between Worlds,* 13, 12.

15. James Newman, "The Myth of the Ergodic Videogame: Some Thoughts on Player-Character Relationships in Videogames," *Game Studies* 2, no. 1 (July 2002), www.gamestudies.org/0102/newman/.

16. Bartle, *Designing Virtual Worlds,* 130.

17. Castronova, *Synthetic Worlds,* 72.

18. Turkle, *Life on the Screen,* 178.

19. Bob Rehak, "Playing at Being: Psychoanalysis and the Avatar," in *The Video Game Theory Reader*, ed. Mark J.P. Wolf and Bernard Perron (New York: Routledge, 2003), 123.

20. Filiciak, "Hyperidentities," 92.

21. Castronova, *Synthetic Worlds,* 25, 77–78.

22. Roger Caillois, *Man, Play, and Games,* trans. Meyer Barash (Urbana: University of Illinois Press, 2001), 87–88.

23. Taylor, *Play Between Worlds,* 117–118.

24. Taylor, *Play Between Worlds,* 111–112.

25. Mia Consalvo, "Hot Dates and Fairy-Tale Romances: Studying Sexuality in Video Games," in *The Video Game Theory Reader*, ed. Mark J.P. Wolf and Bernard Perron (New York: Routledge, 2003), 190.

26. Taylor, *Play Between Worlds*, 98.

27. Henry Jenkins, "'Complete Freedom of Movement': Video Games as Gendered Play Spaces," in *From Barbie to Mortal Kombat: Gender and Computer Games*, ed. Justine Cassell and Henry Jenkins (Cambridge: MIT Press, 1998), 291.

28. Kenneth J. Gergen, *The Saturated Self: Dilemmas of Identity in Contemporary Life* (New York: Basic Books, 1991), 7.

29. Gergen, *The Saturated Self*, 16.

30. Tari Lin Fanderclai, "MUDs in Education: New Environments, New Pedagogies," *Computer-Mediated Communication Magazine* 2, no. 1 (January 1, 1995), 8.

31. Fanderclai, "MUDs in Education," 8.

32. Fanderclai, "MUDs in Education," 8.

33. Daniel Terdiman, "Campus Life Comes to Second Life," *Wired*, September 24, 2004, www.wired.com/gaming/gamingreviews/news/2004/09/65052.

34. Terdiman, "Campus Life Comes to Second Life."

35. Castronova, *Synthetic Worlds*, 110–111.

36. Synthetic Worlds Initiative, *Arden: The World of William Shakespeare FAQ Version 1.2*, http://swi.indiana.edu/ardenfaq.pdf.

37. Synthetic Worlds Initiative, *Arden: The World of William Shakespeare FAQ Version 1.2*.

38. Castronova, *Synthetic Worlds*, 252–253.

39. Elizabeth Kolbert, "Pimps and Dragons; How an Online World Survived a Social Breakdown," *New Yorker*, May 28, 2001, 88.

40. Jack M. Balkin, "Virtual Liberty: Freedom to Design and Freedom to Play in Virtual Worlds," *Virginia Law Review* 90, no. 8 (December 2004), 2047, 2090.

41. F. Gregory Lastowka and Dan Hunter, "The Laws of Virtual Worlds," *California Law Review* 92, no. 1 (January 2004), 73.

42. Balkin, "Virtual Liberty," 2045, 2046.

43. Eric Hayes, *Playing It Safe: Avoiding Gaming Risks*, www.us-cert.gov/reading_room/gaming.pdf.

44. Balkin, "Virtual Liberty," 2071.

45. Julian Dibbell, *Play Money: Or, How I Quit My Day Job and Made Millions Selling Virtual Loot* (New York: Basic Books, 2006), 15, 16.

46. Dibbell, *Play Money*, 16.

47. Raph Koster, *Raph Koster's Website*, "Declaring the Rights of Players," www.raphkoster.com/gaming/playerrights.shtml.

48. Koster, *Raph Koster's Website*.

49. Koster, *Raph Koster's Website*.

50. Koster, *Raph Koster's Website*.

51. Human Constitutional Rights Documents, "Declaration of the Rights of Man and of the Citizen," www.hrcr.org/docs/frenchdec.html.

52. Taylor, *Play Between Worlds*, 38.

53. Taylor, *Play Between Worlds*, 36.

54. Dibbell, *Play Money*, 68.

Chapter 9

1. Alexander Galloway, *Gaming: Essays on Algorithmic Culture* (Minneapolis: University of Minnesota Press, 2006), 107–108.

2. "Quake Blows Away Design Problems," *BBC News,* October 21, 2000, http://news.bbc.co.uk/1/hi/education/982346.stm.

3. Mark Brayfield, "It's a Mod, Mod Game World," *Computer Bits* 14, no. 2 (February 2004): www.computerbits.com/archive/2004/0200/gamemods.html.

4. Steven Levy, *Hackers: Heroes of the Computer Revolution,* www.echonyc.com/~steven/hackers.html.

5. David Kushner, "The Mod Squad," *Popular Science,* July 2002, www.popsci.com/popsci/computerselec/0678d4d03cb84010vgnvcm1000004eecbccdrcrd.html.

6. MIT Program in Comparative Media Studies, "Opening Remarks," an unedited transcript from "Computer and Video Games Come of Age: A National Conference to Explore the Current State of an Emerging Entertainment Medium," February 11, 2000, http://web.mit.edu/cms/games/opening.html.

7. Kushner, "The Mod Squad."

8. Talmadge Wright, Eric Boria, and Paul Breidenbach, "Creative Player Actions in FPS Online Videogames," *Game Studies* 2, no. 2 (December 2002): www.gamestudies.org/0202/wright/.

9. Wright, Boria, and Breidenbach, "Creative Player Actions in FPS Online Video-games."

10. Kushner, "The Mod Squad."

11. Galloway, *Gaming,* 112, 113.

12. Kushner, "The Mod Squad."

13. Brayfield, "It's a Mod, Mod Game World."

14. Celia Pearce, "The Player with Many Faces: A Conversation with Louis Castle," *Game Studies* 2, no. 2 (December 2002): www.gamestudies.org/0202/pearce/.

15. Pearce, "The Player with Many Faces."

16. Galloway, *Gaming,* 111.

17. Kushner, "The Mod Squad."

18. Angela McFarlane, "The Best Pictures Are Often on Radio," *Times Education Supplement,* June 18, 2004, www.tes.co.uk/section/story/?section+Archive&sub_section=Online+Education&story_id=396657&Type=0.

19. Peter Wiemer-Hastings and Judy Robertson, *Teaching Composition Using Role Play and Feedback from Multiple Agents,* http://reed.cs.depaul.edu/peterwh/SS/aied2001.pdf.

20. Learning Games Initiative, *Aristotle's Assassins,* www.mesmernet.org/lgi/index.php.

21. The Education Arcade, *Revolution,* www.educationarcade.org/revolution.

22. "This Revolution Will Be Digitized, Texturized," *In Medias Res: The Newsletter of the MIT Comparative Media Studies* (Spring 2004), 1, 12.

23. The Education Arcade, *Revolution.*

24. Will Wright, "Dream Machines," *Wired* 14, no. 4 (April 2006), www.wired.com/wired/archive/14.04/wright.html.

25. MIT Program in Comparative Media Studies, "Opening Remarks."

26. Galloway, *Gaming,* 124–125.

27. Galloway, *Gaming,* 126.

❖ Glossary ❖

Adventure game—The defining emphasis of the adventure game genre is a focus on puzzle solving and story. They are typically single-player games. Adventure games are some of the earliest examples of computer games, the most famous of which are *Adventure* (1976) and *Zork* (1980), text-based adventure games in which players type commands and receive feedback solely by text. Modern examples include *The Longest Journey* (1999) and the *Myst* (1993) series, both mouse-driven graphical games where players can see the effects of their actions in real changes to the game world.

AI (Artificial Intelligence)—In games, AI refers to the intelligence that controls all computer movements in a game. In a first-person shooter, this would be all enemy and allied movement not controlled by the player. Modern games demonstrate better AI by performing more complex and realistic maneuvers, while adapting to situations created by the player.

Aristotelian narrative—The format of most stories. Character goals and events turn story into plot. Events at the start cause the events in the middle, which cause the events in the end.

ARPANET (Advanced Research Projects Agency Network)—The precursor to the Internet, initially conceived in 1962 and first deployed in 1969.

Atari 2600—Initially released in 1977 as the Video Computer System (VCS), the Atari was the first wildly successful videogame console to be released. It was first called the Atari 2600 in 1982 and was officially retired by Atari on January 1, 1992.

Avatar—The character that a player controls in a role-playing or action adventure game. In many role-playing games, the player determines the character's appearance and attributes at the outset and chooses character modifications and enhancements throughout the game.

Bitmap—A flat type of computer image. Backgrounds, walls, sky, and especially textures are typically created as bitmap images and are not directly able to be changed or manipulated by players.

Bullet time—First made popular by the film *The Matrix,* bullet time refers to the slowing down of time for a character. Time slows to the point where one can easily watch bullets in the air and move out of the way. The effect was first brought into the gaming world in *Max Payne* (2001), though others have since emulated it.

Catharsis—The emotional release felt through playing videogames. Most commonly, this is considered the release of aggression on computerized targets. Catharsis was first defined by Aristotle as a "purging" of emotional tension that builds through the course of a tragic narrative.

Cel-shading—Special type of computer graphics designed to look like less complex hand-drawn animation. This is much more prevalent on console games than computer games. Some cel-shaded games that received critical acclaim and high sales include *The Legend of Zelda: The Wind Waker* (2001) and *Tales of Symphonia* (2004), both exclusive to Nintendo's GameCube.

CGI (computer-generated imagery)—Digitally synthesized images, usually three-dimensional images, created for games. Videogames use real-time generated CGI for characters and any objects that change and move in the game world.

Console—A console, as opposed to a computer, is a dedicated gaming machine. Historically, consoles cannot run typical business applications. They have specialized controllers that are not transferable between systems. They do not require any additional specialized hardware and plug directly into a television set for video and sound output. As of 2008, the current generation of videogame consoles includes Microsoft's Xbox 360, Nintendo's Wii, and Sony's PlayStation 3.

Counterfactuals—"What-if" scenarios of real world events, also called alternate history. Popular premises include: "What if the South won the Civil War?" "What if Hitler were never born?" and "What if the Cold War escalated instead of ending?" Some historians employ counterfactuals to teach lessons of historical cause and effect.

Countergaming—Gaming that breaks conventional standards of interface, design, style, or gameplay. For example, Nintendo's *Eternal Darkness: Sanity's Requiem* (2002) would cause error screens to display, making the console appear to have crashed or having the word "VIDEO" superimposed on the top of the screen like the video settings display on many TVs. Countergaming also refers to the practice of modifying commercial videogames by video artists, hackers, and amateur designers in order to make a subversive statement.

Diegesis—The act of telling, rather than showing. In gaming, this refers to the parts of the game that tell the story and directly impact the story as opposed to elements that are parts of the rules, such as a character's hit points or other derived statistics of which a character in the story would be unaware.

Easter Egg—A secret in a game that usually references pop culture, other games, or in-jokes from the developers. *Max Payne* (2001) refers to the movie and TV series *Buffy the Vampire Slayer,* and *Grand Theft Auto: San Andreas* (2004) has small references to a glass company called "Max Payne," as two examples of Easter Eggs.

Edutainment—Also called educational entertainment, edutainment is software created to amuse as well as teach. *Reader Rabbit* (1989), a game to teach typing and reading; *Where in the World Is Carmen Sandiego* (1985), teaching geography; and the more recent *Big Brain Academy* (2005), teaching a multitude of subjects, are all edutainment software.

ESA (Entertainment Software Association)—The trade association of the gaming industry. It was founded in 1994 as the Interactive Digital Software Association and renamed in 2003. The association's primary purposes include fighting copyright infringement in the gaming industry, fighting censorship and regulation of games, and putting on the annual Electronics Entertainment Expo (E3).

ESRB (Entertainment Software Ratings Board)—The ESRB creates, applies, and enforces ratings in videogames. Much like the Motion Picture Association of America (MPAA), which has a ratings system for movies, the ESRB has ratings for games from "Childhood" to "Mature," with a stringent set of guidelines that must be met for a game to fall under each rating.

EULA (End-User Licensing Agreement)—The EULA is, in essence, a contract between a game company and the end-user. While seldom read by any end-user, the EULA routinely states that publishers are not responsible for damages the software causes to a computer, that the user will not pirate the software, and that the software will not be used for anything illegal or malicious.

First-person shooter (FPS)—First-person shooters are a game type in which the player assumes the role of the protagonist, seeing the game world through the protagonist's eyes. *Wolfenstein 3D* (1992) is considered to be the first success of the genre. Other well-known first-person shooters include *Doom* (1993), *Quake* (1996), *Half-Life* (1998), and *Halo* (2001).

Flash game—A game created for play on the Internet using Macromedia/ Adobe's Flash software. These games are typically shorter and much simpler than full PC or console games.

Game controller—Any input device used to control a game. For consoles, the controller is usually a console-specific gamepad. For PCs, the controller can be the mouse and keyboard combination, a joystick, a racing wheel, or other additional hardware.

Game designer—The person who creates the initial idea and model for a given game. They may or may not play a significant part in the final development of the game. Sid Meier of Firaxis and Will Wright of Maxis are two of the most respected and famous designers in the industry.

Game engine—The core technology behind any game. Games are typically developed using a base graphics and physics model already in place, so that developers can focus more on game design and less on the core technology behind the game. *Max Payne 2* (2003) utilizes the Havok physics engine, developed by Havok. *Doom 3* (2004) has a graphics engine developed specifically for the game. *Quake 4* (2005) licensed and used the *Doom 3* engine.

Game producer—The person, or group of people, overseeing the development of a game. They are responsible for the overall quality of the game and can handle everything from art direction to licensing negotiations.

Game world—The game world or storyworld describes the particular universe where the game unfolds. This refers to all the physical laws that the universe obeys. All the *Star Wars* games take place in the established worlds of *Star Wars*, and the *Neverwinter Nights* series takes place in the established *Dungeons & Dragons* world of Faerun.

God game—A game that casts the player in a divine or world-controlling role. *Black & White* (2001) gives the player godly powers to help or terrorize villages and be worshipped or feared accordingly, while *SimEarth* (1992) allows players to develop a world and foster its growth with no acknowledgement of divine presence from the inhabitants.

Gold farming—Players who repeat tasks in MMORPGs for the purpose of acquiring wealth or particular items for the express purpose of reselling them for real-world currency are referred to as farmers or gold farmers. These players tend to change the nature of the in-game economy. Many publishers will deactivate accounts used for such purposes and ban gold farmers.

Interactive fiction (IF)—Stories in which the user controls the direction as the story progresses. These text-only adventure games allow players to input commands to journey through a game world in the way they choose, allowing the story to unfold based on their decisions. The *Zork* (1980) series is one example of interactive fiction.

Isometric projection—The visual technique used to display images of three-dimensional objects in only two dimensions. The objects do not dynamically change size, as in true three-dimensional games. They remain at fixed angles. Games that use a "top down" view, such as *Fallout* (1997) and *The Sims* (2000), use isometric projection principles.

IGDA (Independent Game Developers Association)—The IDGA promotes professional growth for developers, builds communities between developers, and acts as an advocate against government regulations in games, much like the ESA. The IDGA's primary duties are centered on improving the quality of life for developers.

Immersion—In gaming, immersion represents the degree to which a gamer becomes engrossed in a game. This can range from losing track of time, to intense focus, to actually believing—while playing the game—that the gamer is really the main character and is inside the game world.

Interactivity—A player's in-game actions and the game's level of response both relate to interactivity. When a player uses objects in the world, whether picking up an object or shooting an enemy, they are interacting with the world. Highly interactive worlds allow objects to be used as they would be in the real world, enable more intricate and detailed conversations with characters, and ensure better reactions from enemies and allies.

Leveling—The act of gaining power in a role-playing game is referred to as leveling or leveling up. Players gain new powers and abilities to better handle the more powerful foes they are certain to encounter and gain the rarer and more valuable treasures and items.

Ludology—The study of gaming from a social, psychological, or literary perspective.

Machinima—Utilizing already developed games to create animated stories. The technique was made most popular by Rooster Teeth studios in their hit series *Red vs. Blue: The Blood Gulch Chronicles* (2003), utilizing the *Halo* (2001) game to create their story, adding only voiceovers and an occasional bitmap image to the work.

Magic circle—The magic circle, a term introduced by the Dutch sociologist Johan Huizinga, is the imaginary reality that a player enters when playing a game.

Main quest—The main quest in a game is what would also, in literature, be called the primary story arc. It is the portion of the game that a player must complete to win the game. Main quests are typically linear. Events must be handled in more specific order to advance the plot. Elements of the main quest cannot be skipped. RPGs are the genre most commonly divided into main quests and side quests. MMORPGs typically do not have a main quest.

Media convergence—The blending of different communications media or the expansion of capabilities of technological devices, such as a cell phone that you can use to watch TV or to browse Web sites.

MHz (megahertz)—Computing power as measured by the processor's clock speed. A higher clock speed typically indicates a faster processor. The clock speed of personal computers was factored highly and directly into game performance for many years. In recent years, more focus has been placed on processor architecture.

Military-entertainment complex—A play on the term "military-industrial complex," the military-entertainment complex refers to cooperative projects between those in the entertainment industry and those in the military. The game *America's Army* (2002) was produced by the U.S. military.

Minigames—Games within games. Any activity in a game that deviates from the main gameplay is considered a minigame. *The Elder Scrolls IV:*

Oblivion (2006) has a minigame to pick locks. *Grand Theft Auto: San Andreas* (2004) has arcade consoles throughout the world that allow minigames to be played.

MMORPG (massively multiplayer online role-playing game)—Online games that employ RPG principles of character creation, leveling, and advancement. They are massive persistent worlds that foster large communities of players. An Internet connection is required to play any MMORPG. The first modern MMORPG was *Ultima Online* (1997), still played today.

Mod—A third-party modification or add-on to a game. Mods can be as simple as changing a strand of dialogue or as complex as changing the nature of the game.

MOO (MUD object-oriented)—Like a MUD (see next definition), but players in a MOO can utilize programming techniques, specifically object-oriented programming, to create new objects, new rooms, new creatures, or change the way the MOO interface works.

MUD (multiuser dungeon/domain/dimension)—An online, text-based world. Users log in and play in an RPG-style game in a social environment. Descriptions are given in text only. MUDs resemble a blending of classic adventure games, such as *Zork* (1980), and MMORPGs.

Mythopoesis—Literally translated from Greek as "mythmaking." The creation of modern myths over a short time by one or few authors, as opposed to evolving over time through word of mouth, such as the ancient myths. Modern examples include *The Lord of the Rings* saga and the *Star Wars* saga. In games, some of the comparable stories would be the *Ultima* series and the *Final Fantasy* series.

Narrative franchise—The spread of a narrative throughout many games and other forms of media. The game *Halo* has expanded to encompass many books, two sequels, and a potential movie. The *Star Wars* and *Lord of the Rings* franchises include films, novels, television shows, and games.

Narratology—The study of the theory, history, and formal aspects of narrative.

Nonlinear narrative—Linear games must be completed in a specific sequence. There is no jumping between levels or going back and forth. Non-

191

linear games, while forcing players to begin at the beginning and typically end at the ending, allow the player to move through different parts of the main quest or take side quests at nearly any point before the endgame, without destroying the storyline.

NPC (nonplayer character)—Characters that are not the main character or avatar. Some NPCs can be controlled by the player, but are still not considered to be the player character. NPCs range from innkeepers and merchants to allies and antagonists.

PDP-1 (Programmed Data Processor-1)—The name of the first computer to play a game. The first-ever computer game, *Spacewar!,* was played for the first time on the PDP-1 in February 1962.

Photorealism—The quality of an image that appears as lifelike as a photograph. In a game, photorealism refers to graphics that so much resemble reality that it is impossible to tell whether an image was taken as a screenshot or printed from an actual photograph.

Pixel—The basic unit of display for computer monitors. A single pixel is extremely tiny. Millions of pixels are displayed together in different colors to create a full image.

Player character—The character that the player controls in a game.

Polygonal modeling—An approach to creating computer models by building objects out of smaller shapes. The OpenGL and Direct3D utilize this method.

Procedural rhetoric—How arguments are constructed in videogames; the term "procedural," when used in a gaming context, refers to the way computer software is created and how it follows sets of rules.

Raster graphics—A method for creating computer-generated images using an arrangement of pixels.

Resolution—The total pixels displayed on the screen by width and height. Standard resolutions have a 4:3 ratio for standard or an approximately 16:10 ratio for widescreen. A typical resolution is 1024 x 768 or 1600 x 1200 pixels.

RPG (role-playing game)—RPGs are typically defined by having broad, sweeping storylines. They have both a main quest and many side quests and follow a nonlinear narrative style. Additional characteristics include detailed character creation, leveling, and XP moving toward advancement. RPGs more often are single player only, though MMORPGs are designed to force players to create groups.

RTS (real-time strategy)—The focus of RTS is battlefield simulation from a "top down" or general's perspective. The player controls their entire faction in battle. RTSs typically have several different playable factions, multiple resources needed to build different units necessitating careful resource management, and options to play online with other people.

Screenshot—An image from a game depicting what went on in the split-second it takes to get a still image. Usually the "print screen" button will create a screen shot.

Serious games—Games not designed solely for entertainment. Edutainment games are considered serious games, as are games developed for advertising and military and professional training.

Server—In gaming terms, a central hub that players log into so that they can play games together. Many networked games allow players to create a personal server on their computer that players can log into. Additionally, many companies maintain servers to host games and allow players to network across the globe. MMORPGs are hosted exclusively online. Players must log into the particular server where their character is stored in order to play.

Side quest—Side quests are the parts of a videogame story that have little to no impact on the final outcome, from a story perspective. They can be skipped entirely and players will still be able to advance the main quest. Side quests provide additional gameplay and usually provide additional story (whether relating to the main quest or not), additional experience, or more powerful items than would be found in the main quest. MMORPGs are composed almost entirely of side quests.

Source code—The basic code that developers write to make a game. This includes everything programmed into the game world, including the main interactions, the AI, and the algorithms that control things like grass movements in the wind. The code tells the game how everything should interact when all the pieces are put together and translated from something that can be understood by humans to the binary language that can be understood by the computer.

Texture mapping—The process of applying pre-built 2D textures to 3D objects. Texture-mapping technique is the reason that walls and floors were fairly uniform in classic games like *Wolfenstein 3D* (1992) and *Doom* (1993), due to repeating the placement of the same texture across the system.

Uncanny valley—The "uncanny valley" is a theory relating to the field of robotics and computer images of human beings. The simplified theory is that the more realistic robots or computer-generated images of people become, the better people will react to them. At a certain point, however, people will react strongly *against* them until they reach a level that accurately mimics humans. This dip in reaction is the "uncanny valley." When machines or images enter this state, people tend to see them more as corpselike or zombielike, or, in other words, things to be feared. At the time of the theory's conception in 1970 by the Japanese robotics researcher Masahiro Mori, it was not possible to create lifelike robots.

Vector graphics—Using basic shapes and forms such as points, lines, and curves to create graphics. Vector graphics appear clearer on screen than other types of graphics and can be scaled up and down without loss of quality. They are particularly important in digital art.

Virtual reality (VR)—Virtual Reality is a technology designed to allow a user complete, or near complete, immersion in a computer-generated world. Most people think of wearing a set of glasses and bulky gloves that allow them to be in the world and feel what is going on. Currently, VR games are used mainly for pilot and combat training. Commercial VR games are not in wide production due to the high cost of VR technology and the lack of necessary processing power in consumer-level hardware.

XP (experience points)—Players in role-playing games are granted XP for solving quests, killing foes, and various other achievements. XP is a measure of player progress in a game and how close the character is to leveling. Games such as *Neverwinter Nights* (2002) use a fixed XP system where the character suddenly gains power after acquiring enough XP to level. Others, such as *Dungeon Siege* (2002), utilize a dynamic system in which characters gradually become more proficient in whatever skills they have focused on using.

❖ Videogame Bibliography ❖

Activism. Dev. Persuasive Games. Persuasive Games, 2004.

Adventure. Des. William Crowther and Don Woods. Dev. William Crowther and Don Woods. CRL, 1976.

Adventure. Des. Warren Robinett. Dev. Atari. Atari, 1978.

Aeon Flux. Dev. Terminal Reality. Majesco Games, 2005.

Akalabeth: World of Doom. Des. Richard Garriott. California Pacific Computer, 1980.

America's Army. Dev. U.S. Army and Secret Level. U.S. Army and Ubisoft, 2002.

Asteroids. Des. Lyle Rains and Ed Logg. Dev. Atari. Atari, 1979.

Asteroids Deluxe. Des. Dave Sheppard. Dev. Atari. Atari, 1980.

Asteroids Hyper 64. Dev. Syrox Development. Crave Entertainment, 1999.

Baldur's Gate. Des. Ray Muzyka. Dev. BioWare. Black Isle Studios/Interplay, 1998.

Battlezone. Des. Ed Rotberg and Owen Rubin. Dev. Atari. Atari, 1980.

Big Brain Academy. Dev. Nintendo. Nintendo, 2005.

Bioshock. Dev. 2K Boston and 2K Australia. 2K Games, 2007.

Black & White. Des. Peter Molyneaux. Dev. Lionhead Studios. Electronic Arts Games, 2001.

Blasteroids. Dev. Atari Games. Image Works, 1987.

Border Patrol. www.resist.com/racistgames/playborderpatrol/borderpatrol.htm, 2006.

Breakout. Des. Nolan Bushnell, Steve Bristow, and Steve Wozniak. Dev. Atari. Atari, 1976.

Brothers in Arms: Earned in Blood. Dev. Gearbox Software. Ubisoft, 2005.

Brothers in Arms: The Road to Hill 30. Dev. Gearbox Software. Ubisoft, 2005.

Catechumen. Dev. N'Lightning Software. N'Lightning Software, 1999.

Charlie Church Mouse Bible Adventures. Dev. LifeLine Studios. LifeLine Studios, 2002.

The Chronicles of Narnia: The Lion, the Witch, and the Wardrobe. Dev. Sony Entertainment and Nintendo. Nintendo, 2005.

The Chronicles of Narnia: Prince Caspian. Dev. Traveller's Tales. Disney Interactive Studios, 2008.

The Chronicles of Riddick: Escape from Butcher Bay. Dev. Starbreeze Studios and Tigon Studios. Vivendi Universal Games, 2004.

City of Heroes. Dev. Cryptic Studios. NCsoft, Level Up! Games, and Interactive Brazil, 2004.

Civilization III. Dev. Firaxis Games. Infogrames, 2001.

Civilization IV. Dev. Firaxis Games. 2K Games, 2005.

Command and Conquer: Renegade. Dev. Westwood Studios. Electronic Arts Games, 2002.

Counter-Strike. Dev. Valve Software. Vivendi Universal, 1999.

Darfur Is Dying. Des. Susana Ruiz. Dev. Susan Ruiz, Ashley York, Mike Stein, Noah Keeting, and Kellee Santiago. Reebok Human Rights Foundation, 2005.

Dark Age of Camelot. Dev. Mythic Entertainment. Abandon Entertainment and Vivendi Universal Games, 2001.

Death Race. Dev. Exidy. Exidy, 1976.

Destroy All Humans! Dev. Pandemic Studios. THQ, 2005.

Deus Ex. Des. Warren Spector and Harvey Smith. Dev. Ion Storm. Eidos Interactive, 2000.

Donkey Kong. Des. Shigeru Miyamoto. Dev. Nintendo. Nintendo, 1981.

Doom. Des. John Romero. Dev. id Software. id Software, GT Interactive, Activision, Atari, and Sega, 1993.

Doom II: Hell on Earth. Des. John Romero. Dev. id Software. id Software, GT Interactive, Virgin Interactive Entertainment Limited, Activision, and Tapwave Incorporated, 1994.

Doom 3. Dev. id Software. id Software, Activision, and Aspyr Media, 2004.

DRIV3R. Dev. Reflections. Atari, 2004.

Dungeon Siege. Des. Chris Taylor. Dev. Gas Powered Games. Microsoft Game Studios, 2002.

E.T.: The Extra-Terrestrial. Des. Howard Scott Warshaw. Dev. Atari. Atari, 1982.

Ehud's Courage: The Cunning Blade. Dev. Davka Corporation. Davka Corporation, 2004.

The Elder Scrolls III: Morrowind. Dev. Bethesda Game Studios. Bethesda Softworks and Ubisoft, 2002.

The Elder Scrolls IV: Knights of the Nine. Dev. Bethesda Softworks. Bethesda Softworks, 2006.

The Elder Scrolls IV: Oblivion. Des. Todd Howard. Dev. Bethesda Game Studios. 2K Games and Bethesda Softworks, 2006.

Enter the Matrix. Des. David Perry. Dev. Shiny Entertainment. Atari and Warner Brothers Interactive, 2003.

Eternal Darkness: Sanity's Requiem. Des. Denis Dyack. Dev. Silicon Knights. Nintendo, 2002.

Eternal War: Shadow of Light. Dev. Two Guys Software. Two Guys Software, 2003.

The Ethics Game. Des. Pakorn Tancheron. Khondee, 2006.

EverQuest. Dev. Sony Online Entertainment. Sony Online Entertainment, 1999.

Fable. Des. Peter Molyneux. Dev. Lionhead Studios. Microsoft Game Studios, 2004.

Far Cry. Dev. Crytek. Ubisoft, 2004.

F.E.A.R. Des. Craig Hubbard. Dev. Monolito Productions and Day 1 Studios. Vivendi Universal, 2005.

Final Fantasy. Des. Hironobu Sakaguchi, Masafumi Miyamoto, Yoshitaka Amano, Kenji Terada, Nobuo Uematsu, and Nasir Gebelli. Dev. Square. Square, 1987.

Frontrunner. Dev. Lantern Games. Lantern Games, 2004.

Full Spectrum Warrior. Dev. Pandemic Studios. THQ, 2004.

The Godfather: The Game. Dev. Electronic Arts Redwood Shores Studios. Electronic Arts, 2006.

Gospel Champions. Dev. Third Day Games. Authentic Software, 2007.

Grand Theft Auto: San Andreas. Dev. Rockstar North. Rockstar Games, 2004.

Grand Theft Auto III. Dev. DMA Design. Rockstar Games, 2001.

Grand Theft Auto: Vice City. Dev. Rockstar North. Rockstar Games, 2002.

Habitat. Des. Chip Morningstar and Randy Farmer, et al. Dev. Lucasfilm Games, Quantum Link, and Fujitsu. Quantum Link and Fujitsu, 1986.

Half-Life. Dev. Valve Studios. Sierra Studios, Electronic Arts, and Valve, 1998.

Half-Life 2. Des. Gabe Newell. Dev. Valve Corporation and Electronic Arts. Vivendi Universal Games and Valve Corporation, 2004.

Half-Life 2: Lost Coast. Dev. Valve Corporation and Electronic Arts. Vivendi Universal Games and Valve Corporation, 2004.

Halo: Combat Evolved. Dev. Bungie Studios. Microsoft Game Studios, 2001.

Harry Potter and the Chamber of Secrets. Dev. Amaze Entertainment and Eurocom. Electronic Arts and Warner Bros. Interactive, 2002.

Harry Potter and the Goblet of Fire. Dev. Electronic Arts UK. Electronic Arts, 2005.

Harry Potter and the Order of the Phoenix. Dev. Electronic Arts UK. Electronic Arts, 2007.

Harry Potter and the Philosopher's Stone. Dev. KnowWonder Digital Mediaworks, Warthog, Griptonite, and Argonaut. Electronic Arts, 2001.

Harry Potter and the Prisoner of Azkaban. Dev. KnowWonder Digital Mediaworks and Electronic Arts. Electronic Arts 2004.

The Howard Dean for Iowa Game. Des. Ian Bogost and Gonzalo Frasca. Dev. Persuasive Games. Persuasive Games, 2003.

Hulk. Dev. Radical Entertainment. Vivendi Universal Games, 2003.

James Bond 007: Everything or Nothing. Dev. Electronic Arts. Electronic Arts, 2004.

Jet Set Radio. Dev. Smilebit. Sega, 2000.

John Kerry Tax Invaders. Dev. Republican National Committee, 2004.

Katamari Damacy. Des. Keita Takahashi. Dev. Namco. Namco, 2004.

King Kong. Des. Michael Ancel. Ubisoft, 2005.

Left Behind: Eternal Forces. Dev. Left Behind Games. Left Behind Games, 2006.

The Legend of Zelda: The Wind Waker. Des. Eiji Aonuma, Shugeru Miyamoto, and Yoshiyuki Oyama. Dev. Nintendo Entertainment Analysis and Development. Nintendo, 2004.

The Longest Journey. Des. Ragnar Tørnquist and Didrik Tollefsen. Dev. Funcom. Empire Interactive Entertainment, Egmont, KE Media, and Micro Application, 1999.

The Lord of the Rings: The Return of the King. Dev. Hypnos Entertainment. Electronics Arts, 2003.

The Lord of the Rings: The Two Towers. Dev. Stormfront Studios. Electronic Arts, 2002.

Making History: The Calm and the Storm. Dev. Muzzy Lane Software. Muzzy Lane Software, 2007.

Marble Madness. Des. Mark Cerny. Dev. Atari. Atari, 1984.

Max Payne. Dev. Remedy Entertainment. Gathering of Developers, 2001.

Max Payne 2. Dev. Remedy Entertainment. Rockstar Games, 2003.

Medieval: Total War. Dev. Creative Assembly. Activision, 2002.

Medieval II: Total War. Dev. Creative Assembly. Sega, 2006.

Men of Valor. Des. John Whitmore. Dev. 2015, Incorporated. Vivendi Universal Games, 2004.

Meridian 59. Dev. 3DO Studios. 3DO Studios, 1996.

Milieu. Des. Alan E. Kleitz. Dev. Alan E. Kleitz, 1978.

Missile Command. Des. Dave Theurer. Dev. Atari. Atari, 1980.

Mitzvah Man. Dev. Torah Educational Software. Torah Educational Software, 1997.

Mono. Dev. Binary Zoo Studios, 2005.

Mortal Kombat. Des. Ed Boon and John Tobias. Dev. Midway Games. Acclaim Entertainment, 1993.

The Movies. Des. Peter Molyneaux. Dev. Lionhead Studios. Activision, 2005.

MUD1. Des. Richard Bartle and Roy Trubshaw. Dev. Richard Bartle and Roy Trubshaw, 1977.

Myst. Des. Robyn Miller and Rand Miller. Dev. Cyan, Incorporated. Brøderbund, Midway, and Mean Hamster Studio, 1993.

Neverwinter Nights. Dev. BioWare. Infogrames and Atari, 2002.
Neverwinter Nights 2. Dev. Obsidian Entertainment. Atari, 2006.
Night Trap. Dev. Digital Pictures. Digital Pictures, 1992.
Ōkami. Des. Hideki Kamiya. Dev. Clover Studios. Capcom, 2006.
Ominous Horizons: A Paladin's Calling. Dev. N'Lightning Software. N'Lightning Software, 2002.
Oregon Trail. Dev. Minnesota Educational Computing Consortium, Brøderbund, and The Learning Company, 1985.
Pac-Man. Des. Toru Iwatani, Hideyuki Mokajima San, and Toshio Kai. Dev. Namco. Namco and Midway Games, 1979.
Pencil Whipped. Des. Lonnie Flickinger. Dev. ChiselBrain Software. ChiselBrain Software, 2000.
Peter Jackson's King Kong: The Official Game of the Movie. Dev. Ubisoft Montpelier Studios. Ubisoft, 2005.
Pirates of the Caribbean. Dev. Akella. Bethesda Softworks, 2003.
Pirates of the Caribbean: At World's End. Dev. Amaze Entertainment and Eurocom. Buena Vista Games, 2007.
Pirates of the Caribbean: Dead Man's Chest. Dev. Amaze Entertainment and Griptonite Games. Buena Vista Games, 2006.
Pitfall! Des. David Crane. Dev. Activision. Activision, 1982.
Planetfall, Des. Steve Meretzky. Dev. Infocom. Infocom, 1983.
The Political Machine. Dev. Stardock. Ubisoft, 2004.
Pong. Des. Allan Alcorn. Dev. Atari. Atari, 1972.
Quake. Des. John Romero, John Carmack, American McGee, Sandy Petersen, and Tim Willits. Dev. id Software. GT Interactive, 1996.
Raiders of the Lost Ark. Des. Howard Scott Warshaw. Dev. Atari. Atari, 1982.
Reader Rabbit. Dev. The Learning Company. The Learning Company, 1989.
Red vs. Blue: The Blood Gulch Chronicles. Rooster Teeth Production, 2003.
Resistance: Fall of Man. Dev. Insomniac Games. Sony Computer Entertainment America, 2006.
Revolution. Dev. Education Arcade. Education Arcade, 2004.
Rez. Des. Tetsuya Mizuguchi. Dev. United Game Artists. Sega, BigBen Interactive, and Sony Computer Entertainment, 2001.
Rise to Honor. Dev. Sony Computer Entertainment America. Sony Computer Entertainment America, 2004.
Riven. Des. Robyn Miller and Rochard Vander Wende. Dev. Cyan, Incorporated. Brøderbund Software, 1997.
Rome: Total War. Dev. Creative Assembly. Activision and Sega, 2004.
Rome: Total War: Barbarian Invasion. Dev. Creative Assembly. Activision and Sega, 2005.
Scepter of Goth. Des. Alan E. Klietz. Dev. Alan E. Klietz. Interplay, 1984.
Second Life. Des. Linden Research, Incorporated. Dev. Linden Research, Incorporated. Linden Research, Incorporated, 2003.
September 12: A Toy World. Dev. Newsgaming. Newsgaming, 2003.
Shogun: Total War. Dev. Creative Assembly. Electronic Arts, 2000.
SimCity. Des. Will Wright. Dev. Maxis. Brøderbund and Maxis, 1988.
SimEarth. Des. Will Wright. Dev. Maxis. Maxis, 1990.
The Sims. Des. Will Wright. Dev. Maxis. Electronic Arts, 2000.
The Sims 2. Des. Will Wright, et al. Dev. Maxis. Electronic Arts, 2000.
SOCOM: U.S. Navy SEALs. Dev. Zipper Interactive. Sony Computer Entertainment, 2002.

Space Invaders. Des. Tomohiro Nishikado and David Yuh. Dev. Taito Corporation. Midway, 1978.

Spacewar! Des. Steve Russell. Dev. Steve Russell, 1968.

Special Force. Dev. Hezbollah, 2003.

Spheres of Chaos. Dev. Iain McLeod, 1992.

Spider-Man. Dev. Treyarch. Activision, 2002.

Spider-Man 2. Dev. Treyarch and The Fizz Factor. Activision and MacPlay, 2004.

Spider-Man 3. Dev. Treyarch and Vicarious Visions. Activision, 2007.

Star Wars: Battlefront. Dev. Pandemic Studios. LucasArts, 2004.

Star Wars: Battlefront II. Dev. Pandemic Studios. LucasArts, 2005.

Star Wars: Bounty Hunter. Dev. LucasArts. LucasArts, 2002.

Star Wars: The Clone Wars. Dev. Pandemic Studios. LucasArts, 2002.

Star Wars: Episode III: Revenge of the Sith. Dev. The Collective Incorporated and Ubisoft. LucasArts, 2005.

Star Wars: The Force Unleashed. Dev. LucasArts and Krome Studios. LucasArts, 2008.

Star Wars: Galaxies. Dev. Sony Online Entertainment. LucasArts, 2004.

Star Wars: Jedi Starfighter. Dev. LucasArts. LucasArts, 2002.

Star Wars: Knights of the Old Republic. Des. David Falkner, Steven Gilmour, Casey Hudson, Derek Watts, Drew Karpyshyn, James Ohlen, and Preston Watamaniuk. Dev. BioWare. LucasArts, 2003.

Star Wars: Knights of the Old Republic II: The Sith Lords. Dev. Obsidian Entertainment. LucasArts, 2004.

Starcraft. Des. James Phinney and Chris Metzen, et al. Dev. Blizzard Entertainment. Blizzard Entertainment and Sierra Entertainment, 1998.

Stubbs the Zombie in "Rebel Without a Pulse." Dev. Wideload Games. Aspyr Media, 2005.

The Suicide Bombing Game. www.newgrounds.com/portal/view/50323, 2005.

Super Mario Bros. Des. Shigeru Miyamoto. Dev. Nintendo. Nintendo, 1985.

Take Back Illinois. Dev. Persuasive Games. Persuasive Games, 2005.

Tales of Symphonia. Des. Kosuke Fujishima and Takashi Hasegawa. Dev. Namco Tales Studio. Nintendo, 2003.

Team Fortress II. Des. John Cook and Robin Walker. Dev. Valve. Valve, 2007.

Team Fortress Classic. Des. Valve and id Software. Dev. Valve Corporation. Sierra Entertainment, 1999.

Tempest. Des. Dave Theurer. Dev. Atari. Atari, 1980.

Tetris. Des. Alexey Pajitnov, 1985.

XIII. Dev. Ubisoft. Ubisoft, 2003.

Tom Clancy's Ghost Recon. Des. Brian Upton. Dev. Red Storm Entertainment. Ubisoft, 2001.

Tom Clancy's Ghost Recon: Advanced Warfighter. Dev. Ubisoft and Red Storm Entertainment. Ubisoft, 2006.

Tom Clancy's Rainbow Six. Des. Brian Upton. Dev. Red Storm Entertainment. Red Storm Entertainment, 1998.

Tom Clancy's Splinter Cell: Stealth Action Redefined. Dev. Ubisoft Montreal and Ubisoft Shanghai. Ubisoft, 2002.

Tomb Raider. Des. Toby Gard, Paul Douglas, Martin Iveson, and Nathan McCree. Dev. Core Design. Eidos Interactive, 1996.

Transformers. Dev. Traveller's Tales and Vicarious Visions. Activision, 2007.

True Crime: New York City. Dev. Luxoflux. Activision, 2005.

Ultima IV: Quest of the Avatar. Des. Richard Garriott. Dev. Origin Systems. Origin Systems, 1985.

Ultima Online. Des. Raph Koster, et al. Dev. Origin Systems and Electronic Arts. Electronic Arts, 1997.

Under Ash. Dev. Dar al-Fikr. Afkar Media, 2001.

Under Siege. Dev. Dar al-Fikr. Afkar Media, 2005.

Unreal Tournament 2003. Des. Cliff Bleszinski. Dev. Epic Games and Digital Extremes. Atari, 2002.

Velvet-Strike. Des. Anne-Marie Schleiner, Brody Condon, and Joan Leadre. Dev. Anne-Marie Schleiner, 2002.

Viewtiful Joe. Des. Hideki Kamiya and Atsushi Inaba. Dev. Capcom Production Studio 4. Capcom, 2003.

The Warriors. Dev. Rockstar Toronto. Rockstar Games, 2005.

Where in the World Is Carmen Sandiego? Dev. Brøderbund Software. Brøderbund Software, 1985.

Wolfenstein 3D. Des. John Romero and Tom Hall. Dev. id Software. Apogee Software, 1992.

World of Warcraft. Des. Rob Pardo, Jeff Kaplan, and Tom Chilton. Dev. Blizzard Entertainment. Vivendi Universal, 2004.

Zaxxon. Dev. Ikegami Tsushinki. Sega, 1982.

Zork. Des. Tim Anderson, Mac Blank, Dave Lebling, and Bruce Daniels. Dev. Infocom. Infocom, 1980.

❖ Bibliography ❖

Aarseth, Espen J. *Cybertext: Perspectives on Ergodic Literature.* Baltimore: Johns Hopkins University Press, 1997.

Aarseth, Espen J. "The Dungeon and the Ivory Tower: Vive La Difference ou Liaison Dangereuse?" *Game Studies* 2, no. 1 (July 2002). www.gamestudies.org/0102/editorial.html.

Aarseth, Espen J. "Genre Trouble: Narrativism and the Art of Simulation." In *First Person: New Media as Story, Performance, and Game,* edited by Noah Wardrip-Fruin and Pat Harrigan, 45–55. Cambridge: MIT Press, 2004.

Afkar Media. www.afkarmedia.com/en/index.htm.

Annenberg Media. "Modernist Portraits." *American Passages: A Literary Survey.* www.learner.org/amerpass/unit11/context_activ-4.html.

Aristotle. *The Art of Rhetoric.* Translated by Hugh Lawson-Tancred. New York: Penguin, 1991.

Aristotle. *Poetics.* Translated by Malcolm Heath. New York: Penguin, 1996.

Augustine. *Confessions.* Translated by R.S. Pine-Coffin. New York: Penguin, 1961.

Balkin, Jack M. "Virtual Liberty: Freedom to Design and Freedom to Play in Virtual Worlds." *Virginia Law Review* 90, no. 8 (December 2004): 2043–2098.

Barbican Gallery. *Game On—Tour.* www.barbican.org.uk/artgallery/event-detail. asp?ID=4964.

Barthes, Roland. "The Death of the Author." In *The Norton Anthology of Theory and Criticism,* edited by Vincent B. Leitch, et al., 1466–1470. New York: Norton, 2001.

Bartle, Richard. *Designing Virtual Worlds.* Berkeley: New Riders, 2003.

BBC. *Simon Schama's Power of Art.* "Van Gogh." www.bbc.co.uk/arts/powerofart/vangogh.shtml.

Blackman, W. Haden. "Collaborative Connections: Teamwork Unleashed," May 1, 2007. www.lucasarts.com/games/theforceunleashed/#/diary/.

Bogost, Ian. "Frame and Metaphor in Political Games." *Proceedings of the DiGRA 2005 Conference: Changing Views—Worlds in Play.* www.digra.org/dl/db/06276.36533. pdf.

Bogost, Ian. *Persuasive Games: The Expressive Power of Videogames.* Cambridge: MIT Press, 2007.

Bogost, Ian, and Gerard LaFond. *Persuasive Games.* www.persuasivegames.com/.

Bogost, Ian, and Gonzalo Frasca. "Videogames Go to Washington: The Story Behind *The Howard Dean for Iowa Game.*" In *Second Person: Role-Playing and Story in Games and Playable Media,* edited by Noah Wardrip-Fruin and Pat Harrigan, 233–246. Cambridge: MIT Press, 2007.

Boyd, Clark. "Darfur Activism Meets Video Gaming." *BBC News,* July 6, 2006. http://news.bbc.co.uk/2/hi/technology/5153694.stm.

Brayfield, Mark. "It's a Mod, Mod Game World." *Computer Bits* 14, no. 2 (February 2004). www.computerbits.com/archive/2004/0200/gamemods.html.

Caillois, Roger. *Man, Play, and Games.* Translated by Meyer Barash. Urbana: University of Illinois Press, 2001.

Castronova, Edward. *Synthetic Worlds: The Business and Culture of Online Games.* Chicago: Chicago University Press, 2006.

Catechism of the Catholic Church. New York: Doubleday, 1995.

"Cathedral Row over Video War Game." *BBC News,* June 9, 2007. http://news.bbc.co.uk/2/hi/uk_news/england/manchester/6736809.stm.

Chee, Florence, Marcelo Vieta, and Richard Smith. "Online Gaming and the Interactional Self: Identity Interplay in Situated Practice." In *Gaming as Culture: Essays on Reality, Identity, and Experience in Fantasy Games,* edited by J. Patrick Williams, Sean Q. Hendricks, and W. Keith Winkler, 154–174. Jefferson, NC: McFarland, 2006.

"Church Wants Cash for 'Sick' Game." *CNN.com,* June 11, 2007. www.cnn.com/2007/TECH/fun.games/06/11/sony.manchester/index.html.

Clinton, Hillary Rodham. "Senators Clinton, Lieberman Announce Federal Legislation to Protect Children from Inappropriate Video Games." *Statements & Releases,* November 29, 2005. http://clinton.senate.gov/news/statements/details.cfm?id=249368&&.

Colayco, Bob. Review of *Ghost Recon: Advanced Warfighter. GameSpot,* March 8, 2006. www.gamespot.com/xbox360/action/tomclancysghostrecon3/review.html?om_act=convert&om_clk=gssummary&tag=summary;review.

Consalvo, Mia. "Hot Dates and Fairy-Tale Romances: Studying Sexuality in Video Games." In *The Video Game Theory Reader,* edited by Mark J.P. Wolf and Bernard Perron, 171–194. New York: Routledge, 2003.

Crabtree, Shona. "Finding Religion in Second Life's Virtual Universe." *Washington Post.com,* June 16, 2007. www.washingtonpost.com/wp-dyn/content/article/2007/06/15/AR2007061501902.html.

Davis, Ryan. Review of *The Movies. GameSpot,* November 8, 2005. www.gamespot.com/pc/strategy/movies/review.html?om_act=convert&om_clk=gssummary&tag=summary%3Breview&page=2.

Dee, Jonathan. "Playing Mogul." *New York Times Magazine,* December 21, 2003. www.sachsreport.com/Playing%20Mogul.htm.

Dibbell, Julian. *Play Money: Or, How I Quit My Day Job and Made Millions Selling Virtual Loot.* New York: Basic Books, 2006.

Dodig-Crnkovic, Gordana, and Thomas Larsson. "Game Ethics—Homo Ludens as a Computer Game Designer and Consumer." *International Review of Information Ethics* 4 (2005): 19–23.

Dy, Bernard. Review of *Brothers in Arms: The Road to Hill 30, Military History,* October 2005, 69.

Dy, Bernard. Review of *Medieval: Total War, Military History,* June 2003, 68.

Ebert, Roger. "*E.T.: The Extra-Terrestrial,*" rogerebert.com, March 22, 2002. http://rogerebert.suntimes.com/apps/pbcs.dll/article?AID=/20020322/REVIEWS/203220304/1023.

Ebert, Roger. "Games vs. Art: Ebert vs. Barker." *rogerebert.com,* July 21, 2007. http://rogerebert.suntimes.com/apps/pbcs.dll/article?AID=/20070721/COMMENTARY/70721001.

Ebert, Roger. "Why Did the Chicken Cross the Genders?" *rogerebert.com,* November 27, 2005. http://rogerebert.suntimes.com/apps/pbcs.dll/article?AID=/20051127/ANSWERMAN/511270302.

The Education Arcade. *About the Education Arcade.* www.educationarcade.org/about.
The Education Arcade. *Revolution.* www.educationarcade.org/revolution.
The Education Arcade. *Revolution.* "Mechanics." www.educationarcade.org/node/119.
The Education Arcade. *Revolution.* "Student Testing." www.educationarcade.org/revolution/testing.
The Education Arcade. *Revolution.* "Summary of Findings." www.educationarcade.org/revolution/testing/findings.
Erard, Michael. "In These Games, the Points Are All Political." *New York Times,* July 1, 2004. http://query.nytimes.com/gst/fullpage.html?sec=technology&res=9C01E4DD1338F932A35754C0A9629C8B63.
Eskelinen, Markku. "Towards Computer Game Studies." In *First Person: New Media as Story, Performance, and Game,* edited by Noah Wardrip-Fruin and Pat Harrigan, 36–44. Cambridge: MIT Press, 2004.
Evans, Richard J. "Telling It Like It Wasn't." *Historically Speaking: The Bulletin of the Historical Society* 5, no. 4 (March 2004). www.bu.edu/historic/hs/march04.htm.
Fanderclai, Tari Lin. "MUDs in Education: New Environments, New Pedagogies." *Computer-Mediated Communication Magazine* 2, no. 1 (January 1, 1995): 8.
Filiciak, Miroslaw. "Hyperidentities: Postmodern Identity Patterns in Massively-Multiplayer Online Role-Playing Games." In *The Video Game Theory Reader,* edited by Mark J.P. Wolf and Bernard Perron, 87–102. New York: Routledge, 2003.
Frasca, Gonzalo. "Simulation Versus Narrative: Introduction to Ludology." In *The Video Game Theory Reader,* edited by Mark J.P. Wolf and Bernard Perron, 221–236. New York: Routledge, 2003.
Frasca, Gonzalo. "Videogames of the Oppressed: Critical Thinking, Education, Tolerance, and Other Trivial Issues." In *First Person: New Media as Story, Performance, and Game,* edited by Noah Wardrip-Fruin and Pat Harrigan, 85–94. Cambridge: MIT Press, 2004.
Galloway, Alexander. *Gaming: Essays on Algorithmic Culture.* Minneapolis: University of Minnesota Press, 2006.
Galloway, Alexander. "Social Realism in Gaming." *Game Studies* 4, no. 1 (November 2004). www.gamestudies.org/0401/galloway/.
GamePolitics.com. "Church of England Condemns Sony over Cathedral Setting in *Resistance: Fall of Man.*" http://gamepolitics.com/2007/06/10/coe-bashes-sony-over-manchester-cathedral-setting-in-resistance-fall-of-man/.
Gardner, John. *The Art of Fiction: Notes on Craft for Young Writers.* New York: Vintage, 1991.
Gee, James Paul. *What Video Games Have to Teach Us About Learning and Literacy.* New York: Palgrave Macmillan, 2003.
Gergen, Kenneth J. *The Saturated Self: Dilemmas of Identity in Contemporary Life.* New York: Basic Books, 1991.
Goroff, David B. "The First Amendment Side Effects of Curing Pac-Man Fever." *Columbia Law Review* 84, no. 3 (April 1984): 744–774.
GovTrack.us. *Statements on Introduced Bills and Resolutions—The United States Senate, Section 60,* December 16, 2005. www.govtrack.us/congress/record.xpd?id=109-s20051216-60&bill=s109-2126.
"Grand Theft Auto." *60 Minutes,* produced by Mitch Weitzner, narrated by Ed Bradley. CBS, March 6, 2005.
Greene, Richard Allen. "Christian Video Game Draws Anger." *BBC News,* December 14, 2006. http://news.bbc.co.uk/2/hi/technology/6178055.stm.
Grossman, Cathy Lynn. "Faithful Build a Second Life for Religion Online." *USA Today,* April 1, 2007. www.usatoday.com/tech/gaming/2007-04-01-second-life-religion_N.htm.

Gygax, Gary. "On the Influence of J.R.R. Tolkien on the *D&D* and *AD&D* Games." *The Dragon* 95, March 1985, 12–13.

Haraway, Donna. "A Manifesto for Cyborgs: Science, Technology, and Socialist Feminism in the 1980s." In *The Norton Anthology of Theory and Criticism,* edited by Vincent B. Leitch, et al., 2266–2299. New York: Norton, 2001.

Hayes, Eric. *Playing It Safe: Avoiding Gaming Risks.* www.us-cert.gov/reading_room/gaming.pdf.

Heim, Michael. "Alternate World Disorder." *Mediamatic* 8, no. 4 (1996): 3.

Herman, Edward S., and Noam Chomsky. *Manufacturing Consent: The Political Economy of the Mass Media.* New York: Pantheon, 1988.

Heyward, David. *Videogame Aesthetics: The Future!* http://modetwo.net/users/nachimir/vga/.

"Hezbollah's New Computer Game." *WorldNetDaily,* March 3, 2003. www.worldnetdaily.com/news/article.asp?ARTICLE_ID=31323.

Holson, Laura M. "Out of Hollywood, Rising Fascination with Video Games." *New York Times,* April 10, 2004. www.nytimes.com/2004/04/10/technology/10GAME.html?ex=1396929600&en=871fe925a859ddc9&ei=5007&partner=USERLAND.

Huizinga, Johan. *Homo Ludens: A Study of the Play Element in Culture.* Boston: Beacon, 1955.

Human Constitutional Rights Documents. "Declaration of the Rights of Man and of the Citizen." www.hrcr.org/docs/frenchdec.html.

Ince, Steve. *Writing for Video Games.* London: A.C. Black, 2006.

International Game Developers Association. *Foundations of Interactive Storytelling.* www.igda.org/writing/InteractiveStorytelling.htm.

Jacobs, Steven. "Writesizing." *Game Developer,* November 2004, 21.

Jenkins, Henry. "Art Form for the Digital Age." *Technology Review,* September 2000. www.technologyreview.com/InfoTech/wtr_12189,294,p1.html.

Jenkins, Henry. "'Complete Freedom of Movement': Video Games as Gendered Play Spaces." In *From Barbie to Mortal Kombat: Gender and Computer Games,* edited by Justine Cassell and Henry Jenkins, 262–297. Cambridge: MIT Press, 1998.

Jenkins, Henry. *Convergence Culture: Where Old and New Media Collide.* New York: New York University Press, 2006.

Jenkins, Henry. "Game Design as Narrative Architecture." In *First Person: New Media as Story, Performance, and Game,* edited by Noah Wardrip-Fruin and Pat Harrigan, 118–130. Cambridge: MIT Press, 2004.

Jenkins, Henry. "Games, the New Lively Art." In *Handbook of Computer Game Studies,* edited by Jeffrey Goldstein and Joost Raessens, 175–192. Cambridge: MIT Press, 2005.

Johnson, Steven. *Everything Bad Is Good for You: How Today's Popular Culture Is Actually Making Us Smarter.* New York: Riverhead, 2005.

Johnson, Steven. "SimCandidate: Videogames Simulate Sports, Business, and War. Why Not Politics?" *Slate,* December 16, 2003. http://slate.com/id/2092688/.

King, Geoff, and Tanya Krzywinska. *ScreenPlay: Cinema Videogames Interfaces.* London: Wallflower, 2002.

Kolbert, Elizabeth. "Pimps and Dragons: How an Online World Survived a Social Breakdown." *New Yorker,* May 28, 2001.

Koster, Raphael "Raph." *Raph Koster's Website.* "Declaring the Rights of Players." www.raphkoster.com/gaming/playerrights.shtml.

Kroll, Jack. "'Emotional Engine'? I Don't Think So." *Newsweek,* March 6, 2000, 64.

Kushner, David. "The Mod Squad." *Popular Science,* July 2002. www.popsci.com/popsci/computerselec/0678d4d03cb84010vgnvcm1000004eecbccdrcrd.html.

Lane, Anthony. "Creating Monsters." *New Yorker,* May 24, 2004, 97–98.

Lastowka, F. Gregory, and Dan Hunter. "The Laws of Virtual Worlds." *California Law Review* 92, no. 1 (January 2004): 3–73.

Learning Games Initiative. *Aristotle's Assassins.* www.mesmernet.org/lgi/index.php.

Left Behind Games. "About Left Behind: Eternal Forces, The PC Game—Mainstream Media FAQ." www.leftbehindgames.com/pages/faq.htm.

Leggat, Graham. "Chip Off the Old Block." *Film Comment* 40 (2004): 26–29.

Lerner, Jeremy. "Religion Goes Digital in Faith-Based Computer Games." *Columbia News Service,* March 1, 2005. http://jscms.jrn.columbia.edu/cns/2005-03-01/lerner-religiousgames/.

Lenoir, Tim, and Henry Lowood. "Theaters of War: The Military-Entertainment Complex." www.stanford.edu/class/sts145/Library/Lenoir-Lowood_TheatersOfWar.pdf.

Lepore, Jill. "The Meaning of Life." *New Yorker,* May 21, 2007, 38–43.

Levy, Dan. "Lucas' Presidio premiere," *San Francisco Chronicle,* June 26, 2005. www.sfgate.com/cgi-bin/article.cgi?f=/c/a/2005/06/26/BAGTQDF4RU1.DTL.

Levy, Steven. *Hackers: Heroes of the Computer Revolution.* www.echonyc.com/~steven/hackers.html.

Lindley, Craig A. "The Semiotics of Time Structure in Ludic Space as a Foundation for Analysis and Design." *Game Studies* 5, no. 1 (2005). www.gamestudies.org/0501/lindley/.

Loftus, Tom. "God in the Console: Looking for Religion in Video Games." *MSNBC,* August 20, 2003. www.msnbc.msn.com/id/3078392/.

Lucas, George. "Future of Entertainment," *Hollywood Reporter,* September 13, 2005. www.hollywoodreporter.com/hr/search/article_display.jsp?vnu_content_id=1001096310.

Lucasfilm, Ltd. "Letterman Digital Arts Center: A New Vision for the Digital Arts," June 24, 2005. www.lucasfilm.com/press/presidiopreview/index.html?page=2.

Lunenfeld, Peter. "Game Boy." *Art & Text* 68 (2000): 37–38.

Lyndon, Troy. "The World Is Primed for Christian Video Games." *GameDaily BIZ,* November 28, 2006. http://biz.gamedaily.com/industry/myturn/?id=14572.

"Marge vs. the Monorail." *The Simpsons.* Episode no. 71. Fox Network, January 14, 1993.

Markkula Center for Applied Ethics. "Video Gaming: Playing with Ethics?" November, 29, 2005. www.scu.edu/ethics/publications/submitted/video-game-panel.html.

Martin, William. "Game On: Videogames, Popular Culture, and the New Aestheticism of Interactivity." *Art Criticism* 20, no. 1 (2005): 86–97.

McFarlane, Angela. "The Best Pictures Are Often on Radio." *Times Education Supplement,* June 18, 2004. www.tes.co.uk/section/story/?section+Archive&sub_section=Online+Education&story_id=396657&Type=0.

McMahan, Alison. "Immersion, Engagement, and Presence: A Method for Analyzing 3-D Video Games." In *The Video Game Theory Reader,* edited by Mark J.P. Wolf and Bernard Perron, 67–86. New York: Routledge, 2003.

McNamara, Tom. "GDC 2004: Warren Spector Talks Game Narrative." *IGN.com,* March 26, 2004. http://pc.ign.com/articles/502/502382p1.html.

McNeill, William H. "Counterfactuals and the Historical Imagination." *Historically Speaking: The Bulletin of the Historical Society* 5, no. 4 (March 2004). www.bu.edu/historic/hs/march04.htm.

Megill, Allan. "The New Counterfactualists." *Historically Speaking: The Bulletin of the Historical Society* 5, no. 4 (March 2004). www.bu.edu/historic/hs/march04.htm.

MIT Program in Comparative Media Studies. "The Future of Games." An unedited transcript from "Computer and Video Games Come of Age: A National Conference to Explore the Current State of an Emerging Entertainment Medium," February 11, 2000. http://web.mit.edu/cms/games/future.html.

MIT Program in Comparative Media Studies. "Games as Interactive Storytelling." An unedited transcript from "Computer and Video Games Come of Age: A National Conference to Explore the Current State of an Emerging Entertainment Medium," February 11, 2000. http://web.mit.edu/cms/games/storytelling.html.

MIT Program in Comparative Media Studies. "Opening Remarks." An unedited transcript from "Computer and Video Games Come of Age: A National Conference to Explore the Current State of an Emerging Entertainment Medium," February 11, 2000. http://web.mit.edu/cms/games/opening.html.

Modelina, Jamil. "Hard-Boiled Developer: Luxoflux's Peter Morawiec on Bringing Classic Story Genres to Life." *Game Developer,* March 2004, 12.

Montfort, Nick. *Twisty Little Passages: An Approach to Interactive Fiction.* Cambridge: MIT Press, 2003.

More, Thomas. *Utopia.* Translated by Paul Turner. New York: Penguin, 1965.

Morris, Chris. "The Greatest Story Never Played." *CNNMoney.com,* July 6, 2005. http://money.cnn.com/2005/07/06/commentary/game_over/column_gaming/index.htm.

Murray, Janet H. *Hamlet on the Holodeck: The Future of Narrative in Cyberspace.* Cambridge: MIT Press, 1997.

Muzzy Lane. *Education.* "Why Games?" www.muzzylane.com/education/.

Muzzy Lane. *Making History: The Calm and the Storm.* "Assessment and Discussion Questions." www.making-history.com/downloads/Making_History/The_Calm_and_the_Storm/assess_discuss_questions.pdf.

Muzzy Lane. *Making History: The Calm and the Storm.* "FAQ: The Calm and the Storm." www.making-history.com/content_packs/calm/faq.php#a5.

Nash, Susan Smith. *"The Ethics of Video Game-Based Simulation."* E-Learning Queen, August 25, 2004. http://elearnqueen.blogspot.com/2004_08_25_archive.html.

"The New Force at Lucasfilm," *BusinessWeek,* March 27, 2006. www.businessweek.com/innovate/content/mar2006/id20060327_719255.htm.

The New Media Consortium and the Educause Learning Initiative. "The Horizon Report—2006." Stanford, CA: Creative Commons, 2006.

Newman, James. "The Myth of the Ergodic Videogame: Some Thoughts on Player-Character Relationships in Videogames." *Game Studies* 2, no. 1 (July 2002). www.gamestudies.org/0102/newman/.

Newman, James. *Videogames.* New York: Routledge, 2004.

Ocampo, James. Review of *Rome: Total War. GameSpot,* September 23, 2004. www.gamespot.com/pc/strategy/rometotalwar/review.html.

Ochalla, Bryan. "Are Games Art? (Here We Go Again . . .)." *Gamasutra,* March 16, 2007. http://gamasutra.com/features/20070316/ochalla_01.shtml.

Papert, Seymour. "Does Easy Do It? Children, Games, and Learning." *Game Developer,* June 1998, 88.

Pearce, Celia. "The Player with Many Faces: A Conversation with Louis Castle." *Game Studies* 2, no. 2 (December 2002). www.gamestudies.org/0202/pearce/.

Plato. *Gorgias.* Translated by Chris Emlyn-Jones and Walter Hamilton. New York: Penguin, 2004.

Plato. *Laws.* Translated by Trevor J. Saunders. New York: Penguin, 2004.

Plato. *The Republic.* Translated by Desmond Lee. New York: Penguin, 1987.

The Poetic Edda. Translated by Carolyne Larrington. Oxford: Oxford University Press, 1996.

"Police Positive in Shooting Probe." *BBC News,* September 11, 2006. http://news.bbc.co.uk/2/hi/uk_news/england/manchester/5332918.stm.

Poole, Steven. *Trigger Happy: Videogames and the Entertainment Revolution.* New York: Arcade, 2004.

Poole, Steven. "Virtual Aesthetics." *Modern Painters* 14, no. 2 (2001): 76–77.

Prensky, Marc. *Digital Game-Based Learning.* New York: McGraw-Hill, 2001.

"Quake Blows Away Design Problems." *BBC News.* October 21, 2000. http://news.bbc. co.uk/1/hi/education/982346.stm.

Reeder, Sara. "Computer Game Ethics." *Compute!* 137, January 1992, 100.

Rehak, Bob. "Playing at Being: Psychoanalysis and the Avatar." In *The Video Game Theory Reader,* edited by Mark J.P. Wolf and Bernard Perron, 103–128. New York: Routledge, 2003.

Review of *Ghost Recon: Advanced Warfighter. Groovalicious Games,* June 22, 2006. www. groovgames.com/display.cfm?id=321.

Reynolds, Ren. "Playing a 'Good' Game: A Philosophical Approach to Understanding the Morality of Games." *International Game Developers Association.* www.igda.org/ articles/rreynolds_ethics.php.

Robinett, Warren. "Foreword." In *The Video Game Theory Reader,* edited by Mark J.P. Wolf and Bernard Perron, vii–xix. New York: Routledge, 2003.

Ryan, Marie-Laure. *Narrative as Virtual Reality: Immersion and Interactivity in Literature and Electronic Media.* Baltimore: Johns Hopkins University Press, 2001.

Sambeteanu, Ioan. Review of *Elder Scrolls IV: Oblivion. Softpedia,* April 14, 2006. www. softpedia.com/reviews/games/pc/The-Elder-Scrolls-IV-Oblivion-Review-21532.shtml.

Sandor, Ellen, and Janine Fron. "The Future of Video Games as an Art: On the Art of Playing with Shadows." *Playing by the Rules: The Cultural Policy Challenges of Video Games.* http://culturalpolicy.uchicago.edu/conf2001/papers/sandor.html.

Schneider, Mary Beth. "Bayh vs. Video Game Violence." *The Indianapolis Star,* December 2, 2005, A1.

Shepard, Cyn. *4-20: A Columbine Site.* "AOL User Profiles." www.acolumbinesite.com/ profiles2.html.

Sicart, Miguel. "The Ethics of Computer Game Design." *Proceedings of the DiGRA 2005 Conference: Changing Views—Worlds in Play.* www.digra.org/dl/db/06276.55524. pdf.

Slovin, Rochelle. "Hot Circuits: Reflections on the 1989 Video Game Exhibition of the American Museum of the Moving Image." In *The Medium of the Video Game,* edited by Mark J.P. Wolf, 137–154. Austin: University of Texas Press, 2002.

Smith, Greg M. "Computer Games Have Words, Too: Dialogue Conventions in Final Fantasy VII." *Game Studies* 2, no. 2 (2002). www.gamestudies.org/0202/smith/.

"Sony Apologises over Violent Game." *BBC News,* June 15, 2007. http://news.bbc.co.uk/2/ hi/uk_news/england/manchester/6758381.stm.

Sparks, Gregg. "Political Video Game Simulates 2004 Election." *Wisconsin Technology Network,* March 24, 2004. http://wistechnology.com/article.php?id=695.

Squire, Kurt. *Replaying History: Learning World History through Playing Civilization III.* "Abstract." http://website.education.wisc.edu/kdsquire/dissertation.html.

Stables, Kate. "Run Lara Run." *Sight & Sound* 11, no. 8 (2001): 18–20.

Synthetic Worlds Initiative. *Arden: The World of William Shakespeare FAQ Version 1.2.* http://swi.indiana.edu/ardenfaq.pdf.

Takahashi, Dean. "The Ethics of Game Design." *Game Developer,* December 2004, 14–19.

Tanner, Lindsey. "Is Video-Game Addiction a Mental Disorder?" *MSNBC,* June 22, 2007. www.msnbc.msn.com/id/19354827/.

Taylor, T.L. *Play Between Worlds: Exploring Online Game Culture.* Cambridge: MIT Press, 2006.

Terdiman, Daniel. "Campus Life Comes to Second Life." *Wired,* September 24, 2004. www.wired.com/gaming/gamingreviews/news/2004/09/65052.

"This Revolution Will Be Digitized, Texturized." *In Medias Res: The Newsletter of the MIT Comparative Media Studies* (Spring 2004): 1, 12.

Theodore, Steve. "Uncanny Valley." *Game Developer,* December 2004, 43–45.

Thompson, Clive. "Going into Godmode in Left Behind." *Wired,* November 6, 2006. www.wired.com/gaming/gamingreviews/commentary/games/2006/11/72071.

Thompson, Clive. "Why a Famous Counterfactual Historian Loves Making History with Games." *Wired,* May 21, 2007. www.wired.com/gaming/virtualworlds/commentary/games/2007/05/gamefrontiers_0521.

Thomson, David. "Zap Happy: World War II Revisited." *Sight & Sound* 11, no. 7 (2001): 34–37.

Turkle, Sherry. *Life on the Screen: Identity in the Age of the Internet.* New York: Simon and Schuster, 1995.

Turner, Dorie. "Orangutans Play Video Games at Zoo Atlanta." *MSNBC,* April 11, 2007. www.msnbc.msn.com/id/18064686/.

United States Army. *America's Army.* "Parents Info." www.americasarmy.com/support/faqs.php?t=9&z=59#59.

United States House of Representatives. *Violence in Videogames: Hearing Before the Subcommittee on Telecommunications and Finance,* June 30, 1994. Washington, DC: GPO, 1994.

United States Senate. *The Impact of Interactive Violence on Children: Hearing Before the Committee on Commerce, Science, and Transportation,* March 21, 2000. Washington, DC: GPO, 2003.

United States Senate. *Marketing Violence to Children: Hearing Before the Committee on Commerce, Science, and Transportation,* September 13, 2000. Washington, DC: GPO, 2003.

"The Values in Video Games." *Religion and Ethics Newsweekly,* May 30, 2003. www.pbs.org/wnet/religionandethics/week639/cover.html.

Vargas, Jose Antonio. "Way Radical, Dude." *Washington Post,* October 9, 2006. www.washingtonpost.com/wp-dyn/content/article/2006/10/08/AR2006100800931.html.

Veale, Jennifer. "Where Playing Video Games *Is* a Life." *Time,* May 14, 2007. www.time.com/time/world/article/0,8599,1620799,00.html.

"Video Game Battles Satan." *WorldNetDaily,* June 15, 2006. http://worldnetdaily.com/news/article.asp?ARTICLE_ID=50658.

Waldron, David. "Role-Playing Games and the Christian Right: Community Formation in Response to a Moral Panic." *Journal of Religion and Popular Culture* 10 (Spring 2005). www.usask.ca/relst/jrpc/art9-roleplaying.html.

Waugh, Eric-Jon Rössel. "Worlds Are Colliding!: The Convergence of Film and Games," *Gamasutra*, December 12, 2005. www.gamasutra.com/features/20051212/waugh_01.shtml.

The White House. "President Reiterates Goal on Homeownership," June 18, 2002. www.whitehouse.gov/news/releases/2002/06/20020618-1.html.

Wiemer-Hastings, Peter, and Judy Robertson. *Teaching Composition Using Role Play and Feedback from Multiple Agents.* http://reed.cs.depaul.edu/peterwh/SS/aied2001.pdf.

Wolf, Mark J.P. "Abstraction in the Video Game." In *The Video Game Theory Reader,* edited by Mark J.P. Wolf and Bernard Perron, 47–66. New York: Routledge, 2003.

Wolf, Mark J.P. "Inventing Space: Toward a Taxonomy of On- and Off-Screen Space in Video Games." *Film Quarterly* 51, no. 1 (1997): 11–23.

Woolf, Virginia. "Mr. Bennett and Mrs. Brown." In *Collected Essays,* vol. 1. New York: Harcourt, 1969.

Wonderland. "SXSW: Will Wright Keynote." South by Southwest Interactive Festival, 2007, Austin, TX, March 13, 2007. www.wonderlandblog.com/wonderland/2007/03/sxsw_will_wrigh.html.

Wright, Talmadge, Eric Boria, and Paul Bridenbach. "Creative Player Actions in FPS Online Videogames." *Game Studies* 2, no. 2 (December 2002). www.gamestudies.org/0202/wright/.

Wright, Will. "Dream Machines." *Wired* 14, no. 4 (April 2006). www.wired.com/wired/archive/14.04/wright.html.

WNYC New York Public Radio. "Joystick Nation." *On the Media,* December 19, 2003. www.onthemedia.org/yore/transcripts/transcripts_121903_joystick.html.

❖ Index ❖

❖ About the Author ❖

Harry J. Brown is Assistant Professor of English at DePauw University in Greencastle, Indiana, where he teaches courses in American literature and new media. He completed his doctorate at Lehigh University in 2003. His first book, *Injun Joe's Ghost: The Indian Mixed-Blood in American Writing,* was published in 2004. He resides in Greencastle with his wife and two daughters.